PRINCE
Not So
CHARMING
Cinderella's Guide to
FINANCIAL INDEPENDENCE

KATHLEEN GRACE, CFP®, CIMA®

New York

PRINCE Not So CHARMING
Cinderella's Guide to FINANCIAL INDEPENDENCE

Published in New York, New York, by Morgan James Publishing. Morgan James and The Entrepreneurial Publisher are trademarks of Morgan James, LLC. www.MorganJamesPublishing.com

The Morgan James Speakers Group can bring authors to your live event. For more information or to book an event visit The Morgan James Speakers Group at www.TheMorganJamesSpeakersGroup.com.

Nothing contained in the book Prince Not So Charming® should be misconstrued as investment, financial, legal, tax or other professional services advice, but is general information only. Nor is the information provided in the book being offered by United Capital Financial Advisers, LLC, its parent, or its subsidiary entities. You should seek the services of a competent professional before beginning any improvement program. The story and its characters and entities are fictional. Any likeness to actual persons, either living or dead, is strictly coincidental.

Certified Financial Planner Board of Standards Inc. owns the certification marks CFP®, CERTIFIED FINANCIAL PLANNER™, CFP® (with plaque design), and CFP® (with flame design) in the United States, which it awards to individuals who successfully complete CFP Board's initial and ongoing certification requirements. Investment Management consultants association (IMCA®) is the owner of the certification marks "CIMA®" and "Certified Investment Management Analyst®." Use of CIMA® or Certified Investment Management Analyst® signifies that the user has successfully completed IMCA's initial and ongoing credentialing requirements for investment management consultants.

A free eBook edition is available with the purchase of this print book.

CLEARLY PRINT YOUR NAME ABOVE IN UPPER CASE

Instructions to claim your free eBook edition:
1. Download the BitLit app for Android or iOS
2. Write your name in **UPPER CASE** on the line
3. Use the BitLit app to submit a photo
4. Download your eBook to any device

ISBN 978-1-63047-634-2 paperback
ISBN 978-1-63047-635-9 eBook
Library of Congress Control Number:
2015908964

Cover Design by:
Rachel Lopez
www.r2cdesign.com

Interior Design by:
Bonnie Bushman
The Whole Caboodle Graphic Design

In an effort to support local communities and raise awareness and funds, Morgan James Publishing donates a percentage of all book sales for the life of each book to Habitat for Humanity Peninsula and Greater Williamsburg.

Get involved today, visit
www.MorganJamesBuilds.com

Habitat
for Humanity®
Peninsula and
Greater Williamsburg
Building Partner

PRINCE Not So CHARMING

With all my love, this book is dedicated to my mother, Margaret Grace, for all she endured in order to keep our family together. And to my beautiful daughter, Margaret Katherine, who I thank God for each and every day! May she grow up to be a confident, proud, financially and emotionally independent woman while maintaining her sweet and loving disposition.

And to all the women who find or have found themselves with a prince who is not so charming. May you have the strength and fortitude to make a change to be empowered and independent!

Table of Contents

Acknowledgements

I am truly blessed to have so many wonderful, talented people in my life who have contributed in one way or another to this book. I have no doubt that without their patience, understanding, encouragement, and help, I could not have persevered.

I thank my writer and friend, Donna Peerce, for her creativity in helping to weave this beautiful, romantic tale and for her undying patience with my edits and reedits. Without her, this story would have never come to life. Donna, you made this so much fun!

Thank you to the women in our firm and in our industry who improve the lives of those in their communities, as well as clients, each and every day. And thank you to our fearless leader, a tremendous role model and visionary.

Hugs and kisses to all my fabulous loving friends and to my loyal business partner and best friend, whose immense love and compassion has seen me through some dark days. Thank you for your encouragement to turn this idea into reality in order to make a difference in the lives of other women.

My deepest gratitude to my dear friend Lawrence Ineno, writer and editor, for being so gracious and understanding—you are a true prince! Thank you for your patience in working with this obsessive-compulsive, perfectionist Virgo and your dedication and resolve to shepherd this project.

Introduction

For over twenty years, I have worked with countless women who represent a wide range of experiences and backgrounds. What I have found is that, regardless of whether someone is a corporate executive or stay-at-home mom, a woman's dream of finding her own Prince Charming is near universal. We all wish for that perfect love! But after hearing story after story of disappointment and heartbreak in relationships, I have come to the unfortunate conclusion that Prince Charming exists only in fairy tales.

Despite the professional boundaries that women continue to break through as we become CEOs of Fortune 500 companies, senators, state governors, high-profile athletes, and military leaders, women continually fall prey to the consequences of what I call the "Prince Charming syndrome."

Many of us are cast under the spell of finding the "perfect mate"—someone who will fulfill us romantically, financially, and emotionally. In and of itself, there is nothing wrong with this aspiration. After all, the union between two people who love one other is the bedrock of our society. The issue, however, comes when women cede control of their financial lives and emotional well-being to someone else. I am referring not just to women who are financially dependent on a breadwinner or have little monetary means on their own or both. I am also including doctors, lawyers, business leaders, and others in prominent roles within their professions and communities. I have also met professionals and business owners that are victims of verbal or physical abuse.

Listening to heartbreaking stories motivated me to provide tools to empower women. By combining the insight I have gained working with clients who represent diverse backgrounds with my experience as a CERTIFIED FINANCIAL PLANNER™ professional, I have reached the following three conclusions:

1. **Giving Prince Charming full financial control also hands over your power.** When someone has control over your financial future, you are vulnerable to a financial crisis. Counting on Prince Charming to pay the bills exposes you to being controlled financially or otherwise. Knowledge and involvement in the daily expenses and income will help prevent becoming a victim.

2. **Anything can happen to Prince Charming, so be prepared.** He can die, become disabled, be a spendthrift, or simply turn out to be a jerk. Relationships may be perfectly romantic in the beginning. The unfortunate truth is that they often come to an end—given the current divorce rate is over 50 percent.

3. **When you are financially independent, you are better equipped to deal with the emotional devastation of a breakup.** Getting over the loss of Prince Charming, in and of itself, is tough enough. But it is exponentially more difficult when you are dealing with a breakup *and* being broke.

Rather than view these as gloom-and-doom relationship realities, I see them as a call to action to fully embrace our current societal role. In fact, it seems we are at an unprecedented historical moment. Take women of my mother's generation, for example. At the time, they were obligated to follow cultural and societal roles that kept them at home, or if they were part of the workforce, they earned paltry wages. Fast-forward to today: we are educated, well compensated, and thus free to take on near-endless opportunities in our personal and professional lives.

Prince Not So Charming® was written to entertain, inspire, and shed light on the consequences of giving one's power to a boyfriend, spouse, or significant other. Although the story is a work of fiction, its message rings true to all of us who have loved, lost, and hope to love again. Lastly, my wish is that this book plays a modest part in the paradigm shift that I see taking place in society today—one where women have unprecedented opportunities to lead romantically, financially, and emotionally fulfilling lives. I am thrilled to embark on this journey with you, and I sincerely hope this book will motivate and inspire positive change. Together, we can begin making a difference in the world, starting today.

Chapter 1

*H*elp me!" *she screamed. Cinderella stood on a cliff overlooking jagged rocks and an endless sea. She was running away from something dark and menacing, but she could not identify exactly what the frightful figure was. Her toes gripped the cliff's edge, and her heart pounded so hard she could hardly form a thought. In an instant, Cinderella's footing gave way, and she slid down the cliff, saved only by a branch that stuck out from a crevice. She clung to it with all her might as her legs dangled in midair. "I can't hold on much longer!" she cried to the heavens.*

Cinderella bolted upright. Sweat beaded on her forehead, and she felt the safety of the mattress beneath her. The morning sun and the birds chirping outside signaled that the nightmare was over. For months, Cinderella—Cindi for short—had been experiencing dreams like these. *I'm probably just stressed out*, she told herself.

Like the fairy-tale character, Cinderella Patterson had flowing blond hair, porcelain skin, and clear blue eyes. Many people admired her for her kindness, and she worked hard to create a happy life for her seven-year-old daughter,

Kaitlyn, and herself. A single mom, Cindi lived with Kaitlyn in a cozy house near the coast of southern Florida. Lush palm trees lined the street leading up to 23102 Marina Circle.

According to those closest to her, Cindi led an idyllic life. But like the classic fairy tale's Cinderella, she faced many challenges. Cindi played multiple roles: She was a single mom, a loyal friend, a fashion designer, and a business owner. While juggling her varied responsibilities, she tried to maintain a social life, though it became more difficult with each passing day.

Her daughter, Kaitlyn, brought her joy and unconditional love. Her best friend, Anne, provided her much-needed support. During tough times, she sobbed in Anne's embrace, unabashedly expressing her sadness. Other times, she and Anne sat with each other in their pajamas, surrounded by fluffy pillows and fashion magazines, while talking about life's ups and downs, sipping Cakebread, and nibbling on fine chocolates. They spent countless hours analyzing their relationships and wondering if they would ever find the man of their dreams. Both wanted to find that special someone, each one's version of Prince Charming, who would bring them love and happiness.

As far as work was concerned, ever since Cindi was a little girl, she had dreamed of designing elegant evening wear. In fact, she was only seven years old when she began filling notebooks with sketches of beautiful gowns. It was a dream she had held onto throughout her fashion-design courses in college. After her studies, a series of lucky career breaks bolstered her belief in her design skills. At one point, she had aspirations to be the designer for A-list celebrities. Recently, however, her confidence had diminished.

Over the past few years, Cindi's self-esteem had reached an all-time low, which caused a lack in creativity. She was embarrassed to admit it, but it had been a long time since she had designed a dress that she was truly proud of. To her disappointment and frustration, her latest designs were unimaginative and lacked the sparkle and flair that had made her previous collection so extraordinary. Her current state gnawed at her, as did the endless stream of questions and doubts that kept her awake at night. *If I can't come up with fresh ideas, how long will I be able to stay in business? And if I go out of business, what will that mean to my daughter and me?*

Cindi often thought that finding love again would provide the inspiration she desperately needed. But her options seemed limited. She tried to encourage herself by recalling her mother's words of wisdom: "There's a lid for every pot." At the same time, she began doubting whether she would ever find the perfect fit.

Her list of concerns weighed heavily on her the evening she met Anne at their favorite Miami restaurant, Las Palmas. They sat at their usual table on the outdoor terrace, sipping the restaurant's famous pomegranate margaritas.

"You okay tonight?" Anne asked. "You seem distracted."

Cinderella could always count on her best friend's ability to sense when something was wrong. "I'm just worried," Cindi sighed, shrugging her shoulders. "You know, the usual stuff. Worried about my business. Worried about how blocked I am. Worried about making sure Kaitlyn gets a good college education and, of course, worried I'm never going to date or fall in love with anyone again."

Anne smiled. "Oh, you'll date again. The question is: Will you date anyone who deserves you?"

Cindi felt fortunate to have a friend like Anne. Friday-night margaritas with her best friend were the highlight of her week. Together, they'd spent many hours venting about work, comparing notes on the challenges they faced, and dishing about the men—or the lack of them—in their lives.

"Sweetie, you're going to need a superman to keep up with you!" Anne said. "He's going to have to be creative, driven, beyond smart, and great with kids because that angel of yours deserves a dynamite dad. He's gotta be drop-dead gorgeous—and, of course, amazing in bed!"

"Cheers to that!" Cinderella said as she raised her margarita in the air. The two clinked their frosty beverages. "And more to the point, the kind of man who will treat me with respect—a real partner in life."

"In other words, utterly charming," Anne said.

"*Prince* Charming," Cindi added, "if he exists."

"Seriously," Anne said, raising an eyebrow, "I'm not sure he exists ... at least, I haven't found him yet. And even if he does, he's not going to rescue you. That's why I think you should focus on yourself and creating fabulous clothes again. It's your gift. And no man, Prince Charming or otherwise, is going to help you do that. But he might *inspire* you!"

They laughed in sync.

"You're right. I don't actually expect someone to sweep in on a white horse and make everything better. Besides, I'm sick of dating. In fact, I'm over it," Cinderella said.

She had been on only a handful of dates since her divorce. At Anne's insistence, she tried meeting men online, but the results were disappointing: Nearly every guy was uninteresting, unattractive, or just plain boring. While she did not expect all of them to be GQ models or as good looking and athletic as David Beckham, she also didn't want a couch potato who thought a fun night was getting wings and beer at Applebee's while watching ESPN. *Where are the Renaissance men? Sexy, smart, handsome, chivalrous, and romantic men who know how to sweep a girl off her feet and make her feel like the most amazing and beautiful woman in the world. Maybe they're make-believe and only exist in fairy tales,* she decided. *Or maybe I'm just too picky.*

"This is no good. We have to find a way to boost your self-esteem," Anne said.

"I'm not sure there's any hope for me," Cindi said.

Anne frowned. "I hate your ex for making you doubt yourself. You've bought all the nonsense Richard said about you—hook, line, and sinker. You're one of the most creative, and talented women I know. Any man would be lucky to have you in his life. And, you have a figure to die for."

"He used to call me fat," Cindi said. She'd always been curvaceous, and she wished she were more willowy and tall, like Anne.

"What are you talking about?" asked Anne. "You're beautiful and voluptuous, and men love that! Contrary to the fashion world, men love curves."

"I appreciate your support; I really do. But you're my best friend," Cindi said. "You're supposed to say those things."

"Sure, I'm biased, but I'm also the first one to tell you areas in your life that need attention. In fact, right now, that area is *you*. You need to be the strong woman you are, Ms. Cinderella," Anne said.

Cindi smiled. But it was followed by a hint of sadness. "I really thought I'd made it through the worst of it," said Cindi. Tears began to fill her eyes. She thought by now she had overcome the dreadful things Richard had said and done.

"Don't be so hard on yourself. You were married to him for years and raised a daughter together. You can't expect to get over something like that overnight. And it's totally understandable for it to impact other areas of your life, too," said Anne.

"You're right. I guess the emotional toll has been affecting my creativity in ways I haven't even been aware of."

"Richard is nothing but a self-centered, egotistical loser who doesn't deserve your attention. Even *thinking* about him is giving him an ounce of control," Anne said.

Cindi had sailed into "happily ever after" with the wrong man. He seemed like the perfect mate. But a mere three years into their marriage, she discovered that he had been cheating on her with a younger version of her.

When she confronted her husband, Richard didn't even bother hiding his infidelity. Instead, he told her that she didn't own him and that, because he was the breadwinner, she had no right to tell him what to do. She knew she owed it to her daughter and herself to divorce. But the divorce wasn't easy and only intensified Richard's worst qualities. In fact, there were times when Cindi had been afraid for her safety when he went into his rages.

To make matters worse, Richard sullied her name with vicious lies to their mutual friends. According to his accounts, he was a victim of a jealous and painfully insecure wife who demanded that he work harder in order to feed her insatiable spending appetite. She had heard through mutual friends that he repeatedly called her a dumb, talentless woman who couldn't succeed without clinging to the coattails of someone successful and rich like him. By the time he was finished with her in court, Cindi believed she was worthless.

At five feet seven inches tall, Cinderella was stunning but didn't know it, which in Anne's mind only added to Cindi's appeal. Her best friend rested her hand on Cindi's arm.

"Sweetie," Anne said, "no wonder you're having a hard time designing beautiful things. You can't expect to be creative until you feel confident and comfortable in your own skin."

Cindi felt tears well in her eyes. *Dammit, don't cry*, she told herself. She was tired of feeling inadequate.

Their waiter arrived at the table and took their food order.

"The only one who's holding you back is *you*," Anne continued. "It's time to shoot for the stars! Design the next Academy Awards gown for the diva *du jour*. Now's the perfect time, *before* you get involved with someone new. That way, you'll enter a relationship from a place of power and as a real partner—a confident person who already has a fabulous life."

"You're so right," Cindi said. "But sometimes I feel overwhelmed. If I'm not creating new designs, I have no product to sell. And if I have no product, how can I grow my business? I've been supporting myself for several years without Richard's help, and I think I've done a pretty good job. At the same time, it is so stressful that sometimes I feel like giving up."

Cindi licked some salt off the rim of her margarita glass and put it down. "I guess that's where the Prince Charming fantasy comes in," she confessed. "It would be nice to have a partner to share the burden, the bills, maintaining the house, and Kaitlyn's school stuff."

"No doubt, it would be nice to have a *good* partner in life," Anne said. "I think of it more like a bonus—if it happens, great. But it shouldn't stop us from having a fabulous life *now*."

"I agree. Then again, I thought Richard would make an excellent partner, and look how he turned out," Cindi said.

"Hey, let me tell you a secret. As you know, I work with dozens of high-powered, successful women. They seem to have the whole world at their fingertips. But what's surprising is even the most sophisticated and beautiful women are under the spell of believing that Prince Charming exists, and most of them are trying to find him. Sometimes I wonder if the fairy tales have done us more harm than good."

Anne was a talented financial planner. She was passionate about creating the connection between being an accomplished woman and maintaining financial literacy. In other words, she believed that women needed to know how to take care of themselves financially, mentally, emotionally, and physically before finding a partner in life.

"Believe me," Cinderella said, "based on the recent batch of sketchy characters I met on the dating site, I'm not expecting to find Prince Charming anytime soon."

Anne grinned. It was one of her characteristic big smiles that lit up her entire face. Cindi's best friend had a gorgeous smile. Her long brown hair was thick and luxurious, and the rich color matched her large eyes, which always shone with excitement as if she'd just made an amazing discovery. Anne was one of the strongest, most independent women Cindi knew.

"Now that's what I like to hear," Anne said. "You don't *need* Prince Charming!"

Just then the waiter appeared with their Mexican sampler. Right away, both women began nibbling on their favorite appetizers while enjoying their evening together. As the sky darkened, the terrace filled with more diners.

"I'll tell you something funny, though," Cindi said, brushing her silken hair out of her eyes. "You know I've practically given up on finding Prince Charming—but it just so happens that I'm going to a ball tomorrow night."

Chapter 2

Every February, Florida's biggest charities combined to host the Brave Cherubs Charity Ball, a star-studded, black-tie affair to raise money for children battling cancer. It was held at Vizcaya Museum and Gardens. The event was lavish—tickets started at $500—and the guest list comprised the state's *Who's Who*, including entrepreneurs, artists, executives, lawyers, actors, pro athletes, philanthropists, local politicians, and photographers whose images would appear in the week's society pages. The gala was the place to see and be seen while rubbing elbows with power players.

Which is exactly why, if left to her own devices, Cindi would have avoided the ball altogether. This was the first ball she'd been to since the breakup, and she was only attending because her publicist had ruthlessly twisted her arm. "You gotta go! It will be good to network and promote the label!" he said. As a designer, Cindi had made a name for herself around town. But times were hard for all luxury goods, and if the charity ball was the best way to make lucrative business contacts, then so be it.

In the past, it was her ex-husband who had always insisted they go. Richard's net worth was well over fifty million dollars, and what better place to flaunt it than at the Brave Cherubs Charity Ball? Never mind that he didn't actually devote his time or money to any charities. For Richard—a shallow, ego-driven entrepreneur—everything in life was purely for show. Unfortunately, by the time Richard revealed his true nature, Cindi had already taken her marriage vows.

To her dismay, it turned out that their marriage was just another way for Richard to impress others, which meant that the relationship itself wasn't important to him. When she suspected he was cheating, she hired a private detective to discover his midday trysts with his administrative assistant. How tacky and cliché. Her husband was having an affair with his employee, and he didn't even have the decency to hide it. Cindi's friends had all agreed that it was one of the worst ways to find out your husband was cheating—by having a private investigator—a perfect stranger—show you the video footage.

Richard had a tendency toward emotional abuse during their marriage. His bullying tactics, however, sank to new depths during the divorce. Despite his breathtaking net worth, Richard's goal was to give Cindi and Kaitlyn the bare minimum. Thus, in order to achieve his goal, Richard had retained a divorce lawyer as underhanded and ruthless as he was.

Meanwhile, Cindi was the opposite of Richard. She was loyal and faithful to her loved ones. She threw her heart and soul into her relationships. And what she'd chosen to do—what she'd been trying to do—was create a stable, happy life with her husband and daughter. Despite all of Richard's faults, she loved him ... or so she thought, especially in the beginning.

Their divorce proceedings were lengthy and full of heartbreak and trauma. Richard's lawyer bullied Cinderella, threatening to strip her of all her parental rights if she didn't agree to his terms. The thought of her little girl living with her volatile, emotionally abusive father was so horrible that Cindi signed away what she was entitled to. In the end, the settlement left her with nearly nothing.

She consoled herself by saying that at least she had full custody of her child. And her dignity. Or did she?

Thankfully, because of her age, her daughter wasn't aware of the ugliness of their unraveling marriage. Cindi had protected her as much as possible. And when they separated and Richard took their little girl for his weekend visits, he was cordial and kind. In fact, he tended to shower her with gifts and tried his best to show Kaitlyn that he was the superior parent.

But all the stress caused Cindi to fall into depression. Overnight, her title of wife was replaced by *divorcée*, a term she despised. She found herself a single mom, supported by a paltry income and a struggling business. This was hardly the life she had envisioned for herself and her daughter. To her, the divorce was a failure—*her* failure. She questioned everything that had gone wrong: *Why couldn't I make Richard happy? Why would he ever want to cheat on me when I had tried so hard to be the perfect wife and mother?*

The night of the ball, Cinderella sat in front of her vanity, pinning her blond hair in a French twist. No, this wasn't the life she'd planned, but it was still her life. Her daughter was healthy, and she was blessed with good friends.

"Kater-tater!" she called.

Her daughter didn't respond.

"Kaitlyn?"

She heard a pair of tiny footsteps bounding down the hall, followed by silence, which was broken the moment her daughter somersaulted and plopped on her mother's bed. Her landing was followed by giggles.

"Yes, Mommy?" Kaitlyn asked, cocooned in the comforter and catching her breath.

In the mirror, Cindi watched her daughter. She had a cherub's face: round cheeks, crystal-clear blue eyes, and perfect pink lips, framed by a head full of blond curls. She had the best features of both of her parents: her bright eyes and blond hair from her mom, and her chiseled jawline from her dad. Fortunately, she'd inherited her mom's personality, which meant that Kaitlyn didn't exhibit any of her father's arrogance.

Cindi's friends had been telling her for years that Kaitlyn should be a model. But there was an unspoiled gentleness to her—such a sweet, wholesome innocence that Cindi couldn't bear the thought of dragging her to fashion shows and photo shoots.

"I was wondering," Cindi said, pointing to her hair, "If I might have a little help with this French twist."

Kaitlyn's face brightened. "Yes!" she shouted. "Let me get my hair kit." Her daughter bolted out of the bedroom to grab her prized possession. For her seventh birthday, Cindi had given her daughter a hairstyling kit, which Kaitlyn now considered her most treasured gift.

She had spent hours trying her wild creations on her mom, including, but not limited to, ponytails, side ponytails, braids, French braids, and pigtails. There was even one foray into the 1980s theme of "bigger is better," which resulted in a teased look that gave them both the giggles.

Cindi stared into her mirror, squinting, then smiling, trying to make the lines around her eyes disappear. She was by no means old, but at thirty-five, she could see laugh lines forming around her mouth. She liked to remind herself that those wrinkles expressed the mountains of joy she'd experienced, once upon a time.

Cindi lightly poked at the skin under her eyes. In her twenties, she'd sworn she would never do Botox, but now that she could see new lines on her forehead and around her eyes—a side effect of the stress of getting her business running and her divorce—she was seriously considering it.

Kaitlyn ran into the room, cheery as ever, and flopped onto the bed, her hairstyling kit tumbling open in the process. There was no way Cindi could feel depressed when Kaitlyn was so cheerful.

"Butterfly or banana?" Kaitlyn asked, digging through her assortment of hair clips.

Cindi shrugged. "Maybe we should try them both and see which one looks better."

A grin spread across Kaitlyn's face. She eagerly hopped on her mother's vanity and got to work, sweeping Cindi's hair back into a French twist with the skill and finesse of someone much older.

As she looked at her daughter in the mirror's reflection, Cindi's heart filled with joy. Kaitlyn was a ray of sunshine who added bountiful warmth and goodness to her life. Yet something was still missing. And though she didn't want to be like some of Anne's financial clients who were constantly in search of their elusive Prince Charming, she longed for a partner to share her life. She couldn't help the fact that she was raised that way. Her mother and father had been devoted to one another, and she wanted to experience the same partnership and commitment she'd witnessed in them.

In fact, when Cindi loved someone, she gave 110 percent. She aspired to be the best partner, friend, and lover possible. And she wanted someone who would return her commitment. Now that the marriage was over, deep down she wished to meet her Prince Charming. She wanted him to be kind, loving, and loyal. She dreamed of being swept off her feet and falling head over heels in love. *Didn't all women want that?* she asked herself.

"Mommy," her daughter said.

"Yes, Kater-tater?"

Kaitlyn crossed her arms over her chest and stuck out a pouty lip. "I can't make your hair look pretty when you're frowning like that."

A quick look at her reflection in the mirror revealed that her daughter was right. She had a large patch of wrinkles on her forehead.

"I'm sorry," Cindi said with a sigh. "I didn't realize I was frowning. I must have been distracted." She pulled her daughter onto her knee. "You've got to have good material to work with, don't you? How else will you get me ready for the ball?" She smiled, kissing Kaitlyn once on each cheek, then three times on the tip of the nose—their secret, special kiss.

"I'm going to make you look like a princess, Mommy," said Kaitlyn.

"Then I hope you can work your magic because I'll need it tonight," Cindi said, laughing.

Kaitlyn swooped her mother's hair in the back and inserted a shimmering butterfly clip. As Kaitlyn styled her mom's hair, she chattered about school friends. Before long, Cindi had forgotten her troubles.

Kaitlyn always had an ability to lift Cindi out of even the darkest state. Richard had given her the most precious gift in the world, their daughter.

"Is Daddy going to be at the ball?"

The question was like a dagger that pierced her heart. She tried to breathe normally so her daughter would not detect her sorrow. "I don't think so. Not this year."

"Then who will you dance with, Mommy?" Kaitlyn asked.

It was an innocent question, and it made Cindi's stomach sink. The thought hadn't even occurred to her. Who *would* she dance with?

She looked at her daughter in the mirror. "Who says I need someone to dance with, Kater-tater?"

Kaitlyn shook her head, as if this was the silliest question in the history of the world. "Of *course* you need someone to dance with. You're a princess, and you need a prince!"

Suddenly, Kaitlyn jumped up and sprinted out of the room, yelling, "I know what you need!" She returned and walked straight to the vanity where her mom sat. Kaitlyn held a glittering silver charm bracelet in front of her mother's face.

"You can wear it," she said, "if you promise to be careful."

Richard had given the bracelet to Kaitlyn for Christmas last year, and it was her pride and joy. It made Kaitlyn feel grown-up and special to own such a fancy piece of jewelry.

Cinderella was touched. She held out her left hand as Kaitlyn fastened the bracelet onto her slender wrist.

"It's pretty! It looks *perfect* on you," Kaitlyn said.

"Oh, this is so special," said Cindi. "I'll be honored to wear it. But first, I have an idea."

She rustled through her jewelry box and pulled out a silver bracelet of her own—one that her father had given her when she was a little girl.

She unclasped it and slid it on her daughter's tiny wrist. "Your grandpa gave me this when I was about your age. Now you and I have matching bracelets," said Cindi.

Cinderella stood up and examined herself in the mirror. She wore a floor-length, off-the-shoulder blue dress that had an overlay of shimmering sequins and featured a plunging neckline. Two years ago, she had designed the gown, which accentuated her slender waist and ample bosom. And Kaitlyn was right. The charm bracelet looked lovely with her dress. To her surprise, Cinderella felt beautiful.

She hugged her daughter. "My hair looks perfect."

Cindi leaned over and finished applying her lipstick. It was a deep, rich red—aptly named "Poison Apple." The color brightened her pale face as she pressed her full lips together and took one last look at her reflection. Inside, she could still recall the sting of Richard's cruelty—the way he used to criticize her appearance. At this moment, however, she thought, *Not too bad, Cindi, not too bad.* To her surprise, she actually *wanted* to go and enjoy herself. The woman who hardly ever put on lipstick, the single mom divorcée, wanted to laugh, to mingle, and to dance.

Kaitlyn was giddy. "Mommy, you look bee-you-ti-ful! Just like a real princess, and my bracelet will make you lucky.

You'll see." Cindi smiled. "Maybe it will," she said. "You just never know."

Chapter 3

*J*acquie, Kaitlyn's favorite babysitter, arrived right on time. Kaitlyn always looked forward to their adventures together.

Cinderella reviewed her notes with Jacquie. "Dinner's in the fridge. TV *only* after homework's done. I shouldn't be gone very long. I'll text you when I'm on my way home," she said.

Jacquie nodded. "Got it. Now where's the little princess?"

Kaitlyn flew into the living room, completing the perfect somersault on the carpet near the sofa. She giggled and then asked, "Doesn't Mommy look beautiful?"

"Stunning," said Jacquie.

"Thanks, Jacquie," Cindi said. "That's sweet. It's not every day that I go to a ball! Now, you two have fun. I'll be back before you know it." Cindi hugged Kaitlyn and headed to the door. "And, girls, go easy on the cookies."

"Wait, Mommy!" Kaitlyn shouted. "Don't forget your purse!"

"Oh, thanks," Cindi said. She had designed it from the same sapphire blue silk she had used for her gown, and it was one of her favorites.

In the first months after the divorce, Cinderella had experienced a burst of creativity unlike anything she had ever known. She lined the walls of her studio with exquisite creations. After tirelessly marketing her line of fall dresses, she arranged two distribution deals with buyers who began selling her work immediately. From those contacts, she was introduced to a buyer whose client list included the hottest celebrities. She knew that if the buyer liked any of her pieces, he would bring them to the attention of his high-profile clients, catapulting Cindi to a level of success she had always dreamed of.

She now found herself with solid business experience and fantastic contacts. All she had to do was design incredible dresses. Perhaps it was the pressure of this new possibility that was daunting, or the fact that Cindi was still struggling with her self-doubt, brought on by her divorce. Whatever the case, at the moment, she needed to rely on her artistry to remove the block. If she didn't have something to show her celebrity buyer soon, she might lose that contact forever.

Despite these recent anxieties, she had to admit that tonight she did feel a little beautiful. When she'd designed the gown that currently draped her body, she had envisioned it as a one-of-a-kind masterpiece that would turn heads. It made her feel like "a real princess," just as Kaitlyn had said.

Cindi carefully stepped into her Honda Accord, started the engine, and eased out of the driveway. The car was one thing she kept. It was nothing luxurious, but it was dependable and solid. And Cindi loved it.

As Cindi pulled up to the Vizcaya Museum and Gardens—Vizcaya for short—she shook her head in disbelief at how over-the-top the ball was. A long line of cars queued in front of the valet stand. There were Mercedes, Porsches, Maseratis, and even a chauffeured Rolls-Royce. The irony, of course, was that the event was ostensibly to raise money for children's cancer research. Cindi couldn't help but think of how much money they were wasting on opulent dining and entertainment, let alone the gowns and jewelry.

A valet in a white tuxedo approached Cinderella's car and opened her door. "Welcome, Miss," he said, offering his arm as she stepped out of the car.

"May I say that you look lovely tonight?" he said.

"Why, thank you," Cindi said. She knew he probably said this to all the ladies but enjoyed the attention nonetheless. He escorted her to the garden terrace entranceway.

"Have a wonderful evening," he said as he departed to park her car.

Cindi stood at the entrance of the lush gardens. She hesitated. Her mouth was dry, her hands trembled, and she felt her heart pound. She looked down at Kaitlyn's charm bracelet, which reminded her that she was loved and she had nothing to worry about. Still, she wasn't sure whether she should go inside. She wondered who would be there and, specifically, if Richard would show up. Stepping timidly through the threshold, she took a deep breath and said to herself, *Okay, Ms. Cinderella, just go in and enjoy yourself. Remember, this is a networking opportunity.*

As she stepped into the grand space, she found herself swept up by the magical ambience. The Vizcaya Museum and Gardens, a national historic landmark located in Miami, featured a main house, ten acres of formal gardens, and a lush native forest. For the gala, the garden had been transformed into a stunning Arabian-themed paradise. The main area was enclosed in a huge Bedouin tent with luxurious draped silks overhead that created a ceiling. Palm trees lined the periphery, and colorful velvet tapestries hung on the sides of the terrace. Soft pillows were piled on chairs with low couches and Persian carpets spread out on the ground. At one of the open ends of the tent, elegant white tablecloths covered the tables. Lanterns hung in the palm trees, giving off a soft, ethereal light. Female servers were dressed like belly dancers, and the male wait staff wore harem pants and scarves. The scent of spicy Moroccan food wafted through the air.

Male guests dressed in their finest tuxes, and women, wearing beautiful, expensive evening gowns and jewelry, mingled through the crowds. To her surprise, Cindi didn't see anyone she knew. What she did see, at one end of the garden, was a massive dance floor surrounded by strings of lights. She hoped that one of her male friends had come so she would have someone to dance with. The evening was almost perfect and would have been even more so had she been with someone she loved.

Hundreds of thousands were spent annually to make the soirée an event to remember, and this year was no exception. A full band was already playing on a stage at one end of the veranda. As Cinderella watched a couple dancing, she felt a pang of longing. Although she hated to admit it, she was slightly embarrassed that she didn't have a date.

Despite her saddened state, Cindi put a smile on her face, took a glass of champagne from a waiter, and ambled through the crowd, aware of every step and every breath she took. Numerous men noticed her and smiled. *Remember,* she told herself, *you're here to network with business contacts. And if some of your friends show up, you'll surely have someone to dance with.* So far, however, she hadn't seen anyone she knew.

Suddenly, someone caught her eye. A tall man, well over six feet, with luscious, thick, wavy dark hair stood under an ornate tapestry. A nearby lantern highlighted his brawny physique. Cindi noticed that he was wearing an Ermenegildo Zegna dark gray suit with Cartier cufflinks and Italian leather shoes.

Cindi held her breath. *Good Lord, he's gorgeous!* she thought to herself. And not just boy-next-door gorgeous. No, he was the kind of handsome man who could be on the cover of *GQ* magazine, in a Halston ad, or a leading man in a movie.

He balanced a plate of Moroccan lamb shish kebabs precariously in one hand and a glass of champagne in the other. His dark hair rested carelessly over his forehead, which only added to his sex appeal.

Cindi could see that he was well built, with broad shoulders and narrow hips. He had a strong jawline, square chin, and tanned skin, perfectly suited for an *Arabian Nights* novel. She wasn't usually the type to stare, but she couldn't take her eyes off him. And then, to her astonishment, he began heading directly toward her. Her heart pounded harder with each step he took.

"Your beauty is captivating," he said by way of introduction. "I hope you will excuse the intrusion ... I just had to see if you were real."

What did he say? Could this be happening? she asked herself.

Cindi attempted to speak, but the words remained lodged in her throat. At the moment, she thought of movie stars who rivaled his looks but was unable to think of their names. And there he was, talking to her.

"A faint blush becomes you." He held her gaze. "Is this your first time at the ball?"

Finding her voice at last, Cindi said, "Oh, no. I used to come every year with my husband."

As soon as the words left her mouth, she regretted them. She'd been talking to this stranger for mere seconds, and she'd already broken dating rule number one: No mentioning exes. Clearly, she was out of practice when it came to talking to beautiful men.

"I mean *ex*-husband," she said.

He smiled. "No further explanation needed. I used to come to the ball with my wife ... *ex*-wife." He extended his hand.

"I'm Paul Francis," he said.

"Cinderella," she said, marveling at the firmness of his handshake. "But my friends call me Cindi."

"Mmmm ... Cinderella? How apropos," he said, clutching her soft hand. "You do look like a modern-day Cinderella. Quite beautiful, if I may say so."

"Thank you, Paul. I ... er ... uh ... I haven't seen any of my friends here yet, and I was just wondering where everyone was," she said.

"Well, I'm here, and I hope to be one of your friends," said Paul. He raised her hand to his lips and kissed it. His penetrating gaze and his deep, rich words promised much, much more than friendship. She felt his lips, soft and tender on her hand. His touch was electrifying—that's the only way she could describe it.

His eyes flashed a mysteriously captivating blue-green. Suddenly, Cindi felt a little lightheaded. It was as if he could read her thoughts and her soul. She feared that she was going to faint.

"Sorry. I'm feeling a little dizzy," Cindi said, feeling self-conscious as she pulled back her hand and broke eye contact. She coughed, trying to regain her sense of equilibrium.

"Too much to drink?" Paul asked.

"That must be it," she said, even though she'd only taken a sip of her champagne.

"Listen, it's kind of stuffy in here. How about we go outside and get some fresh air?" Paul asked.

"I think that's a good idea," she said.

He placed his hand on the small of Cindi's back, sending warm shivers down her spine. She noticed the outline of his biceps and forearms bulging beneath his tux's sleeves. Heat waves coursed through every fiber of her being, and she felt connected to him—as if she could feel his heartbeat.

"After you," he said, guiding her gently toward the door.

Together, they walked out of the Bedouin tent and into a starlit night where all Cindi could think about was how much she wanted to kiss him and allow this prince to do whatever he desired with her body.

Chapter 4

Cinderella had always thought Vizcaya was magical, even without the lavish Arabian decor. In 1914, James Deering, an American industrialist, had chosen this spot to build what was then his private villa. He paid to have authentic tapestries, murals, and frescoes—sourced from opulent castles in Spain and Italy—shipped across the Atlantic Ocean and reassembled on site. The result was a magnificent mix of Mediterranean history tinged with the tropical flavor of Miami. And now, as Cindi and Paul strolled through the lush gardens, she felt overwhelmed by the beauty of both the lavish grounds and her handsome companion.

"So what do you do?" Cinderella asked casually. She felt an urge to get the question out of the way.

"I'm a litigator," he replied.

"That's fascinating. What's it like? I have friends who are lawyers but not litigators," she said.

He ran his fingers through his thick, wavy hair. "Although you'll never hear lawyers describe it this way, litigation is really about telling a good story. Every smaller story is part of a larger one. And it's my job to articulate those stories in the most powerful and persuasive way on behalf of my clients."

"I like the sound of that," she said.

They approached the East Terrace. Paul signaled to the waiter and asked if they might have a table for two.

"Most certainly, sir," the server replied. He led Paul and Cindi to a spectacular spot that overlooked Biscayne Bay.

Paul requested that the waiter bring a bottle of Cristal. He also ordered a sampling of gourmet hors d'oeuvres. The bottle and hors d'oeuvres arrived shortly afterward. The waiter filled Cindi's flute, and she took a slow, deliberate sip. It was the finest champagne she had ever tasted. The tiny bubbles seemed to dance in her mouth.

Surrounded by her date, first-class bubbly, and exquisite hors d'oeuvres, time seemed to stand still. The resonance of Paul's baritone voice was hypnotic. In fact, she imagined that she could listen to it for hours. It was so dreamy she felt as if she were in a trance. *Who is this beautiful man? Where did he come from?* she asked herself as she stared into his eyes.

"Remember the Krup case last year?" he asked, spearing a slice of filet mignon and holding it in front of his mouth. "The horrific media field day?"

"I think so," she said. Her mouth watered while she watched his lips move with every word he spoke. She vaguely remembered the case from the news.

"That was one of mine." He described the case with the mastery of a gifted storyteller.

She nodded, impressed. So far, she'd gathered that Paul was a successful lawyer, and she could see why. He was an expert at weaving a captivating tale. Everything he said sounded so interesting and convincing that she couldn't imagine a jury ruling against him. He was brilliant, funny, self-confident, and completely charismatic.

"You have just a touch of sauce on ..." Paul's voice grew softer as he pointed at her chin, and Cindi felt her face flush.

"Where?" she asked. Cindi clutched her napkin, ready to wipe away the offending sauce. She was embarrassed. Here she was, her first successful dinner since her divorce, and thanks to her clumsiness, she had Béarnaise on her face.

"Here, allow me," he said. He took his napkin and gently dabbed at her chin. Then he took his fingers and brushed back a lock of hair that was dangling over her left eye. His touch sent chills through her. For a moment, she wasn't sure if her heart was still beating.

"You have the most wonderful skin. So exquisitely soft," he said.

"Thank you," she whispered shyly.

She saw a flash in his blue-green eyes that made her knees weaken. He was strong yet vulnerable. Thoughtful and intoxicating. For all his polish, fancy clothes, and professional prestige, he had a boyish charm, which lay just beneath the suave designer veneer. Paul managed to engage her intellect and captivate her heart, all in a single look.

He asked her about her career, and she told him she was a designer and hoped one day to dress celebrities on the red carpet.

"Well, if your creations are anything like you, I'm sure they're spectacular," said Paul.

"Thank you. But I experience creative blocks once in a while, like many in my field," she said.

"I'd love to see some of your sketches sometime," he said.

"Sure," she said. She felt giddy at the thought that they would see each other again. They talked a little more about her career, but she was compelled to cut the conversation short since work had been a difficult subject to talk about lately.

"Cinderella, would you like go back to the ball?" he asked.

"Absolutely not. In fact, I like it here just fine. To be honest, I've been dreading the whole event," she said. She wondered if her answer had been too emphatic.

He nodded in agreement. "A lot of pomp and circumstance, and very little substance, which is why I'm happy I met you and that you joined me here in this magical spot." He looked up at the sky, which seemed like a Van Gogh painting—swirls of dotted light overhead in blue and orange and milky white.

"Fantastic, isn't it? Too bad we never take the time to appreciate the beauty of the world. My God, it's breathtaking," Paul said.

Cindi had thought the same thing many times, but she had never heard anyone else express it. Her heart warmed, and she felt an instant kinship with this man—a person who saw beauty in ordinary things ... and who seemed to see beauty in her.

"I couldn't agree more. Tonight, it all looks especially magical," she said.

Paul boldly reached across the table. "I hope I'm not being too forward, but I would like very much to hold your hand. It's so delicate," he said.

She didn't move. She didn't breathe. Time seemed to stand still.

His hands were large, yet soft and smooth—those of a Renaissance man. Cindi could do nothing more than nod and smile because she was completely distracted by his gentle fingers, which caused her heart to drum so loud she feared he could hear it.

He stroked the inside of her wrist. "So delicate," he whispered. Then he discovered the charm bracelet and tugged on it lightly.

"What's this?" he asked.

"Oh," she said. Instinctively, she thought about Kaitlyn, and a series of guilty thoughts filled her. *Is it inappropriate that I'm out with this handsome man, drinking champagne and holding hands? Is this all too much, too soon?* Cindi felt a pang, the kind that only a mother can feel—that horrible, heavy guilt of not being with your child ... of having fun without her.

Then again, she reasoned, perhaps this was the prince her daughter had wanted her to find.

Be reasonable. No need to feel bad about this, she told herself. She had met the man only an hour earlier, after all. There was no reason to overreact.

Then again, she found herself acting like her girlfriends who start dreaming about their weddings as soon as they meet a nice man.

Meanwhile, she felt the pressure to tell Paul about Kaitlyn. She took a deep breath. "The bracelet's my daughter's," she confessed. So many men had a phobia about responsibility and ran when they learned she had a child. She searched Paul's face for apprehension—any sign of how he felt toward children. But he shared no expression.

"She thought it would bring me luck," Cindi said.

Paul winked. "Did it?"

Cindi smiled shyly. "Maybe."

"How old is your daughter?"

"She just turned seven."

"Seven's a fun age. I've got two myself."

Cinderella's eyes widened. Now this was a surprise. She felt every bit a mother, but she never would have imagined that Paul was a parent, too.

"No kidding!" she blurted out.

"Why? Do I not seem like the paternal type?"

"No, it's just ... well ... you seem so calm and collected, so bachelor-like. As if you don't have a care in the world."

He laughed. "Well, keep in mind, I *am* a bachelor, and my ex-wife has the kids the majority of the time. But I'm also a dad."

"How old are they?" she asked.

"Nine and eleven."

"Great ages," she said.

She couldn't help but imagine their children playing together, building sandcastles, telling each other bedtime stories, sharing ice cream late at night, all of which reminded her of her maternal obligations. She fished inside her purse, pulled out her phone, and glanced at the time.

"Oh my gosh, I hadn't intended on staying very long at this event. In fact, I told my babysitter that I'd be home early," she said.

"I can tell you're a committed mother," Paul said.

"I try. At the same time, my daughter, Kaitlyn, would be the first one to tell me to stay out and enjoy myself," she said.

"I think I would have to agree with Kaitlyn."

She giggled—as clear and light as a bell. It was a sound she hadn't heard come from her own voice in a long time.

"This has been so fun. It really has. I'm so happy I met you. You made my night, Paul."

"And you made mine." His eyes found hers again. "Must you really go?"

"Yes, I really have to. I told the babysitter I'd be back at a reasonable hour, and if I stay out any later, she might start worrying."

"What happens if you don't get home on time? Do you turn into a pumpkin, Cinderella?"

She smiled. "Never heard that one before."

Rising from the table, Paul reached inside his wallet—an elegant Italian leather trifold—and pulled out several hundred-dollar bills. He tossed them nonchalantly on the table. "There, that should cover it."

That's amazing! Cindi thought to herself. Her ex-husband may have been worth fifty million dollars, but he was also notoriously parsimonious. She could never see Richard being so generous, and yet Paul had just dropped four hundred dollars on the table without a care. Either this man was trying to impress her, which she'd seen before, or maybe he was truly generous. She opted to believe he was in fact generous, not cheap like her ex.

Paul took her arm and guided her through the gardens. She wasn't sure if it was the champagne or her prince. Whatever it was, she felt positively giddy.

"You okay to drive?" Paul asked as they approached the valet.

"Yes, thanks," she said. She hated that the night was about to be over.

"I want to see you again, lovely Cinderella," he said.

There was so much self-assurance and confidence in his voice. Her knees grew weak again at the thought of a second date.

"I'd like that," she said. She fumbled nervously through her purse and pulled out one of her business cards. "That's my direct line," she said, pointing to the top number. "But you can call me on my cell anytime."

The valet pulled up, driving her Accord, and when he stepped out, Paul escorted her to the driver's side. He brought her hand to his lips and kissed it, pausing for what seemed like an eternity. He withdrew his hand, and she smelled the scent of his cologne on her hand. The masculine, bold scent made her dizzy.

As she took a seat in her car, he leaned in to kiss her cheek. His lips were soft against her skin. His thick hair hung on his forehead, almost covering his bright blue-green eyes. They sparkled with mischievousness.

Cindi blushed from head to toe. She hadn't felt like this since she was a teenager.

"Your husband was an absolute fool," he whispered, his breath warm against her neck. "*Ex*-husband, I should say. But I'm grateful for it. I would never have met you otherwise. Cinderella, you have completely captivated me."

Before she had a chance to reply, he stood up, closed the door, and motioned for the valet to bring his car. Moments later, a shiny black Range Rover pulled up to the curb. Paul looked at her and waved good-bye. He entered his SUV and waited for her to drive away. She looked at his massive car from her rearview window—chivalry was clearly not dead.

Cindi texted her babysitter and let her know she was on her way home. Her heart fluttered as she put both hands on the steering wheel. *Drive*, she coached herself, finding it next to impossible to focus on anything but her encounter with the prince. She could still smell his cologne on her hand. *Just drive.*

The events of that enchanting evening were a haze—an experience too good to be true, so much so that her mind filled with doubts. Did she really meet Paul Francis? Did she sip Cristal while dining on fine hors d'oeuvres under a moonlit sky? One thing she was certain about was the adrenaline coursing through her body with an excitement and euphoria she hadn't felt in years. Within hours, Cinderella had fallen in love with her prince.

Chapter 5

A late-night stroll through Vizcaya, huh? Sounds magical," said Anne as she took a sip of her pomegranate margarita.

"It really was," Cinderella said. Reminiscing about the incredible night helped remind her that it wasn't just a dream. "Almost too good to be true," said Anne.

"I'll give you that. And you haven't even met him yet. Anne, he is drop-dead gorgeous."

"I get it. You call him *Prince Charming*. I can't wait to meet the guy."

"Oh, and did I tell you? He smells too good to be true, too. I don't know what kind of cologne he wears, but it's so ... so ... masculine, yet sweet."

"I do love a man who smells good," Anne said.

They were tucked away at their usual table, happily sipping margaritas while Cinderella gushed about the new man in her life.

"I just hope you're going to take things slow. This guy sounds amazing, and I'm excited for you. But it's only been a month since you two met," Anne said.

"I agree. But, to be totally honest, I've never met anyone quite like him. It's as though I made a list of all the things I wanted in a man—my own Prince Charming—and poof! Paul Francis, in the flesh."

Anne arched one perfectly shaped eyebrow. "He sounds like quite the catch," she said.

It was the understatement of the year. The past month had passed in a whirlwind. When she wasn't with Kaitlyn or in her studio working on her designs, he was taking her out on the town. He wined and dined her at the city's finest restaurants and took Kaitlyn and her out to theaters and museums. They'd been to Vizcaya several times, which became Kaitlyn's favorite new place.

If it were up to them, Paul and Cindi would spend every waking moment together. He took long lunch breaks from his downtown law office so he could be with her. According to Paul, no one minded at his office. "I'm the boss," he told her.

The problem was the lunches were so opulent and the afternoons passed so quickly in his company that Cindi found herself repeatedly losing track of time. She had been late picking her daughter up from school not just once, but three times. Cindi cringed at the sight of the yellow highlighter each time the annoyed after-school daycare counselor marked her as a "late pickup."

The past few weeks, her lifestyle had taken a dramatically different direction, and she found herself feeling guilty and thrilled at the same time. She had fallen madly, deeply, and wildly in love. And the more time she spent with Paul Francis, the more she felt herself swept away and under his spell.

"He treats me like a princess. Every night of the week, he's taking me to some hot new restaurant. I've never eaten so extravagantly in my life, and I'm convinced that I'm going to gain weight. Don't worry, I know what you're thinking ... but I think he does really well, to tell you the truth."

"Well, even so, he's spending an awful lot of money. You deserve to be pampered—I just hope Paul isn't one of those guys who flaunts his money as if he's loaded when, in reality, he isn't. You just never know, Cindi," Anne replied.

Cindi furrowed her brow. "I *have* noticed that he seems to have no qualms about dropping hundreds of dollars for dinner or an evening out. It's so different from how I am and the way Richard was. It's kind of refreshing. You know how I fret and worry over every little cent."

"That's why you have a nice house, no debt, and a successful business. There's a difference between living well and living extravagantly. You can tell a lot about a man by the way he handles his money, and Paul doesn't exactly sound frugal. A financially irresponsible partner is hazardous to your fiscal health."

"Lighten up, will you? You're off the clock, remember?" Cindi asked.

"You're right. I should be in best friend mode, *not* financial planner mode. It's just hard not to analyze someone's spending habits. I'm always observing people."

Cindi pointed at a tall, impressive building down the street. "See that monolith? His law office is on the thirteenth floor. He makes plenty of money to fund his lifestyle, believe me," Cindi said.

"I'm glad to hear that. And please know that I'm only saying this because I love you to pieces. If he has more money than God and wants to spend it on you and Kaitlyn, then I'm all for it."

"It feels luxurious, and I love it. And you know one of the best parts? I've been creating new designs like crazy. Paul has inspired me! I've sketched five new gowns in the last few weeks. *Five!* It's like a monsoon after a dry spell. They're really good, too, Anne ... my best work in years. One of them in particular is something special."

A smile spread across Anne's face. "I'm so glad to hear it."

"Being with Paul has unlocked all this creative, positive energy. Suddenly, I feel excited about everything. I want to create beautiful new dresses and redecorate my home, and it's all because I feel beautiful. It's a feeling I haven't had in a really long time."

"But do you really think this creative boost of new energy is coming from Paul?" Anne asked. She was reluctant to ask, but she felt it her duty to do so.

"Absolutely. Where else could it be coming from? I figure it's a sign that this is a good long-term match—that he inspires me to be better than I am. Being with Paul fuels the work I love."

"I don't know, Cin," Anne said.

Cinderella folded her arms across her chest. "What do you mean?"

"It's just ... I don't know. Whenever my self-esteem feels as though it's tied to the person I'm dating, I get nervous. For me, true creativity and self-worth always come from within, no matter who is in my outer life," Anne said.

"It *is* coming from within. That's what I'm saying. Paul is helping me be more connected to my true self." Cindi paused. "Honestly, I thought you'd be happier for me. For months, you've been saying you wished I were creating work I was proud of. And now I am. Isn't that a good thing?"

"Of course, it is! I'm thrilled that you're designing again. But the protective part of me is just afraid that things are moving a little too fast. You're already talking about the long term, and it seems a little early to, like, plan the rest of your life with the guy."

Cinderella realized Anne's point. In her imagination, every perfect moment with Paul combined to create a lifetime of perfect moments. Every delightful afternoon added up to a lifetime of delightful afternoons in his presence. Romantic evenings at fancy restaurants and carriage rides through the park strung together into a lifetime of equally romantic evenings basking in the presence of her true love. And in her fantasies, each time she felt inspired to design a new gown, she was building a lifetime of business and artistic success, and finally—*finally*—having someone to share it with.

"I get what you're saying, I really do. I know you're just looking out for me because I've been hurt so much in the past, but it's different this time. I promise," Cindi said.

Despite acknowledging Anne's point, a part of Cindi wished her best friend could just be happy for her. Yes, Anne was an accomplished financial planner and knew everything there was to know about building wealth and stability. And yes, Anne had been her soul mate since high school. They had been through thick and thin together; they'd cried on each other's shoulders before, during, and after their divorces; and although Anne didn't have a daughter of her own, she was practically Kaitlyn's second mom. So as Kaitlyn's godmother, wasn't it her job to be excited about the man who could potentially become Cindi's husband and Kaitlyn's dad?

"I know what you're thinking," Anne said, stirring her margarita slowly with her straw. She did, in fact, always have an uncanny way of identifying exactly what was on Cinderella's mind. "You're asking yourself why I can't just be excited for you. You've finally found love, and now here I am, wanting to burst your balloon."

"Well, yes. That's pretty much exactly what was on my mind," Cindi said.

Anne put her hand on Cindi's arm. "I love you. I never want anyone to hurt you the way Richard did. I just want you to be careful. When someone sounds too good to be true, it's because he probably *is* too good to be true."

"I know," Cindi said. "And I promise you I'm being careful. I want to be sure about this one, so we're going nice and slow. We haven't even ... you know."

Anne smirked. "Really? All those late nights and no ...?"

Cindi shrugged. "Kaitlyn's usually around, and Paul really wants to be respectful, which I appreciate. The fact that he's not pressuring me to have sex makes me feel that he's interested in me for the long term, not for just a couple of nights in the sack."

The reality was that Cinderella wanted to make love with him. Every time she was with him, desire rushed through her body like a tidal wave. He was intoxicating.

"You said he's got two kids?" Anne asked.

"Yes. Nine and eleven. But I haven't met them yet—they're always at their mom's. There seems to be some underlying tension there. He hasn't talked about it much, but I can tell it was an unpleasant breakup. Of course, I can understand that."

Anne nodded. "There's always tension," she said.

Five years earlier, Anne had married an artist who turned out to be financially insolvent, not to mention still married to another woman in a different state—a fact he neglected to mention until after their wedding day. No wonder she was hesitant to trust men. When Anne encouraged her girlfriends to be financially independent, it came from a place of personal experience.

Anne leaned forward over the plate of tortilla chips and salsa. "Paul probably pays hefty alimony and child support, right? How long was he married?" she asked.

"Thirteen years."

"So between his personal and business expenses, he's probably amassed quite a bit of debt. And that's *before* he spends his money so lavishly on you. He might enjoy your company, but I think it's a bit odd that you've been dating a month and he hasn't wanted to have sex with you."

Cinderella bit her lip. On one hand, she wanted her friend to rejoice with her. On the other, Anne was making her think about things she hadn't considered. The rigorous analysis was making her uncomfortable.

"I want you to meet him. I think you'll feel better about all of this once you see how wonderful he is. You'll like him, I promise," Cindi said.

"I sure hope so. Because you only deserve the best, and if I don't think he's worthy of you, I won't be afraid to say so," Anne said.

Just then, Cindi's cell phone buzzed inside her purse.

"I bet that's the devil now," Anne said jokingly.

As usual, she was right. It was a text from Paul. It read:

Hello, gorgeous. Turn around.

"I think he's here," she told Anne.

Cinderella looked over her shoulder and saw Paul walking across the parking lot toward their table. He slipped his phone into his pocket and waved.

"Guess I'm about to meet Prince Charming," Anne said.

Cinderella panicked. "How do I look? I barely have any makeup on!" she said to Anne.

"Fabulous, as always. And if he's as crazy about you as he seems to be, he'll think you look just as sexy in jeans as in a ball gown."

Paul strode across the patio. His olive skin looked bronze against his pale purple shirt and light gray suit jacket. He signaled the end of a long day at the office by loosening his tie and unfastening the top button of his dress shirt. Dark chest hair peeked out over the top.

Cindi's throat went dry. She swallowed hard. She had seen Paul's chest two or three times before when they took Kaitlyn to the beach, and now she ached to see more of him.

"Paul," she said breathlessly. He took her hand in his and kissed it, his lips lingering on her skin.

"You look lovely," he said.

Flustered, she withdrew her hand and gestured toward Anne. "I want you to meet my best friend, Anne."

"So you're the Anne I hear so much about?" he said, turning and taking her hand in his and bringing it to his lips. "A lovely name for a lovely woman."

"Nice to meet you," Anne said. She immediately understood why Cinderella was so smitten. He was gorgeous and charming. But still, she was a little wary for her best friend.

"Please sit down and join us," Cindi said.

"Thanks—I'd be delighted," he said. He pulled out a chair next to Cindi and took a seat.

"So, Paul, don't tell me that you come here for margaritas on Friday nights too."

"My office is just down the street, and it must've been my lucky day to see you two lovely ladies before you walked in," he said.

Cindi beamed. "I'm so glad you two finally get to meet each other!"

She knew that her best friend was sizing him up. But she was also aware that Anne found him incredibly attractive—why else would she have blushed when he kissed her hand? Cinderella felt very proud that this was *her* man.

"Listen. I know this is completely last minute, but I have tickets tonight for a special event, and I wonder if you would do me the honor of being my date," Paul said.

There was nothing she wanted more and was just about to say yes when she remembered her daughter. Cindi had promised Jacquie, her babysitter, that she would return home early tonight. It wouldn't be fair to Jacquie or Kaitlyn to change plans at the last minute.

"I wish I could," Cindi said, regretting having to say no to Paul for the first time. "But I have the babysitter covering for me right now, and I promised Kaitlyn we'd spend some time together tonight. Just us girls."

"The truth is that I already bought tickets for *both* of you! I would love it if you and Kaitlyn would join me," Paul said.

"I'm speechless," Cindi said.

Anne crossed her arms. "What's this "special event" anyway?"

Paul smiled broadly. "Disney on Ice."

Chapter 6

Kaitlyn and Jacquie were watching Disney's *A Little Mermaid* when Cindi arrived home.

"Where's my Kater-tater?" she called. Kaitlyn leapt up and enveloped her in a big bear hug.

"You gals having fun?" Cindi asked.

"We always do," Kaitlyn said.

"How about having even *more* fun? Sweetie, I have a surprise for you," said Cindi.

"Can Jacquie have a surprise with us?" asked Kaitlyn.

"Not this time," said Cindi, winking at Jacquie. "But maybe next time."

"Don't worry about me, Kaitlyn. I have plans with friends tonight. But I think you're awesome for thinking about me," Jacquie said.

Cinderella handed her daughter's favorite babysitter a check and thanked her for all the extra hours she'd put in recently. Jacquie left, and Cindi walked Kaitlyn to the front window.

"Honey, see who's out there?"

"Mr. Paul!" Kaitlyn said, clapping her hands in delight.

"That's right. And guess where Mr. Paul is going to take us tonight?" Cindi asked.

"Where, Mommy, where?" Kaitlyn asked.

"It's a surprise, but I promise you'll love it. So go put on your socks and shoes and comb your hair, and I'll tell you more on our way there," she said.

Minutes later, mother and daughter were buckled up in Paul's Range Rover.

"Ms. Kaitlyn, it's my pleasure to chauffeur you this very fine evening," Paul said, giving her hand a quick peck.

"You talk funny," Kaitlyn said, giggling.

"And Ms. Cinderella, it is my pleasure to have you by my side this evening," he said. He then kissed her hand.

As they drove to the ice rink, he regaled them with his wit, charm, and storytelling skills. Cindi couldn't believe she had ever worried that the connection between Paul and her daughter would be awkward or difficult. *He has his own children. No wonder he's so good with kids,* she told herself.

"Did your mom tell you where we're going?" he asked.

"She said it would be a surprise," Kaitlyn said.

Paul smiled, "I'm taking you to a magical place I know you'd want to go."

There was no traffic as they headed to the Miami Arena—even the streetlights were charmed by his presence.

"The good news is that we've arrived early," Paul said as he pulled into the arena's parking garage, "which means we have all earned ourselves some fine snacks."

"Yay!" Kaitlyn said.

When they were halfway across the parking lot, Kaitlyn spotted the brightly colored Disney on Ice banner waving above the arena. She squealed in delight.

"Oh my gosh, oh my gosh. How did you know I've been wanting to go?" she asked as she jumped up and down.

"Sweetie, maybe Paul remembered you'd mentioned it more than a few times when we'd all gone out," Cindi said laughing.

"That's right. I'm only too happy to oblige my little princess," he said.

Paul sidled up to Cindi and took her hand in his. The tingling feeling she had enjoyed so much over the last few weeks returned the instant he lightly kissed her ear. "Can I offer you a refreshment, my darling?"

"Ah ... yes," she answered, distracted by the chills that ran through her body.

Paul bought them sodas and popcorn, and they walked toward their seats. As they passed each row, Kaitlyn realized how close the seats would be to center stage. But she had never imagined that they would have front-row seats.

"Mommy, I can feel the ice from here," she whispered into Cindi's ear once they were seated.

The performance didn't disappoint. They watched Disney characters from *The Little Mermaid, Tangled, Beauty and the Beast, Snow White,* and the newest addition, *Brave,* skate gloriously across the ice. The stories of these princesses were told with color, music, and dancing.

Paul allowed himself to get swept up in Kaitlyn's jubilation. Cindi's heart overflowed as she watched him. It was romantic—the kind of good old-fashioned romantic that comes when a family enjoys a night out together, children and adults alike. Cindi could not believe that she'd met a man who made both her and Kaitlyn happy. His kindness toward her daughter was another example of how atypical and how different from her stodgy husband he was. Despite being worth tens of millions of dollars, Richard would have never taken his family to Disney on Ice. To him, it would have been a colossal waste of time. "Silly" was how he would describe the mere thought of it.

Kaitlyn cheered through the entire show. Meanwhile, Cindi enjoyed being close to Paul. He held her hand, touched her arm, and leaned over to kiss her neck repeatedly. At first, she felt nervous about romantic displays of affection that took place in front of her daughter, but Kaitlyn was so engaged in watching the skaters that she didn't notice.

"I've been thinking about you. In fact, to tell you the truth, I can't stop thinking about you," he whispered to Cindi.

"Me, too," she whispered back.

"I have a great idea. Maybe we could get away somewhere. Just you and me. Venice, Paris ... anywhere you want," he said.

His offer was unexpected, and she didn't know how to answer.

"What about your work?" she asked.

He shrugged. "They can do without me for a week or two."

She glanced at Kaitlyn. Her attention was still directed completely on the show.

"What about Kaitlyn? And your kids?" Cindi asked.

"I have a lot of freedom because my ex has mine most of the time. As far as Kaitlyn's concerned, you don't think Richard could take her?"

"He has a demanding workload, so we stick pretty strictly to our visitation arrangement. Of course, he'd be fine if I took her anytime, but as far as his schedule's concerned, I can't suddenly ask him to take her for a week. I can probably check with Anne. But even if she could, I don't think I could be gone more than a long weekend," Cindi said. She was nervous Paul would take her answer as a sign of rejection.

"Okay, then we'll simply have to go somewhere romantic locally," he said.

Cindi was relieved that he understood her circumstances, which served to increase her attraction to him. After the performance, the three returned to Paul's car, all holding hands. On their drive home, Kaitlyn shared how she now wanted to become a Disney on Ice performer.

"But honey. You need lots and lots of practice first," Cindi said.

"Then how about ice-skating lessons?" Paul suggested.

Kaitlyn leaned forward between their seats. "Yes, yes, yes! Mommy, how about ice-skating lessons?"

"I think that's a great idea," she said.

"I know a great skating rink that offers high-quality lessons. The owner is a former Olympic bronze medalist. I'd be happy to take care of the lessons, if you'd let me," Paul said.

"Paul, I could *never* ask you to do that!"

"It would be my pleasure, Cindi. Please, allow me to take care of you and Kaitlyn," Paul said.

Anne's words flashed through her mind: *He's spending a lot of money. You can tell a lot about a man by the way he handles his finances.*

Ice-skating lessons required a significant financial and time commitment: transportation to and from lessons as well as the cost of skates, custom costumes, and travel. Cindi wondered whether she should be concerned with how freely he offered to pay for things.

Don't jump to conclusions. What's wrong with Paul being so generous? she asked herself. Besides, the way he proposed his offer was so gentle and loving that it nearly made her cry. She couldn't recall the last time she'd felt so cared for.

When they pulled onto Cindi's street, the palm trees swayed softly in the moonlight. Paul parked the Range Rover at the curb in front of her house.

"Allow me the privilege of walking you ladies to the door," he said. But when he and Cindi turned around, they saw Kaitlyn fast asleep in the backseat.

"Shhh," Paul said, placing his fingers lightly on Cinderella's lips. "I'll carry her in."

"That would be lovely," Cindi said. They walked up the sidewalk, Paul holding a sleeping Kaitlyn in his arms. Cindi couldn't help but notice how his muscles bulged underneath his shirtsleeves. She imagined caressing his strong biceps.

Cinderella unlocked the front door and tiptoed in. She showed Paul to Kaitlyn's room, and together they tucked her in bed. Cindi kissed her daughter on the nose, and Paul switched on the night-light. The two closed the door behind them and walked toward the living room.

Before they reached their destination, Paul began to nuzzle her neck. His scent and touch sent shivers through her body. Cindi bit her lip. She wanted his body close to hers *right now*. Yet she didn't like the idea of being with a man when her daughter was right next door.

"I don't have to stay if it makes you uncomfortable," Paul whispered. "But I would love to have a glass of wine with you before I leave."

"I'd love that. Unfortunately, my wine collection is pretty pathetic—I might have half a Dancing Bear in the fridge," she said.

"That works for me. But only if you want me to stay," he said.

"Of course! It's just that Kaitlyn ... she's right there," she said as she pointed to the room next door.

"I get it," he said.

They kissed as they made their way to the kitchen, and Cindi nearly bumped into a wall—she was so consumed with lust. His lips tasted of salty popcorn, which made her giggle.

Chapter 7

There was a half-full bottle of Dancing Bear in the fridge. She returned to the sofa with the wine and glasses, and Paul sat waiting for her. The top of his shirt was now unbuttoned, which left his beautiful chest in plain view. His jet-black hair was slightly tousled, his eyes glinting blue-green. She set down the glasses on the coffee table, and he filled them with wine. He raised his glass in a toast.

"To you ... to all the beauty you've already brought into my life and all the happiness you'll continue to bring," he said.

She took a long sip. His presence intoxicated her.

Paul gently placed his hand on her leg. His fingertips were like fire, shooting electricity up her leg and through her entire body. Pleasure swept across her thighs, awakening something deep inside her that had been dormant for too long.

He cupped her chin, gently pulling her face forward until it was mere inches from his own. He looked deeply into her eyes, and Cindi could have sworn she saw tears in his eyes.

"Oh, Cinderella. How I have longed for you," he said. He lifted her gently and walked toward the bedroom.

"Can you lock the door behind you—just in case Kaitlyn comes in?" Cindi whispered as they passed the bedroom's doorway.

Paul skillfully reached for the doorknob, carried out her request, and then made his way to the bed where he laid her down.

He kissed her, and she responded by grabbing his shirt and pulling him closer to her. They had kissed before, but tonight was different. His soft lips devoured her, as if he were starving. His name left her lips in a desperate groan.

Is this real? Could this be happening? She'd never experienced anything like it.

He kissed her lips, her throat, and the nape of her neck. His fingers traced the line of her collarbone as he slowly unbuttoned her blouse. After he worked his way down, he kissed the newly exposed flesh, moving slowly and then faster.

She was breathless with desire, trembling at his touch. By the time he had peeled off her shirt and jeans, her body was on fire. She pulled his shirt over his head and settled against his stomach. Cindi ran her fingers over his muscles and lingered when she reached his hipbones. She unfastened his belt, and helped him remove his clothes. Paul responded by placing his hands on her hips and his mouth all over her skin. Paul lifted her body, and she wrapped her legs around him. She leaned into him, melting in ecstasy.

"I love you, my Cinderella," he said.

"I love you, my prince," she told him.

They made love for hours.

Afterward, as they lay curled in each other's arms, they stayed up late talking, laughing, kissing, and snuggling. Cinderella and her Prince Charming's night of love was beyond anything she could have ever imagined.

"You are exquisite, absolutely beautiful in every way," Paul said. He had never felt so comfortable with anyone in his life. Cinderella was kind, loving, thoughtful, and beautiful. She filled a void inside him and gave him a sense of hope about romance that his ex-wife was never able to provide.

That night had been about more than just lovemaking. When Cindi spoke to Paul, she felt as though he was truly listening—the connection between them was honest and authentic. And when he looked into her eyes, she felt as though he adored her. He saw her frailty, her rawness, and her pain. She felt as if she had found a real partner, someone who made her feel worthy, beautiful, and loved.

He slept the remaining hours of the night on the couch. It was better that way for Kaitlyn, he told her. The whole experience had felt like a dream.

The next morning, she was awakened by a strange sound—the clanking of pots and pans. Confused and still half asleep, she threw a robe over her well-worn pajamas and trudged into her kitchen, rubbing her eyes and yawning.

Paul was at the stove frying eggs, and coffee was brewing next to the sink. The sun was already peeking in the windows, casting a cheerful light in the room.

"Mornin', darlin'!" he said, walking away from the skillet just long enough to give Cindi a sensual peck on the cheek. "Hope you like eggs over easy." He strutted through the kitchen wearing the pants he had worn to work yesterday and the purple shirt, which was now wrinkled and untucked. His hair looked deliciously messy.

God, he looks hot, she thought.

"I love eggs over easy," she said, afraid that, if she blinked, what she witnessed might disappear and she would wake up to a reality in which she was cold, alone, and without a handsome man making breakfast in her kitchen.

"Coffee?" he asked.

"Yes, please."

He placed a steaming mug in her hands. It was thick with cream and sugar— just the way she liked. She wondered how he knew this. She sniffed the air and realized she smelled something besides eggs—it was sweeter and more delectable.

"Is that ...?" she asked.

"Waffles. I thought you and Kaitlyn deserved a feast."

Cindi's jaw dropped. "I forgot I even had a waffle iron."

"You do. Took a while to find it, though, and it was a little dusty. This morning, I am treating you and Kaitlyn to a breakfast fit for queens and princesses."

Cindi couldn't believe that she'd met someone who was handsome, brilliant, funny, successful, and great with her daughter, and who made love to her like no one ever had.

Just then, Kaitlyn came flying out of her bedroom wearing her pajamas. She somersaulted onto the sofa that sat in the open room across from the kitchen.

"Waffles!" she cried, her voice muffled from the pile of pillows on the sofa. "Can I have some?"

"Your wish is my command," he said.

As he'd promised, he served up three piping-hot plates of golden waffles, perfectly cooked eggs, and warm syrup. He touched Kaitlyn's face as she stared gratefully at her plate.

Then he turned to Cindi. "You look beautiful," he said. She blushed, feeling a little self-conscious dressed in her frumpy pajamas and wearing no makeup. But to her Prince Charming, that morning she looked as sexy as she did when they first met at Vizcaya. He could make her feel beautiful and full of bliss.

Chapter 8

*T*heir night of lovemaking only strengthened their resolve to spend every opportunity they could together. Whether it was sharing a meal, taking long walks along the shore, or snuggling while watching videos with Kaitlyn, all that mattered was that they were a couple. They had long conversations in which they revealed their most intimate secrets with one another. Cinderella learned that even though Paul seemed confident and self-assured, his divorce had left him feeling like a failure. He shared that his ex-wife had not understood or loved him. Cinderella could relate to his insecurities and assured him that she would never betray him.

"I'm falling more deeply in love with you by the day," Paul told her, and she felt the same way. Yet for Cinderella, there was still something missing. His children were a big part of his life, and she was anxious to meet them. She was certain that Kaitlyn and his kids would get along well. But because his ex-wife had primary custody, the opportunity had not yet presented itself.

At the same time, she worried that his children would not like her as much as Kaitlyn cherished Paul. Overall, however, she was eager to blend her life with his as they sailed into a shared future together.

One night, Paul took her to a five-star restaurant. Their table overlooked the water, and they enjoyed their evening sipping vintage wine and enjoying a dinner of the area's finest seafood. Dates like these would cause her to worry about Paul's lavish spending—a habit that Anne continued to remind her best friend to observe. But it wasn't Cindi's style to confront, so she kept her concerns to herself.

Paul reached for her hand. "I've been doing a lot of thinking, and, if you're open to it, I'd like you to meet my children."

"I would love that," she said.

"Excellent. What about this Saturday? It's my weekend to have the kids," he said.

"Yes, that's perfect."

"Do you think your ex will be okay with this?" Cindi asked.

"I don't think it'll be a problem because Mal will have a busy weekend. She's headed out of town with her boyfriend on Friday," he said.

Mal was short for Maleficent—the nickname Paul had given his ex-wife. Her real name was Mallory. Paul said it was his own private joke when he called her Mal. She never knew what he really meant by it.

Paul told Cindi that Mal did not always make it easy for him to have an amicable relationship with their children, which made arranging visits with them difficult. Sometimes she wasn't there when he came by to get the kids, or she'd schedule activities for them when he was supposed to have them.

According to Paul, her behavior toward him had become worse lately— probably because she had figured out he was dating someone new.

Cinderella took a sip of wine. "What are we planning this weekend?"

"A celebration," he said.

"Oh? And what are we celebrating?" He lifted his glass. "Our children. You. Me. Us." He smiled. "All five of us."

"Sounds lovely. I couldn't be more excited."

"It makes me happy to hear it. Bring two towels, a bottle of sunscreen, and the lovely Miss Kaitlyn, and leave the rest up to me," he said.

"It sounds like a day in paradise."

"Funny you should say that," Paul said, "because our destination for the day is Paradise Beach."

On the day of their family get-together, Cinderella arrived early. The weather outside was glorious, and the beach lived up to its name—white sand and pristine water glistened as far as the eye could see. It was a private beach, and while it wasn't Paul's, it was owned by one of his firm's clients, and the practice's top lawyers had permission to use it. It was a small yet pristine swath of coastline—not littered with tourists and trash.

Cindi slathered Kaitlyn in sunscreen as they waited for Paul and his children. Kaitlyn wrinkled her nose. "I don't like the way this stuff smells," she said.

"But it smells like bananas," Cindi said.

"I don't like bananas, either."

"That's news to me." She finished rubbing in the lotion and wiped the remainder on a towel. "Is something bothering you?"

"I'm scared about meeting Daniel and Isabel. What if they don't like me? What if they think I'm weird?"

"Oh, honey—they're going to love you. Who wouldn't? Everyone else does! You're kind and smart and fun to be with. Now, don't you spend another minute worrying. We're going to have a wonderful day at the beach, all five of us," she said and kissed her daughter on the forehead.

Kaitlyn flashed her most optimistic, hopeful smile, and Cindi's heart melted. She, too, was scared about meeting Paul's children. Unfortunately, she had no one there to reassure *her* that everything was okay. What she did have was a small gift. She had bought Isabel and Daniel a kite—the perfect toy for a day at the beach, or so she thought. Kaitlyn had helped her pick it out at a toy store the day before.

Just then, Cinderella saw Paul's Range Rover pull up in the spot next to her Accord. In the back seat were two small heads. Cindi took a deep breath and turned to Kaitlyn.

"You ready?" she asked.

"Yes," Kaitlyn said, giving her mother a thumbs-up.

Paul politely greeted Cindi with a light kiss.

"Cinderella, I'd like you to meet my daughter, Bella, and my son, Danny. Kids, this is Cindi."

Cindi smiled brightly as the children stepped out of the car. They responded with silent stares. Bella, who was nine, looked Kaitlyn up and down.

"Who's she?" Bella asked.

"This is my daughter, Kaitlyn," Cindi said.

"How old are you?" Danny asked Kaitlyn.

"I'm seven," Kaitlyn answered.

"Huh." Danny wasn't impressed. "Well, I'm eleven."

"Kaitlyn has a lot of older friends, so even at your age, Danny, I think you'll enjoy playing together," Cindi said, eager to ease the tension.

"I'm confident he will," Paul said in a tone that meant *He'd better.* "Now, who wants to see Paradise Beach?" They followed Paul down the winding path that brought them to the shimmering ocean.

"I really hope you'll enjoy it," Paul said.

"Just being outside in the fresh air with you is wonderful. I don't see how I couldn't," Cinderella assured him.

Cindi laid out their towels under a large striped umbrella. While Danny and Bella were initially unfriendly, they decided to join Kaitlyn, who was already knee deep in the pristine water.

From the shelter of the umbrella, Paul and Cindi watched their children play.

"The divorce has been rough on them. They've had a difficult time understanding why Mal and I couldn't stay together. Then six months ago, I dated a woman they weren't too crazy about. They were really angry with me. Daniel, in particular, couldn't stand her. She had a little boy his age, and we thought they'd get along famously, but there was constant jealousy and conflict."

"I'm so sorry. That must have been really rough," Cindi said.

"To be honest, I wasn't in love with her, and she was more interested in getting married. Suffice it to say, dating and being a dad isn't as easy as I thought."

"Makes sense that they're a little hesitant. Thanks for being honest with me about that," she said. Despite her empathetic tone, inside her, anxiety escalated after hearing about the botched experience he had with his last girlfriend.

"Of course, leaving that relationship was the best decision I ever made because it brought me to you," he said. He lifted her hand to his lips and kissed it.

Cindi summoned the kids back to the tent for strawberries and pineapple slices. She had arranged them in little white containers and had even brought colored toothpicks for spearing. The children gobbled them up.

"You're so thoughtful and sweet. And this, after I told you that you didn't have to lift a finger," Paul said.

Cinderella basked in his praise. Then she unveiled the kite, presenting it to Danny and Bella.

Danny blinked. "What is it?"

"It's a kite, stupid. Sorry, sometimes he's a little slow," Bella said.

"I'm not stupid. *Kites* are stupid," Danny said.

"Daniel, don't be rude. Thank Cindi for her gift," Paul said.

"But they *are* stupid! They're for little kids," Danny said.

"What did I tell you in the car?" Paul asked.

"To ... to be respectful," Danny said.

"That's right. Now, apologize and thank Cindi for her gift."

"I'm sorry. Thank you for the gift," said Danny. Cindi heard the words, but they were completely unconvincing. Danny's anger hurt, but Cindi tried not to show it.

"That's okay. It's hard to know what kids are into these days," she said.

Meanwhile Bella was unraveling the kite. "This is cool. Thanks, Cinderella," Bella said.

The three kids wandered onto the dunes with Paul and Cindi close behind them. Paul kept looking at Cindi, shaking his head and smiling. She didn't understand. Finally, she felt compelled to ask.

"You keep looking at me so strangely. What is it?" she asked.

"You're an amazing woman. I feel so lucky, that's all."

She blushed. "It's just some fruit and a kite," she said, suddenly feeling very self-conscious. Her prince pecked her lightly on the cheek and tucked a strand of her hair behind her ear.

"No. *Not* just fruit and a kite. It's proof of your thoughtfulness. Every day I discover more about you that I love. I adore you, Cindi. I hope you know that."

Overwhelmed with emotion, she could only beam and nod.

Paul pointed to their children, who were gleefully unraveling the kite and watching it float softly on an invisible pillow of air.

"I think this is going rather well, don't you?" he asked.

"I think it's going better than I could have possibly imagined," Cindi said, trying to blink back the tears of happiness in her eyes.

"I'm sorry Daniel was such a jerk earlier," he said.

"Don't worry about it. I think boys are just different from girls, and I haven't had much experience with them," she said.

By the end of the day, all five of them were exhausted. They were slightly pink from the sun and blissfully tired. Bella had taken to Kaitlyn, and when Danny saw his sister embracing her, he had reluctantly followed suit. Once the kids climbed into their respective backseats, they fell asleep immediately.

"This was the best day," Cinderella said to Paul.

"I couldn't agree more," he replied, taking her into his arms and kissing her passionately.

She felt the salt in her hair, the wind on her tanned skin, and the warmth of his hard body against hers. She imagined making love with him, right then and there, on the beach with the warm waves lapping softly over them. Never mind if they got drenched when the tide came in; she would peel off his clothing and then kiss every inch of his muscled body. She shook herself back to reality. *This will have to wait. We have our kids to think about,* she reminded herself. He nibbled on her lip and then kissed her lightly on the nose before opening her car door for her.

"Will I see you tomorrow?" he asked.

"I wouldn't have it any other way," she said.

Chapter 9

For most of her life, Cinderella had awakened feeling vaguely disappointed that her dreams had come to an end. But now the alarm clock signaled the start of a day that was better than anything her subconscious could have created in her sleep. Everything with Paul felt so incredibly right—the way they connected emotionally, intellectually, and physically. Neither of them had ever experienced this sort of magic—not with their spouses or former girlfriends and boyfriends.

"Our time together is a gift. Let's not waste one precious moment of it," Paul said.

Sometimes, she looked at Paul, and her eyes welled up with tears. She couldn't believe he was in her life and that he loved her and she loved him. All her trials and tribulations had served a purpose. They had led her right to this man who stood before her. She was filled with gratitude and overcome with a happiness she had never known. Cinderella was confident that she'd found her prince.

Anne eventually warmed to Paul Francis as well. The three of them spent time together, and even Anne grew to appreciate Paul's warmth and charm.

One Sunday morning, Anne met Cindi at one of their favorite neighborhood bakeries for brunch. Paul had his children that weekend and was spending some time alone with them. Cindi had insisted that he do this. She believed that time alone with his kids would make them less likely to resent the new woman in his life.

"So glad to get some girl time with you. How are things going with Paul?" Anne asked.

"Couldn't be better. He just gets me. I really feel like he understands me in a way I never imagined was possible."

Anne reached out and squeezed her friend's hand.

"I'm so happy for you. You deserve this, Cin. You really do."

A broad smile spread over Cinderella's face.

"You do, too," said Cindi.

Anne was too beautiful to be alone. She had so much to offer someone, even though she never seemed to think of a man as a priority. Cindi and Paul had talked about setting Anne up with someone in his circle of friends, but so far the right guy hadn't come along.

"I'm convinced that if there's someone out there for me, he'll find me. I'm not worried," Anne said.

"You're the epitome of strength. And guess what? You'll be proud of me. I've been getting my finances in order, you know, just in case."

"Just in case *what*?"

"Oh, I don't know … in case I merge lives with a certain someone in the near future."

"Are there any plans?" asked Anne. Things had moved extremely fast between Cindi and Paul, and Anne was still a little wary.

"Oh, no. Nothing, really. I've just been thinking a lot about my own finances lately. I feel that I'm in pretty good shape. I own my own home, which not everyone can say, especially in today's economy. All my student loans are paid off—at least Richard did *something* to improve my life—and I'm not in debt. And you'll be happy to know I make a point of saving a portion of my income every year. Frankly, who wouldn't want to marry me? I'm a great catch!" Cindi laughed.

"You *are* a great catch, Cindi, and it's great to see you so happy. I haven't seen you this content in years," Anne said.

"It *is* great. Next, we have to find you your own Prince Charming!"

"If I find him, I'll consider it a big bonus. For now, I'm just enjoying living through you and your fairy tale. Paul really is a gorgeous guy, and he seems so genuinely sincere and nice."

"He really is. I could talk about him all day and night," she said.

Cindi reached for the jam and smeared it liberally on her toast. Then she dropped her knife with a clatter.

"I can't believe I forgot to tell you! I finally turned in a dozen design sketches to Andersen, my celebrity buyer, and he loves them. Absolutely loves them. He thinks I'll have an A-list celebrity buyer soon!"

"That's fantastic!" Anne said.

"If things go well, I might think about selling the house. Get a bigger place, you know, with a bigger room for Kaitlyn and extra rooms for Paul's children when they visit. Maybe even convert an extra bedroom or den into a design studio so I can work more easily from home. As it is right now, I've been using the sunroom, but it's so cramped in there. I was talking to Paul about it just last night. He didn't go for it—he said I didn't need to do that right now when he has a big house that accommodates all the children just fine. He also mentioned that maybe in the future, we could buy a larger house together. He thinks I should get a home equity loan and use that money to splurge on myself and Kaitlyn."

Anne arched one eyebrow. "What kind of splurges?"

"Oh, nothing big. Just some fun stuff, like Jet Skis. He's been taking the kids and me to the beach lately, and we have an absolute blast. But of course, we'd have more fun if we had Jet Skis."

"Sweetie, I'd be cautious of taking out an equity loan unless there's a real home improvement need or some financial emergency. That's a decision that has long-term implications."

"I shouldn't have said anything. I'm sure nothing will come of it. Castles in the sky and all. Paul would probably buy the Jet Skis himself if it wasn't for his alimony and child support obligations, law office overhead, as well as his own home. He makes great money, but he does have a lot of expenses."

Anne nodded. "I'm glad you and Paul are talking about this stuff. A lot of my clients don't discuss money with their partners, although I encourage them to talk about money issues before buying assets together or commingling the assets they already have—like if you and Paul were to buy Jet Skis."

Cindi looked at her friend closely. "You think it's frivolous, don't you?"

"Hey, whatever makes you happy. I think it's great that the lines of communication are open about money, especially regarding your assets and budgets. I always tell my female clients they need to be involved in the day-to-day management of their family's finances. Women tend to sit back and let the men handle financial matters."

"Well, we're not exactly a family yet!" Cindi exclaimed.

"You know what I mean. Honestly, I think it's better to discuss this stuff before you even *think* about getting married. That way, you're dating someone who has the same money values and philosophies as you. All the signs are there from the beginning. And it never works when a frugal person gets together with a spendthrift. There's always friction. You just have to be aware of the signs and know that certain things aren't good for you, no matter how beautifully they're packaged."

Cinderella felt deflated. Perhaps it was best not to mention to Anne that she and Paul had also discussed paying a contractor to do some home improvements on his house—renovations that would not be cheap. At the same time, she'd felt uneasy during both conversations because Paul was insistent on spending thousands of dollars on what essentially amounted to life-sized toys and unnecessary accouterments. But when Cindi loved someone, she did everything in her power to support his dreams. If this was all she had to worry about with Paul, she was lucky. After all, he was accustomed to spending a lot of money.

"Well, anyway, I just thought you'd be proud of me for practicing a little more financial savvy than I used to."

"Very proud. I knew if I nagged long enough, someday, it would rub off," Anne said.

They both laughed, feeling grateful for the other's friendship. Then Anne said, "I'm really happy for you, Cindi. It's wonderful to see you thriving, and I know Paul has had a lot to do with that."

"Yes, he has. And something tells me it only gets better from here on out," Cindi said.

"Just remember, sweetie, that everyone has flaws, even Paul," she said.

"Oh, I know. None of us is perfect, and we certainly have to deal with a lot of issues with his ex. But you have to admit, he's about as perfect as anyone we've ever known!"

Cindi didn't tell Anne that she went to the bank and obtained an equity loan so Paul could buy two Yamaha Jet Skis for the family. Somehow, she knew Anne wouldn't approve ... or understand. Cindi didn't think they needed such expensive equipment, either, and even suggested that they look on Craigslist for some used Jet Skis.

"You never really know what you're getting when you buy used stuff online," Paul said.

When Cindi suggested the cheaper alternative to new Jet Skis, Paul pouted—he didn't exactly argue or raise his voice, but he withdrew from her emotionally and physically. And after they discussed the equity line of credit, he barely kissed her goodnight and turned away from her in bed. This wasn't like him, and she hated it when he was distant.

Cindi decided that it wasn't worthwhile to argue over a silly pair of Jet Skis. As a result, she went along with Paul's plans to purchase brand-new ones. After they bought them, Cindi had to admit they were fun. Paul's mood brightened, and the children thoroughly enjoyed their new toys. The kids didn't bicker, and more important, Paul returned to being the adoring prince Cindi had met at the ball.

Chapter 10

Three months turned into four, and four months turned into five. Before Paul, Cinderella's life could have been described in bland shades of gray. But after meeting her Prince Charming, every day was brimming with vitality and energy, cast in a mosaic of bright, bold colors. Being in love was a powerful potion, unlike any other drug.

Cinderella felt as if she had known Paul much longer than five months. Before meeting him, she thought it would be impossible to get to know someone so well, so quickly. But things were different with Paul; he had given her a new perspective on life.

Even though both were busy with their respective jobs, they spent all their spare time with each other and their children and worked carefully to blend their two families. Despite the couple's intention to create a cohesive family, Paul seemed a bit uncomfortable, even nervous around his kids when Cindi was there. He was also constantly afraid he would accidently say something negative about their mother in front of them. He knew that, from his kids' perspectives, any critical words he expressed about his ex would make him the monster and Mal the innocent victim.

"It's horrible. My ex wants to sabotage whatever relationship I have with the kids. Last year, she told me that tickets to Bella's school play were sold out. Of course, that was a lie. And who ended up looking like the bad guy? Bella was so upset that I didn't show up. What was I supposed to say? It's not fair," he said.

"So what happened this time?" she asked. Cinderella empathized with him. She could see the hurt and frustration in his eyes. Paul recounted what had occurred when he went to pick up Daniel and Bella earlier that evening.

"They're my kids, too. But you wouldn't know it from the way Mal treats me. Today I got there at 5:30, and she yelled at me, telling me I was always late. I swear she told me 5:30, but she said no, it was 5:00. It's always like that with her. Changing the times and then telling me I'm late—that *I'm* the one screwing things up."

"Did the kids think you were coming at 5:00?" Cinderella asked.

"I have no idea. How am I supposed to know what she tells them? The fact is that I was there to pick them up like a good father, and Mal jumped down my throat. Then she goes and tells the kids I'm a bad dad—that I can't keep my word. She takes every opportunity to make me look like the bad guy."

It needled Cindi that he wouldn't give her a straight answer. Had he known he was supposed to pick them up at 5:00, or hadn't he? In her mind, it made a big difference.

Regardless of how she felt, she realized that the most important role she could play would be that of the supportive girlfriend.

"I'm sorry. I know how upsetting this is," she said.

"It's infuriating. I don't care in the slightest if she tries to hurt *me*. I'm a big boy, and I can take it. But what kills me is that she makes me out to be a terrible dad, which in the end only hurts them."

Danny appeared in the kitchen. He had apparently been eavesdropping from the hall.

"If you're talking about how you were late, we already know why. It's because you care about *her* more than us. Mom told us so." Danny glared at Cindi.

She cringed at the thought of being put in the middle of his and Mal's fights.

"Don't you know that you're more important to me than anything else in this world? You and Isabel. Please believe me when I say that," he said.

"Are you saying Mom is lying? Because she says you're the liar!"

"No, Danny, I'm not a liar, and I wouldn't say anything hurtful about your mother. You know that."

"Mom said that's what you'd say," Danny said before storming out of the kitchen.

"Oh, Paul," Cindi said, putting her hand gently on his arm. "I'm so sorry. Your kids don't deserve this, and you don't, either. We have to ignore her as best we can."

He shook his head as if trying to clear it of his memory of the horrible Maleficent. Then he looked at Cindi, and his face brightened.

"Thank God I have you—you outweigh all the hurt and pain she causes me."

"Exes can be horribly toxic. Believe me, I know," she said.

Cindi thought of everything Richard said that still haunted her. Out of nowhere, his words would often come back to her with startling force—snide comments about how she had gained a few pounds or how inept she was. During the divorce, he criticized her for not understanding the many legal documents that the court required them to sign and then used her ignorance to his advantage. He had his attorney make the legalese so dense and esoteric that Cinderella had to pay her lawyer additional fees to help her interpret it.

Paul and Cindi smiled at each other. It was a sad, knowing smile—one born from mutual experience. They had often exchanged divorce war stories, which made them feel closer. Paul told her that women who hadn't been through an ugly breakup would never be able to understand him the way she did.

"I'd never wish the horrors of my divorce on anyone. I'm so thankful that you understand where I'm coming from. I don't even have to explain it to you—you just know," he said.

Cindi hugged him, and his anger melted away. He knew that as long as they had each other, they could survive anything.

When Danny and Bella first arrived after being at their mother's, they were not very friendly. But the more time Cindi spent with them, the more they seemed to warm up to her—despite Mal's anger about Paul's new relationship. There was no question, however, that Kaitlyn adored Paul. They regularly played board games together and even painted, which was Kaitlyn's favorite patime.

Cindi had a hard time believing she had ever worried that her daughter might not like him. On the contrary, she adored him from the start even more so after their trip to Disney on Ice. Paul was the kind of father Cindi had hoped Richard would be. Whereas Richard had considered Kaitlyn to be exhausting, Paul treated her as though she was his own daughter—with respect, attention, love, and a healthy dose of overindulgence. And Kaitlyn wasn't the only one who benefitted from Paul's ability to shower the women in his life with affection.

Whenever Paul offered Cinderella candy or snacks, her initial reaction would be to say, "No thanks." She was concerned about junk food's effect on her thighs. Her rejection gave him an excuse to kiss her on the cheek and tell her how she was flawless—inside and out. She fondly recalled the time he told her, "You could gain five pounds or fifty—it wouldn't change how madly in love with you I am."

Their shared intimacy reached a point where they began to finish each other's sentences. She collected the love notes and poems he left or emailed her—messages that she would print and pin to the walls of her design studio. Tears filled her eyes when she read a recent one:

i carry your heart with me(i carry it in)
by E. E. Cummings

i carry your heart with me (i carry it in
my heart)i am never without it(anywhere
i go you go, my dear; and whatever is done
by only me is your doing my darling)
i fear
no fate(for you are my fate,my sweet)i want
no world(for beautiful you are my world, my true)
and it's you are whatever a moon has always meant
and whatever a sun will always sing is you
here is the deepest secret nobody knows
(here is the root of the root and the bud of the bud
and the sky of the sky of a tree called life; which grows
higher than soul can hope or mind can hide)
and this is the wonder that's keeping the stars apart
i carry your heart(i carry it in my heart)

All my love, Paul

After she dried her eyes, Cindi exploded with inspiration that prompted her to sketch a sumptuous, one-of-a-kind silver gown in a single four-hour stretch. As her romantic life blossomed, her creative life flourished as well. Could this be a sign that Paul was "the one"? *Yes*, her heart answered. *Yes! Yes! Yes!*

This was the man she'd been waiting for—someone who loved her and brought out the best in her. Although they had been dating for months, the sight of him caused a rush of butterflies to fill her stomach—a feeling as intense as the night they first met at Vizcaya. Recently, her thriving relationship even caused Anne to start talking about finding her "Mr. Right." In fact, it seemed as though all of Cindi's friends wanted to be like the perfect couple.

At the six-month point in their romance, Paul handed her a key to his beautiful home, which was located on a scenic canal. Cindi called it an estate, but Paul chose not to use such lofty designations to describe his home. There was no doubt in her mind, however, that it was indeed an estate—and a sprawling one at that. What else would you call a home with a master suite, two large bedrooms for his children, a guest room, four full baths, a media room, and a huge pool? It was a stunning replica of a small Spanish castle, complete with a large medieval wooden front door, a winding spiral staircase in the entry, and an iron gate surrounding the property. It was so impressive that it had even been featured in *Miami Homes* magazine.

The day after receiving a key to Paul's house, Cindi handed him a key to hers. The following Saturday, Paul secretly entered Cinderella's home. He planned an unforgettable evening.

On Saturday evening, Cinderella was attending a student art show at Kaitlyn's elementary school. Kaitlyn had two pieces of artwork on display, as well as a little bowl she had sculpted in pottery class. They had invited Paul to come along, but moments before he was supposed to pick them up, he called to say that he couldn't make it. He told them that something urgent had come up at work. Last-minute cancellations had become more common lately. Cindi tried not to take it personally; she reminded herself that he was a highly sought-after litigator. Still, his actions hurt Cinderella's feelings.

"Put Kaitlyn on the phone," he had said to Cindi earlier that evening.

Cindi tried to eavesdrop on the phone conversation. She edged closer to Kaitlyn, pretending to wipe the kitchen counter. Much to her chagrin, however, she could not hear a word.

Then a massive grin spread across Kaitlyn's face. She kept nodding and answering, "Okay, okay," and then burst into giggles. She finally hung up and handed the phone back to her mom.

"Paul says he's sorry he can't come tonight. But he thinks my pictures will be the best ones in the whole school," Kaitlyn said.

Cinderella knew Kaitlyn had a scrumptious secret and was dying to disclose what was on her mind. *What could he have told her? Maybe he'll show up after all,* she thought.

"That's it? Did he say anything else?" she asked.

"Yes ... maybe," Kaitlyn said.

Cindi could have easily convinced her daughter to divulge the details of their talk. Instead, she chose to embrace the conversation as an example of how they had their own relationship. She enjoyed imagining Paul as a father to her daughter. But if he were truly a big influence in Kaitlyn's life, why would he not be there tonight? Cindi's old insecurities surfaced during times like these. Richard's infidelity made her wary of everyone, even Paul. *There's nothing to fear, and I've got to stop jumping to conclusions. I'm sure there's no other woman in his life. Maybe it has something to do with Mal or the kids*, she thought to herself.

When Cindi and Kaitlyn arrived at the art show, Anne was there waiting for them. Cinderella's best friend initially expressed surprise that Paul hadn't come but then did her best to reassure Cindi.

"Don't worry, sweetie. He's probably got a big case or something else important going on. I'm sure he's just as upset as you that he couldn't make it," she said.

"You're right. It just seems so odd, and I can't help but wonder what happened," Cindi said.

"I wouldn't overthink it," Anne said.

Despite Paul's disappointing absence, Cindi and Kaitlyn enjoyed their evening. Cinderella was impressed by her daughter's talent and proud that she'd inherited her mom's creativity. The two arrived home after the student art show. As Cindi slid her key in the lock, she noticed that the door had not been locked. She immediately felt anxious.

Did someone break in? she asked herself.

When Kaitlyn noticed that the door was unlocked, she smiled. This made Cindi realize that her daughter knew something she didn't. She pushed the door open and was immediately serenaded with "Forget Me Not" by Joy Williams and John Paul White, the duo of The Civil Wars, playing quietly in the background. It was her favorite and one she had played for Paul several times.

I've been awaiting for you
And you've been awaiting for me
Tell me that you'll always be true
And you'll be the only one for me
Forget me not my dear, my darling
Forget me not, my love

Cindi gingerly stepped inside and saw tea lights at her feet and cascading down the stairs. The light was soft and magical—like a thousand stars twinkling throughout the room.

As she made her way through her house, she finally saw him: her Knight in Shining Armor. Paul was standing at the end of her foyer, dressed in an exquisite Brioni suit. His chiseled face was full of hope and expectation. She melted as relief washed over her like a tropical wave.

"Hello, my beautiful ladies," he said, bowing slightly.

Kaitlyn ran to him and wrapped her arms around his waist.

"This was the hardest secret I've ever kept!" Kaitlyn said.

"You did a perfect job," Paul told her.

Cindi was overwhelmed. She had no idea what was taking place. Paul held out his hand to Cinderella and pulled her toward him.

"I ... I ... thought you were busy with work," Cindi said.

"Never mind that. Come with me, my love." He led her up the stairway to the second floor.

"Do you trust me?" he whispered.

"Completely," she replied.

"Then close your eyes."

When they made it to the second floor, he kissed her ear. Her knees were about to buckle.

"Open your eyes," he whispered.

She looked down and saw that the tea lights were arranged in the shape of a message:

Will you marry me?

Kaitlyn was standing beside her and giggled with delight. Paul dropped to one knee and held out a tiny black velvet box in his right hand. He opened it, exposing the largest radiant-cut diamond Cindi had ever seen. He then read her a poem by Elizabeth Barrett Browning:

I love you, not only for what you are,
But for what I am when I am with you.
I love you, not only for what you have made of yourself,
But for what you are making of me.
I love you for the part of me that you bring out;
I love you for putting your hand into my heaped-up heart
And passing over any foolish, weak things
You can't help but dimly see there...
And for drawing out into the light all the beautiful belongings
That no one else had looked quite far enough to find.
I love you because you have done more
Than any creed could have done to make me good,
And more than any fate could have done to make me happy.
You have done it...
Without a touch,
Without a word,
Without a sign.
You have done it by being yourself.
I am yours forever...

Paul paused to wipe a tear from Cindi's cheek and then continued, "You have made me the happiest man in the world. You and Kaitlyn are part of me, and I want to be with you always. Will you marry me, Cinderella?"

Her hands trembled as she slipped the ring on her finger. It fit perfectly.

"Oh, my goodness! It's just beautiful," she said.

"Only the best for you, my darling. So will you marry me?"

He seemed uncertain what Cindi's reaction would be. Meanwhile, Cindi wanted nothing more than to be his wife.

She cupped his face in her hands and leaned down to kiss him. Disbelief and desire overtook her ability to speak.

"Yes," she said, her voice trembling. "Oh, yes."

Chapter 11

"A nne," said Cinderella, "can you meet for coffee this afternoon? I really
need to see you."

"Is everything okay?" Anne asked.

"Everything's perfect," Cindi said.

"Then what is it?" she asked.

"I can't wait to tell you, but I need to share my news in person. It'll be worth
the wait, I promise," Cindi said.

"I can meet after lunch around 2:30," Anne said.

"Great.

How's Starbucks by your office?" she asked.

"Sounds like a plan. But you know it's torture to leave me hanging like this,"
Anne said.

After they wrapped up their conversation, Cindi sat silently in her kitchen,
gazing at the diamond ring on her finger. Kaitlyn had left an hour ago to spend the
day with her friends, and Paul was at the gym.

Cindi wasn't used to receiving such lavish gifts. In fact, Richard hadn't bought her a diamond ring when they married. "It's a total waste of money," he told her and gave her a modest gold wedding band instead. But now, resting on her finger was a breathtaking three-carat, Harry Winston, radiant-cut center diamond with sparking round cut diamonds covering the band, which added brilliance to the custom design. Cindi knew a little about precious gemstones because, in the fashion world, celebrities were always accessorizing their haute couture clothing with designer jewelry. She surmised that the ring must have cost tens of thousands of dollars, and for a moment, the thought overwhelmed her—particularly because she knew he was paying a significant amount every month in spousal and child support. But she shrugged off any guilty feelings by reminding herself that he was a successful litigator.

When Cindi first walked into the kitchen that morning, she found a pot of freshly brewed coffee on the counter and a sweet handwritten poem by her very own Prince Charming tucked inside her favorite mug. In addition to finding the most fitting poems for her, he was also a poet in his own right.

> *You are the sunlight in my life*
> *that warms my heart and soul*
> *with eternal love.*
> *My love always, Paul*

Part of her was still convinced that the past few months had been some sort of prolonged dream—one that she'd wake from at any moment. At the same time, she couldn't deny that what had unfolded was real. It was a life that she previously thought only existed in romantic movies and fairy tales.

After Paul proposed, they toasted their engagement by drinking Cristal and nibbling on chocolate-dipped strawberries. Kaitlyn joined the festivities with a glass of sparkling grape juice. Kaitlyn felt an immense sense of grown-up pride, knowing she'd been part of Paul's secret plan to propose.

For Cindi, the evening had been perfect in every way. She was brimming with a happiness she had not felt since Kaitlyn had been born. When her daughter finally went to bed, Paul escorted Cindi to her bedroom. The silvery light of a full moon accompanied them as they made their way through the house. Now that they were engaged, she was not worried about how Kaitlyn would feel if he spent the night. They were husband and wife-to-be, after all.

Once in her bedroom, they held each other close, and their bodies melted into one as though they were carved from the same piece of clay. There was a passion between them that she'd never experienced before. Their lovemaking was slow, tantalizingly so, and their yearning for each other grew stronger as each moment passed. He slowly and gently kissed her hair, her neck, and her ears, making his way down her velvety body and ending at her toes—his tongue smooth on her skin. His fingers ran up and down her arm, sending shivers through her before he gently caressed each breast. "I can feel your heart beating," he told her. Cindi was convinced that Paul was what she had been missing all her life—her other half.

Their legs intertwined, and their arms clasped one another as if their lives depended on it. *God help me,* she thought. She thought she would never get enough of him. Ever. Marriage was next; it was exhilarating to think that she would experience lovemaking like this every day of her life.

After they made love, they rested in each other's embrace. Paul fell asleep first, and Cinderella gazed at her lover's chiseled face. He was beautiful in every way. "Who are you, and where did you come from, Paul Francis?" Cinderella whispered as he lay sleeping.

It was always in the quiet darkness that Cinderella pondered questions about his past. Yes, she knew about his ex-wife and children and about his stressful job as a litigator, but part of him remained a mystery.

Throughout the last few months, she repeatedly witnessed that as soon as he was on the verge of disclosing an intimate detail about himself, he would abruptly change course. *Is he hiding something?* she wondered. At the same time, she reminded herself that he *was not Richard.*

That afternoon, Cindi met Anne at Starbuck's. Anne sat waiting for her wearing big designer sunglasses, sipping a latte, and reading one of her financial-planning periodicals.

"Hi, Anne! Thanks for carving out time to meet," Cindi said.

"I was glad you called.

It's so beautiful outside that I didn't feel like catching up on work today," Anne said.

After greeting her friend, Cindi approached the counter and placed her order—a simple mocha latte. She returned to the table with her steamy drink.

"So what's the big news? I'm dying to know," Anne said.

"You know how I was upset that Paul didn't show up last night?" Cindi asked.

"I was going to follow up about that. Did you talk to him afterward? By the way, the show was great. Our little prodigy is so talented! Thanks for inviting me."

"Glad you could make it. You know, Kaitlyn thinks of you as her auntie," Cindi said.

"I wouldn't have missed it for the world. So what happened with Paul?" Anne asked.

"That's the reason I wanted to meet with you right away," Cindi said. She then planted her palm at the center of the table. The sunlight shone on the diamond, shooting sparkles that nearly blinded her best friend.

"Oh my God! He didn't ...," Anne gasped.

"Yes, he did! He popped the question last night. That's why he didn't come to the art show. He was at my house, preparing to propose!"

Anne held her best friend's hand in hers and admired the diamond—its facets reflecting a hypnotic light.

"I know what you're thinking: It too fast. But honestly, I feel like I've known him forever."

"Honey, I'm so excited for you! But you're right. I'm in shock right now. It seems like you just met him yesterday."

"I know, but if you think about it, we've actually been together almost every day for six months. And you know how it is at our age—we know much faster when it's the right guy," Cindi said.

"So have you set a date?" Anne asked.

"Not yet. But Paul said he wanted to do it soon. We haven't really talked about any of the details. I mean, it just happened last night, after all," Cindi said.

"I've gotta ask this because she's my number one—does Kaitlyn know yet?"

"She was actually in on the proposal plans. It was their secret. She's crazy about Paul and can't wait to have him as a stepdad," she said.

Cinderella described the evening in full detail: the music, the lights, the champagne, the passionate sex, and the love poem Paul left for her on the kitchen countertop. Anne followed her every word. It sounded perfect. Almost too perfect for Anne's taste. But she said nothing to hamper her best friend's spirits. Not today, at least.

"Are you going to have a big wedding?" Anne asked.

"To be honest, I haven't thought that far ahead yet," said Cindi. "But right now, I think the answer is no. Between his child support, alimony, and mortgage, Paul has a lot of expenses, and as you know, I'm just getting by. Paul did say that he wanted to get married soon, but that was it. If it were up to me, I'd just go to the justice of the peace at the county courthouse and follow it up with a nice honeymoon in New York or something—Manhattan in the autumn ... breathtaking!"

"I agree. I doubt if I'd want a big wedding the second time around, either. You had a nice one with Richard, and although he paid for most of it, it did cost your parents a lot of money," Anne said.

"And I've often regretted that I let my mom and dad spend so much money. It seems like such a big waste now.

God, I wish they were still here," Cindi said. Cindi's parents had died several years ago—her mother from cancer and her father of a broken heart. An only child, Cindi had felt like an orphan after their passing. Their deaths left her numb and empty.

Cindi had inherited the family home and money from their small savings. She sold the house and, then, after paying their remaining debts, invested most of the money in a college fund for Kaitlyn. As for the remaining cash, she used it to start her fashion-design business. The funds couldn't have come at a better time because Richard thought the idea of her business was silly and refused to invest any of his money in it. Richard never believed in her business and always wanted her to be a stay-at-home mom. Paul, on the other hand, thought it was wonderful. In fact, it seemed to him that everything about her was perfect: her talent, her drive, her looks, and Kaitlyn.

Unfortunately, her business wasn't exactly thriving, but she still managed to earn a decent living and was hopeful that she would see an uptick in profits now that she felt inspired to create beautiful designs again. She was certain that both of her parents would be proud of what she had accomplished, which made her miss them even more.

"Your parents were great. Your mom was so much like mine," Anne said. She appreciated how Cindi's mom and dad had welcomed Anne into their family. "Do you think your mom would have liked Paul?" she asked.

"Yes. First and foremost, I think she would have been enamored by his good looks—who *wouldn't* think he's handsome? But Mom was also a good judge of character. Paul's a little flashy, and I'm not sure she would have liked that—you know, the big home, the expensive car, fancy restaurants, and his lifestyle in general."

"You're right, he is quite flashy. But, it's part of his style. And everyone loves Paul—even I warmed up to him. Well, here's to you and your Prince Charming!" said Anne, holding up her cup in a toast.

"Thank you!" said Cindi. The two clinked their lattes. "By the way, I'm assuming you'll be my maid of honor."

"Of course, I will. Just tell me the time and date, and I'll be there," said Anne. Despite any misgivings she had about their marriage, Anne wanted to be a supportive best friend.

That night, Cinderella made lasagna for dinner. Paul had called her and told her he would be over around 7:00 p.m.—it had been a long day at the office, and he looked forward to enjoying a relaxing meal at home.

Considering all his work stress, Cindi wanted to prepare something extra special and decided on her mother's lasagna. It was always a big hit. She thought that perhaps tonight they could set a date and discuss plans for the wedding. Kaitlyn had begged to spend the night with her best friend, Arielle, and Cindi had agreed, knowing it would give her and Paul time alone to do some preliminary wedding planning.

Paul brought over a bottle of Dancing Bear red wine since he knew it was Cindi's favorite. It came from a well-known winery in Napa Valley. Cindi had been partial to it ever since she first sampled it at a food and wine festival.

The moment Paul arrived at Cindi's home, he wrapped his strong arms around Cindi and hugged her from behind.

"Honey, I'm home," he said as he nibbled her neck.

She leaned into him and sighed. "That has a nice ring to it," she said.

"And now that you're going to be Mrs. Paul Francis, you're going to have to get used to it," said Paul.

"Mrs. Paul Francis—that sounds even better!" said Cindi.

"I've missed you all day, love," Paul said.

"Me, too. Did you have a good day at work?" she asked.

"Yeah. I was able to get a lot of work done because it was quiet," he said.

"Glad to hear it," said Cindi. "Oh, and I love the poem you left me this morning. You're a good writer, you know," she said.

He shrugged his shoulders. "When someone inspires me, I just write what's in my heart."

"It's so romantic! You're a man of many talents," she said.

"You're not too bad yourself, gorgeous. Hey, something smells wonderful ... What is it?"

"Lasagna. Completely from scratch. My mother's recipe."

"You certainly know the way to a man's heart. Why haven't you made this before?" he asked.

"Well, we've been busy, and it takes forever. But, if lasagna is all it takes, then I'm going to be in your heart a lot!"

"Love, you're already in my heart. But, I've got to admit, the lasagna is a huge bonus. Here, this wine should go perfect with dinner," he said. "Where's Kaitlyn?"

"She's spending the night with a friend. And yes, the Dancing Bear is perfect. Guess it's just you and me tonight," she said.

"Ah, perfect," he said. "We need to talk tonight anyway."

"About what?"

"We should discuss our wedding."

"I was just talking to Anne about it today," Cindi said.

"What did she say?" he asked.

"She's very happy for us. In fact, I think she might be a little jealous, but not in a mean way," she said.

"She shouldn't be. She's stunning and shouldn't have any trouble finding someone great," he said.

"For her, it's finding the *right* one that's the tough part. She's extremely independent, and not many men measure up. But she thinks you're special," added Cindi.

"I'm glad she approves," he said, laughing.

Tonight was their first dinner together as an engaged couple—the first of many more special evenings to come, Cindi hoped. Paul poured each of them a glass of wine, and Cindi set the food on the table. She lit candles for their special dinner and turned on the music they had listened to last night. She would love that music forever.

The lasagna was hearty, with spinach tucked between layers of pasta and rich cheeses. Cindi served it with a tossed salad and crusty French bread. Paul loved everything.

"My God! I didn't know you could cook like this. You've been keeping secrets from me!" he said.

"I don't have secrets from you, silly! And I don't have many dishes that I cook very well, but this is one of them," Cindi said. In contrast to Paul's hearty appetite, she had held back on eating—her nerves served as an appetite suppressant. But she managed to sip on her wine. The wedding made her anxious. Part of her was worried that he might renege on his proposal. *God, I'm so insecure*, she thought to herself.

"I guess the first thing we should decide is *when* to get married," Cindi said. "Do you want to wait until the springtime since it's already fall and the holidays are around the corner? That would give us a few months to plan everything."

"Spring seems so far away. I'd like to get married right away. An autumn wedding could be nice," he said.

"I ... I think autumn could be nice, but I was just thinking we might need some time to plan."

"What about next month?" asked Paul.

"Wow! That's so soon! But, I guess it could work. After all, the kids will be on fall break, so we could do it then. We definitely don't have to have a big wedding. In fact, I was thinking we could just go to the courthouse and then have a party with the kids and our best friends. Maybe take a quick trip to New York for a honeymoon." She stopped all of a sudden. "Sorry," she said, "I didn't mean to ramble like that."

"You're not rambling, and sure, we could do all that. But I was thinking of something a bit more romantic," he said.

"What do you mean?" asked Cindi.

"How about Italy? A destination wedding," said Paul.

"Italy?" Cindi's mouth dropped. "Italy?" she said again.

"It's romantic, love."

"I've never been. I have a passport—I hope it hasn't expired. Italy does sound romantic. I've always wanted to go there. Have you been?"

"A few times. I think you'd love it. Artistic people love Italy," he said.

"But wouldn't it be expensive?"

"It's our wedding, and what's money when two people are in love? I think we owe it to ourselves to go somewhere really special and stay in a magnificent hotel," he said.

"One thing I'm worried about is that I'm not sure any of my friends could afford it. Of course, Anne could, and she'd go, but what about our kids?" Cindi asked.

"Well, I was thinking about just us ... you know, eloping. Just the two of us—and some nice Italian villagers standing up for us—and then after our honeymoon in Europe, coming back home and having a party with our families and friends," said Paul.

Cindi's mind was swirling. *A wedding in Italy? A honeymoon in Europe? A luxurious hotel!* At the same time, she heard Anne's voice inside her head, which made her think of the enormous expense of such a romantic wedding.

And yet, it sounded deliriously like a fairy tale. And so it was settled. Paul and Cinderella would go to Italy and get married in the fall. Afterward, they would honeymoon in Tuscany and maybe even spend a few days in Paris.

After dinner, they loaded the dishwasher and then retired to the living room. They curled up on the sofa and talked about their wedding.

Our wedding, Cindy thought. She loved the sound of that. In fact, she loved the sound of Paul's voice. Everything he said seemed so magical.

She was trembling as she woke up. She must have had another nightmare. At first, she did not know where she was, and then she saw Paul beside her. She instantly felt calm. *Everything's going to be okay. Paul's right here,* she told herself. He was the love of her life, and likewise, she was his. They were going to have an amazing wedding and a beautiful marriage.

Chapter 12

*T*he next day, Cinderella was working in her design studio, but she was too excited to focus. She had a wedding to plan, after all. With the wedding date set, time was running out, and she needed help. She called Anne, and they met at Las Palmas after work over margaritas.

"You're going to get married in Italy *next month?*" she asked, her mouth open wide in astonishment.

"Yes, and I know there's not much time to spare, but I need your help—if you're willing, of course," Cindi said.

"You know that you can always count on me. I just don't know what the big hurry is. If you waited until spring, you'd have much more time to plan," Anne said.

"I know, but Paul insisted that we get married next month. I'm actually kind of flattered that he doesn't want to wait. And did I tell you that he writes me the most beautiful poems?"

"You've mentioned it a couple of times," said Anne in a worried tone.

"He's just wonderful. To tell you the truth, I'm just as eager as he is to get married quickly."

"He's totally smitten with you, so I bet he'd wait forever if he had to. I'm really happy for you," said Anne.

Cindi licked the salt off the rim of her margarita. "We haven't even talked about our bank accounts or whether he'll move into my house or I'll relocate to his," she said.

"Well, his house is much bigger, isn't it?" asked Anne.

"Yes, but I'm not sure it's big enough for *all* of us. I guess we'll talk about that this week," Cindi said.

"Has he told his kids?" asked Anne.

"No. He has them this weekend and plans to do it then. I'm actually kind of worried about it. What if they don't approve? Their reactions are very unpredictable; they seem to like us one minute, and the next they're angry and withdrawn," said Cindi.

"How could they *not* like you? You and Kaitlyn are great, and you're very good to them," Anne said.

"It's their mother, Mal. I think she interferes with my relationship with Paul. Every time the kids come back, it seems as though she's turned them against us ... or at least that's what Paul seems to think. So I have no idea how they're going to react when they hear we're getting married."

"Maybe they'll accept you more easily now that you're marrying their father. They may have seen you as temporary before. And perhaps that's why Paul wants to go ahead and get married quickly," said Anne.

"It's possible, I guess. Sometimes, they act as if they like us, and then other times, they're just plain disrespectful. Especially Daniel."

"Well, I wouldn't worry about them right now because you've—no, *we've*—got a wedding to plan," Anne said.

"I don't know where to start. I can't even think straight!" Cindi said.

"But first things first. You know I wouldn't let my best friend get married without asking if you've discussed finances with your fiancé," Anne said.

"Honestly, whenever I mention money, he skirts the issue. He seems to have a lot of it. I don't think he'd want to get married in Italy if he had serious money problems, would you?" Cindi asked.

"That's just it. If he's not openly discussing bank accounts, his savings, his credit history, and things like that, it could mean that he's hiding something."

"I'm sure everything's okay. He's a litigator, and he makes good money. I think you and I are just used to how Richard was so secretive and cheap. Paul's completely different. He actually enjoys his money," Cindi said.

"Now that you're getting married, you should be creating short-term and long-term financial goals. Has he ever developed a financial plan or a budget? Or shared credit reports with you? Talking about goals will give you insight into the kind of man you're dealing with. He doesn't seem to be living within his means. I don't think anyone should marry a man who doesn't have a plan because, sooner or later, you'll find out that if he's not going anywhere, you won't be, either. And it's totally okay to discuss these things. You're just protecting yourself."

"We'll do that ... later!" Cindi said. At this point, she knew there was no way she was going to confess to Anne that she had agreed to take out an equity line of credit to buy Jet Skis.

"I know Paul seems wealthy, but sometimes that's just a façade. You said yourself that he has a flashy lifestyle."

"Yes, he is a bit flashy. But I like it. He lets me relax and enjoy myself instead of worrying about every penny I spend. For once, when I go into a restaurant, I don't look at the prices on the menu. It's so liberating! Do you really think he's hiding something, Anne?"

"I'm just thinking of you, Cindi. I don't want you to be blindsided with some major debt that you don't know about. After all, you haven't known him very long."

"Well, I did Google him," said Cindi.

"And what did you find?" Anne asked.

"Not much. He has a Facebook page, but he only has a few friends. Most of them are women, and very attractive ones at that. But that doesn't surprise me. I think he's had lots of girlfriends, although we don't really talk about his dating history."

"Well, you have a dating past, too. Does he ever ask you about your ex-boyfriends?"

"No, not really. Besides, I don't have anyone in my past who's very important. Richard is the only one we ever discuss. And his ex-wife is the only woman he ever talks about."

"What else did you find out?" asked Anne.

"A few articles about some of his legal cases. But nothing about him personally," said Cindi.

"He just seems too good to be true. Don't get me wrong—I'm ecstatic for you, and I like Paul a lot. I do. But here he is, this gorgeous guy who's rich and seems to have a great personality, and you've never even had a fight, have you?"

"No, we haven't. There have been a couple of times when he seemed to be short and was quickly irritated with me, like, if I questioned him too much about his ex-wife or his family or something, but he's never yelled at me or anything like that."

Cindi thought briefly about Paul's sullenness and how withdrawn he could become. For instance, she recalled his reaction when she first refused to take out an equity loan to buy the Jet Skis. But she didn't say anything to Anne about it. Some things just needed to be kept between Paul and her. *And that was just a one-time thing, anyway. He's been nothing but wonderful ever since*, she told herself.

"My parents still fight, and they're crazy about each other. I just question it when couples don't argue. That's all," Anne said.

"Neither of us has ever met someone who was our Prince Charming. But it does happen. I've heard stories about others who fell in love, and everything was perfect. Maybe I'm one of those people. It's as if I won the lottery or something."

"I just worry. You know I'm looking out for you. I'd really encourage you to have a money talk with Paul before you get married. You're joining your lives together, so I think it'd be good for both of you," Anne said.

"I know you're right," said Cindi.

"You don't even know if he has credit-card debt, how much he owes on his house, or things like that. And by all means, you should consider a prenuptial agreement."

"You can't be serious. I don't have enough to warrant having one of those," Cindi said.

"You have more assets than you think: You own your home and have a sizable savings and an account earmarked for Kaitlyn's college education. But more importantly, the subject of the prenup will facilitate a frank discussion regarding each of your financial situations. I can't stress enough the importance of full disclosure," Anne said.

Anne described additional advantages of a prenuptial agreement or at least the benefits of having a talk about one. It provided a framework for how to organize a family's finances, it insulated each partner from the other's debts, and it defined property that belonged to each person prior to marriage, which could protect claims on assets that should pass to children from previous marriages. Further, Cindi had her own business, and the agreement would protect her ownership should the marriage not work. Since more than half of marriages ended, she needed to be realistic about protecting Kaitlyn and herself.

"Honestly, I love Paul, and I trust him. I'm not worried in the least about *my* assets. It might be different if I had millions, but I don't. And just because we haven't talked about our finances doesn't mean he's hiding anything," Cindi said. Her tone took a defensive turn, and Anne knew it.

"I didn't mean to offend you. I'm just looking out for you. You haven't known him very long, and you haven't discussed these issues at all. It just pays to be cautious," Anne said.

"You know I appreciate you. But you don't have to worry about me. Right now, I just need you to help me get this wedding planned," Cindi said.

"Got it. You know I really like Paul. I'm rooting for him for your sake, and I'm going to stop pressuring you about the finances and trust your judgment. Just know that I'm available if you ever need to talk about it. So tell me, where in Italy will the big event take place?" Anne asked. She decided to drop the money talk and bask in her friend's happiness. She didn't want to be thought of as "gloom and doom Anne."

"A small historical church located on the most spectacular vineyard in Tuscany," Cindi said.

"Oh, wow! And are you designing your own wedding gown?" Anne asked.

"Yes, it's one I've been working on for a long time in the unlikely event that I ever found someone to marry. I brought some sketches to show you."

"Oh, I can't wait to see them!" Anne said. She sipped on her margarita and listened to Cindi's animated voice as she talked about her wedding plans, Italy, her dress, and the honeymoon. Cindi showed her sketch of a soft, ethereal wedding gown that was simple yet elegant. The design would perfectly highlight Cindi's long blond hair and blue eyes.

Anne hoped everything would work out for her best friend, but she was skeptical. To her, Paul seemed *too* perfect. *What was he hiding?* At the same time, she questioned whether she was just jaded. Maybe she had been single too long and had forgotten how to abandon herself to passion and love. Goodness knows, she was a workaholic and seldom took time to even go out on a date, much less fall in love.

I should learn to mind my own business, Anne thought.

But Anne had seen enough financial problems with couples to know that marriages today weren't as they were when her parents merged households. She considered how a few decades ago, couples combined their net worth as soon as they traded "I dos." Nowadays, however, it was not so simple. In fact, roughly half of married people had individual accounts. She thought that was smart.

In addition, Anne often counseled clients who were getting married and advised them to have a personal account for day-to-day spending. That way, neither spouse felt as though he or she had to ask permission to buy something personal. She also recommended that couples should establish a joint checking account for household expenses, such as groceries, utilities, and mortgage or rent. As far as big-ticket items were concerned—such as vacations or a new car—it was good to have a joint savings or investment account.

The bottom line was that, no matter what, it was important for Cindi and Paul to have a thorough financial discussion. But that was their business, not hers. From now on, Anne decided she would censor her opinions on Paul's lavish spending because she knew that it was beginning to make her best friend uncomfortable and defensive.

For a moment, Anne wondered if she should plan on secretly placing her favorite book on financial planning into Cindi's airplane carry-on. *Would that be a little pushy? Yes*, Anne decided. Regardless, she felt that her friend was heading for trouble, so she was resolved to carry out her secret plan.

Now that she had decided to stop dispensing her expert advice, Anne needed to concentrate on helping her best friend plan her wedding. And she had to find something perfect for Cindi: something old, something new, something borrowed, and something blue.

Chapter 13

Four weeks had passed, and Paul and Cindi were on their way to Italy to get married. The first-class flight was as opulent and comfortable as Cindi had imagined. "The only way to fly," Paul said when he presented her with the tickets.

They flew into Florence and then drove their rental car to the centuries-old Castello di Barone Ricasoli and vineyard in Tuscany. It was the oldest winery in Italy, and from the brochures, Cindi knew it would be magnificent.

Based on her initial observation, she was convinced that Tuscany had to have been where romance was born. From its rolling hills covered with olive trees and grapevines and its bright yellow fields of sunflowers to its inviting villages with cobblestone streets, the region was the perfect place for them.

The Castello di Barone Ricasoli was a little over an hour from the airport in Florence. The Barone Ricasoli family had invented the famous Chianti Classico. In fact, the name *Ricasoli* has been linked to wine since 1141, when Brolio Castle passed into the hands of the Ricasoli family.

An ethereal mist floated above the hills like gossamer wings. The sun had finally risen from behind Monte Amiata and cleared the countryside as Cindi and Paul drove deep into the green hills in Maremma—the heart of Tuscany—before they reached the castle. Once they pulled up to the castle grounds, they were greeted with lemon, olive, and pear trees that had been cultivated since Roman times. It was October, and the trees blazed with shimmering golds and reds.

Cindi first caught a glimpse of the Castello di Barone Ricasoli as they drove their rented Mercedes up the hill, and it took her breath away. The castle was a medieval structure dating back to 1141. The grand building had suffered attacks in historic battles from the fifteenth to the seventeenth centuries up until the bombings during World War II. Sitting atop a mighty hill, the castle lorded over the 240 hectares of vineyards and olive groves, which was the largest in the Chianti region. It was a timeless beauty with ancient roots and a rich history.

Paul told her he had always wanted to visit the castle and stay in the villa guest house. Cindi assumed he had toured this area with his ex-wife or a previous girlfriend, but she didn't question him.

"Oh, my! This place is exquisite," she said.

"Just wait until you see the guest house. It's not as huge as the castle, of course, but we have our own private place here, and that's where we'll spend our first honeymoon nights. Very romantic."

"Oh my gosh, Paul, I agree. This is so perfect!" she exclaimed.

The past month had been a whirlwind for Cindi, Paul, and Anne. Cindi's best friend had been a lifesaver when it came to planning the details of their trip and wedding abroad. Cindi would never have been able to do it without her.

Paul told his children about their wedding plans. Daniel and Isabella had been excited at first—that is, until they told their mother. Once the kids shared it with Mal, they had come back to Cindi's house sullen and difficult. Cindi tried not to worry about it because she knew it would take time for them to warm to the idea of their father being married to another woman.

Meanwhile, Kaitlyn had continued to be mature about the big change. In fact, she was delighted at the prospect of having a stepfather and siblings. And surprisingly, even Richard had been supportive. "I'm happy you've found someone special," he told her.

During this celebratory time, Cindi chose to focus on the beauty before her rather than countless what-if scenarios regarding the future of their blended family.

The Castello di Barone Ricasoli was ringed by fir trees and set against a backdrop of lush pastures and hazy hilltops—the scene was pure Renaissance. Miles and miles of vineyards and Tuscan villas dotted the horizon. The grounds surrounding the castle and vineyards were open to explore.

Driving up to Brolio Castle, which was one of the most interesting places in the Chianti area, famous for its history and architecture, Paul explained that the beautiful park was called the English Woods. It was created by Baron Bettino Ricasoli in the nineteenth century and featured plants from all over the world. Cindi wished she could bring the English Woods' remnants back home with her to Florida.

Cindi and Paul parked in front of the estate. Paul then led her to the private chapel, which was adjacent to the castle. This was where their wedding would take place. When they entered the church, Cindi immediately recognized that it was an exact replica (albeit a tinier version) of a Roman cathedral. Paul held her hand and whispered, "Do you like it?"

"Oh, Paul. This is the most beautiful place in the world," she said.

The warm air carried the scent of rosemary and thyme through the chapel doors, and the only sounds they could hear were the buzzing of insects. Cindi felt as if she had been transported in time.

"*Benvenuti! Benvenuti!*" the manager said as he stepped into the cathedral to greet them, his voice echoing off the old walls. Then, in broken English, he said, "You must be Mr. Paul and Miss Cinderella!"

"Yes, I'm Paul, and this is Cinderella," Paul said.

"So happy to have you here. I am Roberto, the manager of the Brolio Castle," he said.

"This place is so beautiful! It really feels as though we've stepped back in time," said Cindi.

"Come, let me give you a tour and then allow you to retire to your rooms to rest before dinner," Roberto said.

He led the couple into the entryway of Brolio Castle, where ancient stone walls and floors, flickering oil lamps, and medieval secrets greeted them. Paul and Cindi learned all about the long, rich history of the castle and the renowned Ricasoli family. The clan had warrior origins that dated back to the Middle Ages, and the castle had suffered attacks and destruction in numerous historical battles.

Roberto took them through the magnificent gardens that overlooked the communes of Gaiole and Castelnuovo Berardenga, which comprised valleys, hills, and woods of oak and chestnut trees, 26 hectares of olive groves and 240 hectares of vineyards. Combined, these made up the largest farmland in the Chianti Classico region.

Cindi was glad that she'd brought her Nikon. She snapped what seemed like countless photos of the scenery around her. This place was a true inspiration for artists, designers, dreamers, and lovers. She was already inspired and could hardly wait to create spectacular designs for her spring collection. At that moment, surrounded by breathtaking beauty, she felt as if she were living a dream.

After touring the castle and gardens, Roberto took the couple in a private car through the Ricasoli vineyards and into the cellars where the wines of Barone Ricasoli were born and where the Chianti Classico recipe was created—one that others would attempt to replicate in the years to come. They marveled at the fermentation room and the imposing *barriccaia*, where wines were aged in barrels.

Paul held her hand, and his eyes shone like emeralds as Roberto explained how the vines were harvested and aged. Cindi knew that Paul was in heaven, too. It delighted him to give her this magnificent trip to Italy. Now and then, she couldn't help but worry about the expense, but she tried not to let it interfere with this wonderful moment.

Roberto finally took them to an exclusive wine tasting of the company's Grand Cru. The wine was elegant, robust, and full-bodied. Both Cindi and Paul savored the silky texture on their tongues.

That night, the chef prepared a delicious Italian meal for them at the Osteria del Castello, the restaurant that sat at the foot of the castle. The food was delicious, but Cindi couldn't remember many details about the dinner because she was overwhelmed with the number of courses and the complexity of each dish.

Paul and Cindi slept in separate guest rooms in the four-star hotel, the Tenuta di Rivaco, located in Castellina, which was in the heart of the Chianti hills. Paul believed it would make their wedding night more special when they stayed in the guest villa on the grounds of the Castello di Barone Ricasoli. Cindi agreed, though she could barely stand to be away from him, even for a night. They would be married the next day in the private chapel, with villagers and castle staff members attending. Fortunately for Cindi, Anne had worked closely with Paul and a wedding planner in Italy to arrange the entire wedding so it would be a surprise for the bride. After the wedding, Paul and Cindi would dance under the moonlight in the castle gardens and spend their first night as Mr. and Mrs. Francis in the villa guest house that Paul had been talking about. But Paul would not let Cindi see it just yet. The bride-to-be had to wait until their honeymoon night.

Chapter 14

The next day, Cindi woke to the sounds of gardeners outside. The hum of their laughter and lyrical Italian language swept her in a cocoon of comfort. A cool breeze blew through the window in her room at the Tenuta di Rivaco Hotel, which was surrounded by the Chianti hills. The scent of freshly made bread wafted through the air. Florida seemed like a world away.

She was in Italy, and her reality seemed more like a dream: She was getting married today to a gorgeous man with blue-green eyes, thick black hair, light olive skin, perfect white teeth, a chiseled jaw, and a toned, taut body. When he had a day-old beard, he almost looked like Johnny Depp, but Paul was a much thicker version of the sexy actor. His boyish yet manly face was stunning, and his broad shoulders with thick, toned biceps made it impossible for her to believe this was going to be her husband. On top of that, he was a highly paid professional—a litigator who lived in a magnificent home in a prestigious Florida neighborhood. He was everything she had always dreamed of. And he loved her and Kaitlyn.

She lay in the soft silk sheets for just a moment, snuggling under the comforter, savoring the moment. Workers called out *"Buongiorno!"* to one another, and the birds sang morning melodies. Paul was just down the hall, sleeping in his own private room.

When it was time for the wedding, a driver would take her to the chapel at Castle Brolio, where Paul would be waiting for her. Tonight, after they were married, they would stay at the villa on the grounds of the Castello di Barone Ricasoli for the first night of their honeymoon.

Despite the spectacular wedding, one concern persisted in Cindi's mind. She wasn't sure they could afford this lavish trip, *they* being the operative word since the couple would soon be merging their incomes. *Or will we keep our money separate?* she wondered. She tried not to think about it because she didn't want anything to spoil their vacation, which was as extravagant as that of any A-list Hollywood celebrity. In fact, this was the kind of place George Clooney visited. She recalled reading in a celebrity gossip magazine that George owned a villa overlooking Lake Como in Italy. And there she was at Castello di Barone Ricasoli, living as grandly as any of the stars.

Stop worrying so much! Cindi told herself. Today was just for her and Paul. She had plenty of time to think about her career and money matters once she was back in Florida.

Cindi spent the day getting ready for her wedding, which would take place that night. Fortunately, Anne and the Brolio Castle staff had already taken care of all the event planning—decorating the chapel, selecting the music, coordinating the reception, preparing the food, hiring the photographer, and inviting the local villagers to be their guests. All Cindi had to do was relax and look beautiful, Anne had told her.

A masseuse arrived that afternoon and kneaded the jet lag out of her muscles and then sloughed off any rough, dry skin. When she was finished, Cindi soaked in a rose-petal-lilac bath for so long that her fingers crinkled. After she toweled off, her shoulders shimmered, and she smelled of lilac and roses.

Cinderella walked barefoot onto her private terrace to breathe the sun-drenched air. Even though it was October, in this part of Italy, the days were still warm, and the nights were mild. The sky was the purest blue and dotted with fluffy clouds. From the terrace, she was greeted with a wrought-iron gazebo, shaded by a wisteria plant. Thankfully, Cindi's room was located on the quiet side of the hotel, which meant that all she heard was the soft breeze rustling through the trees.

That afternoon, the chef sent food to her room so she would not have to go to the restaurant—Anne and Paul had thought of everything. Cindi called Kaitlyn and Anne to check on them. They were both excited to hear about Brolio Castle and couldn't wait to see photos from the wedding and honeymoon. Cindi promised to tell them everything.In order to chronicle the events of her trip, Cindi brought a travel journal. When she searched her messenger bag, she discovered the financial planning guide that Anne had placed inside. *I can't believe she put that in there. She must be really worried about me*, Cindi thought.

Cinderella vowed that she would discuss finances with Paul after they returned from their honeymoon. She would prove to Anne and herself that there was nothing to worry about, despite the fact that the mere thought of having a money talk made her anxious. After all, Paul seemed to spend money—to use her mom's expression—as if it grew on trees.

Cindi dressed in the wedding gown she had designed for herself. She looked in the mirror and was overwhelmed with joy and pride at her masterpiece. She hadn't created anything this beautiful ... ever. She could just imagine what the press write-up would be if a model wore this on the runway:

It was an ivory tulle and organza fit-and-flare bridal gown with an impeccably tailored Chantilly lace bodice. Showcasing the model's beautifully sculpted shoulders and ample bosom was a strapless sweetheart neckline and asymmetrical dropped waist with flower detail and a cascading skirt.

Cindi smiled. Her off-the-shoulder, tulle and organza gown looked like a moon goddess's white illusion. It billowed softly from the snug waist and delicately brushed the floor. It was simple yet elegant. When she had modeled it for Kaitlyn, her daughter had become nearly speechless—exceptional behavior for a girl who loved to talk. "Mommy, your dress is so beautiful. You really do look like a princess," she had said.

"Thank you, sweetheart. I think it's just because I'm so happy," she said.

"I am, too! I love Paul!" Kaitlyn said.

"We're going to be very happy together as a family," Cindi said.

For her wedding, Cindi curled her long blond hair and let it fall loosely around her shoulders. She pinned one side and clasped it with a sapphire-studded comb that Anne had lent her, saying it fulfilled the "something borrowed and something blue" wedding requirement. It had been Anne's grandmother's hairpiece, and Cindi loved it.

As for the "something new," Paul had given her a pair of dangling diamond earrings the night before that also featured blue sapphires—her birthstone—in the shape of hearts. He explained that he had coordinated the design with Anne in order to copy the style of the hairpiece. The earrings and hairpiece looked exquisite together.

For her final piece of jewelry, Cindi put on the silver charm bracelet Kaitlyn had let her borrow the enchanted evening when she had first met her Prince Charming. Kaitlyn had insisted she take it to Italy to wear with her wedding gown. The bracelet reminded Cindi of two of the most important events in her life: the evening when she met Paul and the birth of her beautiful daughter. Tears welled in her eyes as she thought of Kaitlyn's joyful spirit and her unending love and belief in all that was good. Cindi wished Kaitlyn could be with her, helping her with her hair and makeup the way she loved to do, but in the end, Paul had convinced Cindi that it would be best if it were just the two of them.

Cindi had bought Paul a designer platinum wedding band—one that he had requested because he loved it so much. She gave it to Roberto, who would hand it to the minister. Everything was effortlessly and easily falling in place.

Just before the sun began to set, one of the hotel staff members came to Cindi's room to notify her that her driver was waiting for her. Cindi had been instructed to leave her luggage behind because the staff would deliver her belongings to the guesthouse at Castle Brolio.

Cinderella walked to the entrance of the hotel, where she met the driver. He then drove her to the chapel at Castle Brolio. After he helped her out of the car, she stepped light-footedly on the cobblestone path, which was lit by torches. She then carefully made her way to the chapel. Her dress trailed gently behind.

Life will never be the same again, a voice whispered inside. *I know*, Cindi said to herself. *I know.*

Cindi was greeted by violin music playing in the chapel. When she stepped into the doorway, the violinist immediately began playing Mendelssohn's "The Wedding March." Her eyes met Paul's. She felt butterflies inside—no one else had ever touched her so deeply. He stood at the altar, wearing a Hugo Boss gray suit. *He's so handsome*, she told herself. When their eyes met, he smiled and motioned for her to come forward. He was her prince and Renaissance man, with whom she was truly, deeply, and madly in love.

As she walked down the aisle carrying a small bouquet of pink roses picked from the garden, her hands trembled slightly. She loved the soft ambience of the candles that were lit throughout the church. Rose petals were scattered on the stone floor, and sunflowers were strewn around the pews and over the altar.

The chapel minister stood next to Paul, waiting patiently for her to come down the aisle. A few of the villagers stood nearby to serve as witnesses, and others sat in the pews along with those who worked at the castle and vineyards. Cindi wished Anne and Kaitlyn could be there, but in a way this was even better. It was a private, sacred moment meant only for the happy couple.

The minister began with the ceremony. Finally, he asked if she would take this man in holy matrimony. He then asked if Paul would take Cinderella in holy matrimony. They exchanged vows.

Her mind was a blur, and her thoughts a hazy dream. At the end of the ceremony, Paul read her a poem he had written:

> *The beauty of life is when two hearts join together.*
> *There is no greater beauty, no greater life than when*
> *Two hearts drink from the same water of life.*
> *Because I have found you, my beauty, my life,*
> *We shall always drink from this same water of life,*
> *And we shall always be the oneness as man and wife*
> *That we never knew before.*
> *We are forever.*

The minister concluded the ceremony by pronouncing them husband and wife. "You may kiss the bride," he said.

Even the witnesses in the church had tears in their eyes as Paul swept Cindi up in his arms, bent her backward, and kissed her passionately.

The violinist played "Canon in D" by Johann Pachelbel as Paul and Cindi floated out of the chapel, hand in hand, to music and fireflies. The wedding marked the beginning of their forever-after.

The reception was held on the villa terrace under a full moon and a thousand stars. A four-piece band played music late into the evening. People they had never met until that day celebrated with them. Everyone dined alfresco on fine Italian food and drank Chianti while dancing until the early hours of morning.

That night, as soon as it was polite, Paul and Cindi escaped to the Agresto, which was one of the most beautiful guesthouses of the Barone Ricasoli estate.

Miles and miles of vineyards that swept from the towers of Siena to Monte Amiata and Radicofani surrounded it. The villa had been recently restored to its original rural Tuscan beauty. The living room was both modern and old-world, with rustic hardwood floors, plush sofas, and a stone fireplace along one wall. The bedroom had wooden beams and showcased a four-post king-size bed, adorned with off-white, linen-covered pillows and a thick, rich satin comforter. A sunken bath was in a corner of the bedroom, and white fluffy bathrobes and towels waited for them. Candles surrounded the newlyweds, creating an otherworldly, medieval chamber.

Paul lifted Cindi and carried her over the threshold of the villa. She was a little tipsy from the delicious Chianti and appreciated his chivalrous gesture.

"Welcome to our new life, Mrs. Paul Francis," he said.

"I'm so happy! I love being Mrs. Paul Francis. A lifetime together," she said. "We have an entire lifetime together!"

"Yes, we do. God, I never thought we'd get away from the reception," said Paul.

"Me, neither, but it was the most beautiful wedding. Anne did a wonderful job, and everyone here is so nice and attentive to every detail. I loved dancing with you. You melt my heart."

"I feel the same way, my love. This really is the perfect place for a small, intimate wedding. I've always wanted to come here, and when I fell in love with you, I knew this was the ideal place to marry you. You are so beautiful, and you look so stunning in your dress," he said.

"It's one I designed. I've been dreaming about it for a long time," she said.

"It's exquisite. But of course, it's even more exquisite because you're wearing it," he said.

"I've dreamed of this forever. You just don't know how much this all means to me," Cindi said.

"I think I do because it means the same to me," he said.

Paul pulled her close and kissed her gently, sweetly, deeply. The fire inside him built, and he began kissing her fiercely. The fire began to burn inside her as well. She started unbuttoning his shirt, her breath hot on his neck. He quickly turned her around and undid the clasps on her gown. It seemed to take forever, but finally she stepped out of the dress, slipped out of her bra, and quickly removed her underwear. She stood naked before him and Paul gasped at her beautiful body. Smooth, silky skin with a small waist, long legs, and luscious breasts, wide blue eyes, and long curly blond hair, all of which made her look like the Cinderella from the fairy tale. With lightning speed, Cindi helped Paul undress. Her heart was in her throat. She wanted him. *Now*. Her body yearned for him.

He gently guided her down on the bed. He kissed her shoulders, then her breasts, then made his way to her stomach. Cindi held her head back and gripped his biceps as she felt his strong, sculpted muscles against her. He pulled her legs to his waist and took her quickly. Cindi held on to him, fastening herself to him as his body rocked with hers. She would have screamed to the heavens in that moment of pleasure, but he covered her mouth with his, devouring her. She clung to him, wanting more.

"You have driven me mad, Cinderella. I don't think I can get enough of you," he said.

When they made love the second time, it was slow and gentle. They took their time and relished every kiss, every stroke, every touch on their bodies. When they made love the third time, it was almost morning.

There they were, a prince and a princess in the most beautiful villa in Tuscany. They had servants attending to their every need and were experiencing the finest that life had to offer. They had no worries. Time stood still for them. They imagined themselves living during the medieval age—reigning over a mighty kingdom. They spent the next two days and nights tucked away in their villa.

On the third day, they left Italy and flew to Paris.

When they arrived in Paris, Cinderella still felt like royalty. It was as if she and Paul had been transported to another world where fashion reigned and their surroundings represented a perfect blend of past and present.

Cinderella had often dreamed of being in the City of Lights during Fashion Week at the Carrousel du Louvre. She had never been to Paris before, and visiting was like a fantasy come true. *Someday I'll be at Fashion Week*, she thought. With Paul, she felt that all her dreams could come true.

When they arrived at Charles de Gaulle Airport, a limousine picked them up and took them to the Four Seasons Hotel George V in Paris. It was majestic and truly designed for royalty. Paul told her they were royalty and that she deserved nothing but the best. Cindi hoped he would always treat her this way. She wanted him to make her feel like a princess, even when they weren't living a fairy tale.

The Four Seasons was located just steps away from the Champs-Elysées. Their suite had a view of the Eiffel Tower and featured a private terrace overlooking the city's historic and chic Golden Triangle. It was nestled among other beautiful streets and buildings. Their room was luxurious, decorated in eighteenth-century tapestries and adorned with a fireplace. It had the thickest silk comforters Cindi had ever felt.

On the first day, they took a private tour of several famous areas, including the Place Dauphine, the Place des Vosges, and Le Pont Neuf, or the New Bridge, which is actually the oldest bridge in Paris. When they reached Montmartre, they exited the limousine and spent the rest of the day exploring the eclectic, creative area, which was bustling with artists and college students. As they wandered through the steep cobbled streets, Paul told her it was one of the most historic and interesting neighborhoods in Paris. Naturally, he had been to Paris before. It seemed that Paul was so worldly; there was nowhere he hadn't traveled and nothing he had not already done. It made Cindi feel insecure at times, but Paul told her, "We will experience the world together, my dear Cinderella. I'll take you everywhere."

"As long as I'm with you, it doesn't matter where I am," Cinderella said. She liked the idea of traveling all over the world and knew it would help inspire her to create beautiful dresses. She also loved to experience different cultures and knew this was just the beginning of a lifetime of adventure.

Resting at the top of the hill in Montmartre was the Basilique du Sacré-Coeur, a beautiful white church. They took a photo of themselves on the steps of the famous building and then bought crêpes at the Place du Tertre. They laughed when they saw the completed work of their portrait, which was sketched by an artist who was working along the sidewalk. Paul bought it for her, and she knew it would be one of her favorite treasures forever.

At night, they strolled hand in hand along the River Seine and browsed some of the designer shops on the Champs-Elysées. The cool winds of autumn had settled on the streets, and crisp, rust-colored leaves were scattered along the sidewalks. As evening settled around them, an orange moon hung low in the sky—so low that Cinderella could almost reach up and touch it.

She understood why Paris was called the *City of Light* and why it was known as a famous place for lovers.

"I've never felt so complete," said Paul, nuzzling her neck and holding her close. "You make me very happy, Cinderella."

"I love you, Paul. I never in a million years thought I would meet someone who was so perfect for me. This is truly the most romantic honeymoon."

That night while they were dining at the exclusive Alain Ducasse au Plaza Athénée on 25 Avenue de Montaigne, Paul gave her a poem he had written:

Those who do not know this love we share,
Pulling us close like the ocean's tide,
Those who do not feast upon the dawn

Or drink in the heady pleasures of the sunset,
Cannot know life the way we know it.
This love I feel for you is beyond the senses,
Beyond the reasons,
Beyond the sun and moon.
You are bound to me,
And I am bound to you.
Forever ...
Love, Paul

"You're a beautiful poet. I only wish I could write the way you do," she said.

"Your poetry is in your designs. That's how you express yourself," he said.

"I never looked at it that way, but of course, that makes sense," she said.

They drank wine and feasted on *pavé de saumon d'Écosse Label Rouge rôti en matelote*, or as the English translation read, "Scottish roasted lamb fillet 'Label Rouge' red wine sauce with onions and herbs." It was delicious. While they ate, they marveled at the multiple chandeliers hanging from the ceiling that sprinkled dazzling light on the white tablecloths adorning each table.

The first night in Paris, Cinderella and Paul soaked in their private Jacuzzi. Mounds of bubbles floated over their skin as they sipped Dom Pérignon. When they made love later, it felt as though they were melding two souls into one. Cindi didn't know if she would ever be able to go back to being ordinary Cinderella again. Paul told her she was transforming into a "goddess of love." She had never been in love like this before. She wondered if she had slipped into a dream or whether she had died and reached heaven.

On the second day, they visited the Louvre. Cindi became transfixed with artwork from the French Impressionists, especially Monet and Manet. She was bursting with creativity and couldn't wait to open her sketchbook. She could not remember the last time she had felt so inspired.

On their third day in Paris, they returned to the Louvre. Seeing all the massive museum would take more than a week, so they chose certain exhibits to explore. While there, they shopped for souvenirs for Anne, Kaitlyn, Daniel, and Isabella.

On the fourth day, they returned to Florida to begin their lives as Prince Charming and Cinderella—or, as the world would know them, Mr. and Mrs. Paul Francis.

Chapter 15

On the flight home to Florida, Cindi continued to revel in her fantasy wedding and honeymoon with Paul. She contemplated every detail, reliving the memories. Throughout the flight, they held hands on the plane and exchanged kisses. They watched in-flight movies, shared earplugs, slept, whispered flirtatious messages to one another, and talked about how grand everything was and how it was the perfect start to their life as Mr. and Mrs. Paul Francis.

Cindi had taken numerous photographs of the Tuscany region and Paris and was excited about designing a new line inspired by her European travels. The wedding photographer had taken photos of Tuscany as well, so Cindi would have plenty of ideas to draw from when creating her next collection.

Once Cindi and Paul returned to Florida, with Paul's financial backing, Anne hosted a magnificent wedding celebration for the newlyweds. The location of the event was Vizcaya, where they first met. Even Paul's children seemed to enjoy it. Cindi met some of the partners and associates from his firm, and they appeared polished, professional, and quite affluent. One woman in particular stood out. Her name was Andrea Parks, and she was clothed in designer attire from head to toe, wearing Manolo Blahnik heels and a Helmut Lang pheasant-print, voile mini-dress that hung effortlessly on her body. She was a tall, skinny, model type who had long, sleek black hair and large almond-shaped brown eyes. Andrea's demeanor was cool when Paul introduced her to Cindi. Later, Cindi mentioned this. "I don't think your associate Andrea likes me very much," she said.

"Why do you say that?" asked Paul.

"She wasn't very warm, nor did she say congratulations or anything. In fact, she barely shook my hand at all. Just said it was nice to meet me, then moved on," Cindi said.

"Don't pay any attention to her. She's a young paralegal at the office. She's only 25 years old. I think she's just intimidated by your beauty," Paul said.

"I'm flattered that you say that, but I doubt very much if that's why she was so cool toward me. She was quite attractive."

"It doesn't matter what she thinks. I'm sure all my partners at the firm adore you. Who wouldn't?"

"That's what you always say. You're just partial, that's all."

Despite Paul's reassurances, Cindi couldn't help but wonder about Andrea. Everyone else went out of their way to extend warmth to Cindi, but not Andrea. Even Anne noticed. "What's up with her?" Anne asked Cindi. "She seems like a snob."

Overall, however, it was a great evening filled with family and friends. It was another wonderful event that Cindi would add to her memories of her dream wedding.

Life settled down for the couple as they adjusted to being married. It was not that difficult since, prior to their wedding, Paul had already spent almost every night with her. But marriage added another layer of commitment to their relationship. No longer did Cindi think about what she and Kaitlyn would do in the future. Rather, she thought about Paul, Kaitlyn, his children, and herself, and what the five of them would do as one blended family. The growth of her family from two to five would put a strain on Christmas gifts, Cindi realized, because now she had three additional gifts to buy, instead of just one. In addition, long-term planning for everything became more complicated.

Paul worked long hours litigating cases. Meanwhile, Cindi designed her new Tuscany-Paris-inspired collection in her studio, determined to "wow" some new celebrity clients.

Cindi couldn't wait to meet Anne at Las Palmas a couple of weeks after they returned from Italy and Paris. She hadn't been able to talk to her much at the wedding party or any other time since they returned to Florida. She had been busy tending to her new designs and to Paul and his kids.

As usual, Anne was waiting for her, sipping a margarita on the terrace of their favorite bar. Anne had her long hair pulled back in a ponytail and looked much younger than her 36 years.

"Sorry I'm late. It's just been hard to pry myself away from my art table. I have so many ideas; I just can't sketch fast enough," Cindi said.

"Marriage becomes you, my friend," said Anne. She noticed that Cindi had a glow in her cheeks and a happy, relaxed, positive energy around her. Anne hadn't seen that before.

"I don't know how to thank you for everything," said Cindi as she motioned to the server to bring her a margarita. The Las Palmas staff knew the best friends well.

"It was so much fun planning everything. I wish I could have been there," said Anne.

"So do I. But Paul thought it would be easier for us just to elope, and despite my doubts, I have to confess that it was beyond romantic, and of course, the wedding party you planned for us was spectacular. I'll never forget it."

"It was the least I could do for my best friend. Don't worry, you'll have your chance to repay me if—or when—I get married." Anne laughed good-naturedly.

"You bet. Even though you weren't there, I couldn't have managed the wedding without you. It was all so ... so ... *magical.*"

"I can't wait to see the photos!"

"I'll have them back from the photographer soon and will show you everything! I brought my camera, so I can show you the photos I took."

"Oh, good. I researched the place online, and I have to say, Paul did an amazing job picking it," Anne said.

"Yes, he did. I don't think I've ever known anyone so incredibly romantic, Anne," said Cindi.

The server brought over Cindi's margarita, and she took a long sip. "Ooooh, that's good," she said.

With a cool breeze blowing through Cindi's hair, she proceeded to tell Anne all about the wedding and honeymoon. Anne sat back and listened, feeling happy for her best friend.

"Paul's the most wonderful person. I have never met anyone as romantic as he is, and he's so sensual in bed."

"Sweetie, I get it! I get it!" laughed Anne. "You can spare me the bedroom details."

"I can't get enough of him. And quite frankly, he can't seem to keep his hands off me, either," Cindi said.

"Oh, you make me jealous. Here I am, just fine being alone, thank you very much, and then you have to go and meet this hunky, romantic prince of a guy and get me all jealous."

"You'll meet your prince someday. After all, if I can meet the man of my dreams, so can you!"

"I wish it were that easy. I think I intimidate a lot of men."

"I'm sure you do. Sadly, men are often threatened by successful, beautiful women like you."

"You're beautiful and successful, too. But you have a sweetness that kind of cripples men."

"I do not!" said Cindi, laughing and shaking her head.

"Yes, you do. And I think that's why men fall in love with you. It's nothing to be ashamed of. You're just a sweetie pie."

"Thanks ... I think," said Cindi, blushing again. "Oh, by the way, I found that financial planning guide in my bag when I was in Italy."

"Oh ... well ... I ...," started Anne. She blushed.

Cindi laughed. "Don't worry! I wasn't offended. In fact, I actually read a little bit of it. It has some great advice."

"I just thought it might help you out. You're such a *creative*—a true dreamer and artist—and a very talented one at that. But sometimes, I'm not sure you're looking out for your best interests financially. I don't have one ounce of artistic talent in my body, but I'm pretty good with money, if I do say so myself!"

They both laughed.

"You and I have always been opposites that way. Your strengths complement mine. Where I can design a dress for you and even decorate your entire house, I'm not always the best when it comes to long-term financial planning. So I understand why you gave me that book—I do."

"You've done quite well with your business, even when it wasn't thriving. And you've been a great provider for Kaitlyn. I guess I've rubbed off on you a little," Anne said.

"Yes, you have. It's because of you that I have anything, really. You've kept me focused on a plan and what I needed in order to be financially independent," Cindi said.

"Did you and Paul have an opportunity to discuss your finances?" Anne asked.

"Not exactly. We weren't away that long in Italy and Paris, and of course that wasn't the time to discuss anything. And since we've been back, it's been one thing after another. Time is flying."

"I know. Thanksgiving will be here soon. But what I've learned is that there's always something going on in life—there's always something to make you think that 'next week' will be a better time. It never is."

"No, really. I promised myself, and I promise you, that I'll have a serious talk with Paul after the holidays."

"Sounds good. By the way, how are you planning to pay for shared expenses? Are you creating a joint account for them?"

"We both still have our separate accounts. Honestly, we haven't even had time to go to the bank and open up a joint account. So far, I'm paying my own house bills, and he's paying his. But, as I said, we've only been home for two weeks. I mentioned to him that we needed to take care of this, and he told me we'd do it soon. He's been working a lot of late nights. And last weekend, he stayed with his kids at his house. He thought it would be better to ease them into our married world."

"He stayed with his kids at his house without you and Kaitlyn?"

"Well, we all had dinner together. But later, he and I both decided that it would be good for him to have some alone time with his kids. We've only been back from Italy for two weeks. It will take them some time to get used to me being their stepmother."

"Mmmm. That's interesting," Anne said.

"What are you thinking?" said Cindi.

"You had such a whirlwind marriage. Have you decided where you'll all live?"

"We've been talking about moving into his house, maybe adding an extra bedroom and a studio for me, then selling my house eventually," said Cindi.

"Are you talking about extensive, *expensive* renovations?" asked Anne.

"Uh, yeah ... I think so. Like $200,000 or so, I think," said Cindi, her face turning bright red.

"And will Paul be funding this, or is it something you'll be doing jointly?"

"We haven't really discussed how it's going to get financed. We probably won't even think about it until after the holidays, though. But don't worry. I know what you're thinking."

What Cindi deliberately omitted was that Paul had, in fact, suggested they use Cindi's home equity line to help fund the renovations or they shop for a newer, bigger home.

"I don't see anything wrong with you selling your home and moving into Paul's. In fact, that might be a good move. But spending a lot on renovations right away could put you in uncomfortable debt. I'd just take it one day at a time. There's no need to hurry," said Anne.

"I don't know what we're going to do yet. As I said, Paul and I haven't discussed it very much."

"You know I'm here to help you, right?" asked Anne.

"Absolutely. And I promise that you'll be the first one I call to get some advice," said Cindi.

Cindi couldn't help but feel guilty about not sharing the information about her equity loan for the Jet Skis or even talk about buying a new house when she knew Anne would *definitely* not approve.

The time flew, as it always did when things seemed storybook perfect. It was already November, and Thanksgiving was right around the corner, and then Christmas would be here. Cindi could barely believe that they had been in Italy and Paris just weeks ago. Already, it seemed like a long-ago dream. But the afterglow of their wedding was still very much with them. The photographer had recently sent them a file of their wedding photos, and Paul and Cindi spent hours selecting the best ones. They were the most exquisite pictures Cindi had ever seen, and Paul said they should be featured in bridal magazines.

As the days went by, Kaitlyn seemed to get along better and better with Daniel and Bella, and they did not argue as much. As long as Cindi gave Paul's children what they wanted, they were easy to get along with. That meant letting them have cold pizza for breakfast and ice cream and soda whenever they wanted. Paul didn't seem to mind, and she didn't feel as though it was her place to impose her parenting style on them. Of course, she did not like giving in to them all the time, but for the time being, she was just trying to make everyone happy. She desperately wanted his children to love Kaitlyn and her.

Paul didn't really favor the idea of renovating his house. He told Cindi that his kids might look at it as an encroachment on their space. He felt that the best solution was to buy a home near the children's mother, and they could all start brand new as a family.

Lately Paul's work was very stressful, which made him a bit short-tempered with Cindi, so she didn't want to add to his burden. He was coming home late at night; his time consumed with brutal court appearances and long spa visits. She had recently learned about his overindulgent spa treatments. Cindi didn't know why she never noticed it before, but two-hour massages *several times a week?* She liked a guy who took care of himself, but this seemed over the top.

When he came home at night, she had his dinner waiting, something he told her that Mal had never done. She was catering to his every whim. But lately, that didn't seem to be good enough.

Chapter 16

*C*indi sat at the kitchen table making a grocery list while sipping a glass of wine. She tried to decide if she should prepare a small ham along with a turkey breast for Thanksgiving. She was cooking for Anne, Paul, and his children. His kids had a very limited palate of pizza, pasta, and any other white starch they could find. But she would try to cook something they liked and make the day as pleasant as possible. The last thing she wanted was for the kids to sulk because there was nothing for them to eat. They were prone to temper tantrums and mood swings at the drop of a hat, and Cindi did everything she could to avoid that.

This year, it felt as though Cinderella had a big family to cook for, and she was both excited and stressed. Paul had called and said he would be home early to help with the preparations. He also told her there was something he'd like to discuss with her. Cindi presumed that he might want to go away for Christmas—with or without the children. It was something he'd mentioned a week or so ago, so it was probably on his mind right now.

After their talk, they would go to the grocery store and then start preparing food for Thursday's dinner. Cindi appreciated Paul's help. In addition to the wedding and honeymoon, they had also been busy in the fall months with school recitals and plays, as well as their demanding careers. But, as she told Anne several times, she and Paul would talk about their finances after the holidays. The bills were getting paid, and so far, her budget looked very much as it did before they married, with the exception of the new home equity loan payment.

For the next few weekends, Paul decided to splurge by going to fancy restaurants as a way to de-stress. Whenever they went out, he paid for everything without question. They always dined at the most expensive restaurants in the area. And as always, women looked twice at Paul. He was very handsome, and they couldn't help it. When she had mentioned it to Paul, he said, "What are you talking about? I don't get upset when men stare at you. Trust me, more guys are looking at you than women at me." Then with a glint in his eye, Paul added, "Are you jealous?"

"No. Not at all. It's only natural that women are going to look at you. I just happen to have married the sexiest man on the planet!" she said.

"I wish I were only half as good looking as you think I am," Paul said.

And with that, he motioned the server to bring more wine. Then he took her hand and kissed it. "I'll never meet another woman as beautiful, sweet, and loving as you. There is no woman in the world who could make me take my eyes off you."

When Paul said things like this, Cindi always melted inside and forgot about any of the little worries she might have been feeling. In fact, every time Cindi started to believe that he was being distant, which in turn made her feel lonely and disconnected, Paul would schedule a date and take her out to dinner or to a romantic movie night. The date nights were always perfect. As always, he was extremely attentive and loving during their evenings together, and she loved every minute of being with him. He would write her poems and shower her with so much attention and affection that she totally forgot about being lonely during those other nights when he went to the spa for hours, worked late, or became critical or short-tempered with her. He had done this before they were married, too—she just had not realized how up and down and self-involved he really was.

Cindi believed that it was true that things did change after marriage. She became more aware of Paul's habits and nuances—his flaws along with his strengths—things she didn't really notice before or else had not paid attention to.

It became obvious to Cindi that there was no way she was going to mention budgets and financial planning while they were out on a special date.

※

Paul came in and shouted, "Honey, I'm home!" He loved to do this, and it made her smile every time.

"I'm in the kitchen working on our grocery list," she said.

Paul threw his briefcase on the hall table and strolled into the kitchen. He kissed her cheek. "Did you miss me?" he asked.

"Always. I'm so glad you were able to get home early," she said.

"Where's Kaitlyn?" he asked as he poured himself a glass of wine and sat down at the table with her.

"She's with her girlfriend. Arielle's mom picked her up after school and was planning on taking them to the school's Thanksgiving festival. Kaitlyn told me I didn't need to come because it was just a bunch of booths and cotton candy. She'll be home by 8:00. I told her she had to help with chores tomorrow to get ready for our guests on Thursday," Cindi said.

"I invited one of my partners at the firm to come, if that's all right with you," he said.

"Of course! We're going to have a lot of food. Who is it?" she asked.

"Do you remember meeting Trevor Stevenson at our wedding party?" he asked.

"Was he the one with dimples and a head of curly brown hair?" asked Cindi.

"That's him. He's single, and his family lives in Canada. I hated the thought of him going out to a restaurant alone."

"He's cute. I'm surprised he doesn't have a girlfriend," Cindi said.

"He got divorced about a year ago, I think. He's been shy about getting back into the dating scene," he said.

"I can understand that," said Cindi.

"Yeah, so can I."

"Well, he's more than welcome. Anne might find him interesting!" she said.

"I was thinking the same thing," Paul said, smiling.

"You mentioned you had something you wanted to talk about," said Cindi.

"Well, here's the thing. I've been meeting with a Realtor named Henry Barnes to discuss our properties, the renovations on my house—things like that," he said.

"Okay," Cindi said cautiously, as if awaiting a new, big expense to fall out of his mouth. "So, what did Mr. Barnes say?"

"Cinderella, you know how expensive these renovations are going to be, right?" he asked.

"Right. I've been wanting to discuss our budget beforehand to see if we could maybe wait a while before proceeding with the renovations. It's just a lot for us to take on so soon after getting married."

"I think I have an alternative plan to the renovations and one that would allow us to be together every day much more quickly," Paul said.

"How?" asked Cindi.

"Our Realtor found this exquisite home just a few blocks from my children's house that would be absolutely perfect!"

"What do you mean?" she asked.

"Well, we could buy this home, and sell our homes, and we'd probably come out way ahead financially. We wouldn't need to do renovations because the house is relatively new, and it would easily fit all of us. We'd never have to worry about adding more rooms."

"What's the price of the house?" Cindi asked, feeling disturbed. *Why would he decide to buy a new house when we had been discussing renovating his?*

"They're asking two million," Paul said without batting an eye. He said it so nonchalantly that the price could have easily been $200,000.

Cindi gasped. "Did you say two million dollars?"

"Yes, and I know it sounds like a lot, but in today's market, I know we could get it for much less than that, and if you saw the property, you would know it's worth every penny!"

"You said it was near your children's house. You mean near Mal's house?" asked Cindi.

"Yes, a few blocks away, which would be perfect for us," said Paul. "The kids would be so close they could walk or ride their bikes over any time. It would help us so much with logistics when we have to take them to and from their activities. And you know, Cin, that area is quite popular—it will just go up in value."

"Paul, I ... I ... don't know what to say," Cindi stammered, stunned that he would suggest they start their lives together within blocks of his ex-wife. "That's so much money!"

"Look, I've already put in an offer because I assumed you'd want what's best for our family. Daniel and Bella would be so much happier if I lived closer to them." His tone was very persuasive and assertive, as if he was arguing his case before a jury. His brows furrowed together, and a demanding—or was it a *commanding*—demeanor flashed across his face. Little rays of light pierced through his eyes. Cindi knew he was about to get angry and sullen. But he quickly caught himself and checked his anger. His facial features smoothed out and took on a pleasant appearance.

Still, she asked him, "You already applied for the loan?" Cindi was shocked that he would do this without talking to her about it first. Her head was spinning.

"Yes, I thought it would be a nice surprise for you. Only thing is, I found out today that you'll need to cosign the loan ... you know, now that we're married. Plus, we'll need a big down payment, which will help reduce the monthly payments and—"

"Wait. You're saying we need a down payment? How much are you planning to put down, and what are you asking from me?" Cindi asked.

"How much can you afford?" Paul said, gently twirling the wine in his glass while he looked down at it, avoiding her eyes.

"Me?" Cindi heard Anne's voice repeating her warning never to cosign a loan without making sure you're on the same page regarding money and always to discuss financial philosophies *before* buying or commingling assets. She wished they had had the "money conversation" months ago, well in advance of getting married.

"Yes, of course, honey. You're going to be able to sell your house, and you have no mortgage," Paul said. He looked up at her with pitiful puppy-dog eyes. "I only have so much right now. If you could help with the down payment and then cosign the loan, we'd be good to go."

"Let's go together to see it first," said Cindi. But she was not happy.

"Absolutely!" said Paul—his demeanor quickly changed, and he flashed a big smile. "I thought we could run by tonight before we go grocery shopping. Cin, it's a mansion! You'll love it!" He was as excited as a small boy opening a present on Christmas.

"I guess I'm just a bit ... surprised," said Cindi. Her head was spinning. She was upset he did not consult her in this major financial decision. In the back of her mind, she could hear Anne gasping and reciting her recent lecture: *Couples tend to polarize around money. Partners tend to assume defensive personalities, which can cause major problems in a relationship.*

"I know, but it's the best kind of surprise, love! I honestly think it's the best solution for our housing situation. So, what do you think? I promise, you're going to love this house and the neighborhood, and most important—Kaitlyn will love it! Remember, this is for *us*—our family," he said attempting to persuade her as if she was a one-woman jury.

"I know, I know. And, well, sure ... I have savings ... I suppose," stammered Cindi. "And I'm sure I'll love it."

His excitement drew her into the idea, or was it more a fear of his disappointment or, even worse, of losing his love?

"Awesome! Come on, let's go see the house!"

The real estate agent met Paul and Cindi and took them through the multimillion-dollar home in the neighborhood where Mal and Paul's two children lived. Cindi's jaw dropped when she first saw it. And she was shocked to find that it was only four blocks from Mal's house. She didn't really like the idea of living so close to his ex-wife. At the same time, what Paul had said about it being easier on the children was true, and in the end, she wanted more than anything to make him happy. *Right?*

The mansion was exquisite. It was more than six thousand square feet and had five bedrooms, six bathrooms, a media room, a workout room, a huge pool and spa, a studio that would be perfect for her, and an office for Paul. It was a relatively new construction that had Spanish-influenced architecture. Inside the house, Cindi especially loved the kitchen-island countertop of lapis lazuli marble. The house was set on a large lot with many trees and a massive swimming pool in the back.

"Isn't it a bit grandiose? Don't get me wrong, I love it, Paul—I just think it's a bit much," she said.

"It's what we need, Cindi," said Paul, slipping his arm around her and guiding her to a kitchen countertop. There, he opened his laptop and showed her a picture from the Multiple Listing Service. "We need a house that doesn't have any memories of either of our exes—a new beginning, our own place. And somewhere the children can call their new home."

"I have to admit, it is special ... really special," said Cindi. Maybe Paul was right. Maybe purchasing a new home—even though it was outrageously expensive—was the best option. A place to call their own and start afresh. After all, they could spend a lot of money renovating Paul's house, and it would still not be as big or wonderful as this house—this mansion! And as Paul said, the property value would absolutely increase, especially given the neighborhood.

She heard a voice inside her head: *Are you trying to convince yourself, Cinderella? This is all happening so fast that you can't even think straight.*

"Since it's like a Spanish castle, we'll call it our Castillo de Amor," whispered Paul in her ear. "Our Castle of Love. I would want nothing less for you, my beautiful wife. You deserve something this beautiful, this grand. You are a princess, my lovely

Cinderella, and this is where you should live." As long as Paul was nibbling on her ear and kissing her neck, she could not deny him anything.

They told the real estate agent that they were in the process of finalizing the loan and would work out the details with him after Thanksgiving.

After touring their Castillo de Amor, Paul and Cindi went to Whole Foods Market to buy everything they needed for Thanksgiving Day. They held hands in the aisles and exchanged kisses when no one was looking. Paul was like a little boy—happy and giddy about his big purchase. He continually thanked Cinderella for agreeing to cosign the mortgage and for contributing to the down payment. He promised to take her to a special dinner over the weekend to thank her. He continually hugged and kissed her in the grocery store and made her feel like the most adored woman in the world.

It was times like these that Cindi knew why she had married Paul. He could be the most romantic man in the world. Sure, he loved spending money, and she would have to address that with him and determine what they should do about their budget. But that would be later. Right now, she had a Thanksgiving dinner to prepare, a Friday meeting with the bank, and a million and one other things to think about.

It didn't help that Paul's hand was between her legs during their drive home.

Chapter 17

"Mommy, what can I do to help?" asked Kaitlyn as Cindi stood in the kitchen, chopping celery for the turkey dressing. Kaitlyn knew when her mother was stressed and needed her support.

Cinderella stopped for a moment and looked around the cozy kitchen and dining area. Even though it was warm outside, her home was furnished with autumn décor and a traditional Thanksgiving look. On the dining table, she and Kaitlyn had placed an ornamental horn on top of a round doily and filled it with mini pumpkins and all the colorful, oddly shaped squash they could find, which gave the table a harvest touch. Then they wound some artificial grapevines through the horn to make it look more festive.

On the dining table, Cindi placed a brown-and-green colored table runner and Pilgrim candlesticks, both of which surrounded a centerpiece of mums and Indian corn that was tied with an autumn bow.

Cindi turned back to Kaitlyn. "Kater-tater, why don't you take Isabella and Daniel to your room and play some video games until everything's ready? That would help me a lot."

"I asked them if they wanted to go to my room and play when they got here this morning, but they said no," said Kaitlyn.

"Well, why don't you ask again?"

Since the moment Isabella and Daniel arrived, their lukewarm expressions made Cindi worry that they resented celebrating Thanksgiving at her house. She thought Mal may have told them that "Paul's new wife" was a horrible person who would try to take their father's time and attention from them. Paul had told Cindi that Mal was just jealous of her. Cindi worked and had a successful career, whereas Mal's career consisted of full days on the tennis court. Paul had mentioned something about Mal having a master's degree, but she chose to spend her time working on her tennis game. He speculated Mal was irritated with Cindi because her own career never kicked off. Cindi wasn't sure if any of his observations were true.

The bottom line was Daniel and Isabella's bad moods were rattling Cindi's nerves. Daniel watched her as she cooked and continually told her she was not preparing things the right way. "My mom doesn't put butter in the mashed potatoes. She said it's too fattening." It was as if, in Daniel's eyes, Cindi couldn't do anything right.

"Well, I like butter in the potatoes. Lots of it, too," she answered.

"And she uses skim milk instead of cream," said Daniel.

"I like the cream because it makes the potatoes creamier," said Cindi. *Why can't Paul take these kids into the other room? I'm going to go out of my mind if they don't get out of here*, she thought to herself, resisting the temptation to express her thoughts out loud.

Kaitlyn finally persuaded Daniel and Isabella to go to her room to play Wii games, and at last Cindi could concentrate on the food preparations. She looked out the window for a moment. The sun was mellow and soft, and a gentle breeze filtered through the trees. She wished she could just kick off her shoes and go outside and sit for a while. *Can I pull this off? Am I trying to do too much—preparing this huge meal, then cosigning a loan tomorrow for a mansion that is way over our budget? Why is Paul so adamant about buying this new house?*

Paul was drinking beer and watching a football game on television with Trevor Stevenson, his associate from the firm. Cindi was perturbed that Paul had resorted to the "man cave," as he called the den, to watch football. It seemed so cliché: *Man watches football while the little lady slaves away in the kitchen.*

For some reason, she had envisioned her prince as being more helpful. She didn't know why she expected that. After all, he had never helped her in the kitchen before. Yes, he was good at making breakfast, but that was the extent of his repertoire. His idea of cooking dinner for her was taking her to a restaurant or ordering takeout.

Ever since Cindi had agreed to cosign the loan to buy the mansion, Paul had been on a roller-coaster high. He was like a kid who had just received a new toy. He had been extraordinarily attentive and loving, often telling her, "You are everything to me, my Cinderella. Without you, I am nothing."

Cindi couldn't help but wonder what Paul would have done if she hadn't agreed to buy the mansion. Lately, she had seen him get angry over little things that didn't seem to matter at all, such as her forgetting to pick up his dry cleaning or not buying the right kind of food and snacks for the kids.

As always, Paul would regain control of his temper and return to the cheerful man she knew and loved, but it alarmed her when she saw those little outbursts of anger that were downright childish and random. Cindi thought about the new house again and had to admit to herself that it was beautiful. She tried not to think about the debt because it gave her a nagging feeling that she had made a decision that she would later regret.

Anne arrived shortly after the children went to Kaitlyn's room. She brought a homemade chocolate pecan pie and a traditional pumpkin pie that both looked as if they came from a bakery.

"Oh, Anne, you're determined to put some weight on me yet!"

"You could use a few pounds," Anne said, laughing. "You've lost weight since you got married. Must be all that sex!"

"Shush. The kids might hear you," Cindi said.

"Sorry! Speaking of kids, where are they?" Anne asked.

"Kaitlyn took them to her bedroom to play video games. They were criticizing my cooking and getting on my nerves here in the kitchen," Cindi said.

"Looks like you need some help. Have you been working all by yourself?" Anne asked.

"Pretty much," said Cindi.

The women heard a rustle in the hallway, and Trevor and Paul emerged from the so-called man cave. Paul introduced Anne to Trevor. He was sweet, a bit shy, and seemed tongue-tied around Anne. When they pulled a couple more beers out of the fridge, Paul and Trevor hurried back to their sacred lair to resume watching football, leaving the women to cook. With the same proficiency she used in her financial planning, Anne whizzed around the kitchen like lightning.

"Anne, as always, you've come to my rescue. I really needed help preparing this Thanksgiving feast," said Cindi.

"Of course! I'm always here for you. I had no idea it would be so much work making dinner for all of us," Anne said.

"It is, but I enjoy it," she said.

"What did you think about Paul's associate, Trevor?" asked Cindi.

"He's pretty cute. You said he's divorced, right?"

"Yes, but it was amicable. And it's been about a year. Paul thought the two of you might hit it off," Cindi said.

"I have to admit, he seems cute. I love those curls and those dimples. He seems kinda shy. I don't think I'm his type," Anne said.

"Honey, you're *everybody's* type!" said Cindi. The two women laughed. "I don't know him at all, but Paul speaks highly of him. Anyway, let's just relax and enjoy ourselves. Trevor has a really nice personality, and who knows? It never hurts to have another friend."

"I agree," said Anne as she finished setting the table with Cindi's fine china and silverware. Anne had to admit that she often wondered if she would ever meet her prince. Paul was so affectionate toward Cindi that it made her long for romance in her life as well. But she wasn't one to force it. She loved her life, and if she met the right man, that would be a bonus.

Once the food was ready, everyone gathered around the dining table. Dressed in jeans and a Miami Dolphins jersey, Paul laughed about being the typical guy who watched football on Thanksgiving Day. He then opened a bottle of wine for the adults and sparkling apple juice for the kids. Trevor was just as good natured and casual in his red-plaid, button-down shirt and jeans. With his curly hair, he looked youthful. He helped Paul with the wine and sparkling apple juice and teased the children about needing to take it easy on the drinking. Even Daniel and Isabella seemed to be happier than they were earlier, which made Cindi happy. She couldn't help but notice that Trevor could barely take his eyes off Anne. If her best friend noticed, she did not let on.

When Cindi looked at the beautifully prepared food on her dining table, she felt a sense of pride. It wasn't easy making the roasted turkey, stuffing, mashed potatoes, sweet potato pie, green bean casserole, cranberry sauce, and cornbread.

Cooking wasn't a natural skill for her as it had been for her mother, and she had felt rather frazzled throughout the afternoon. Cindi pushed her hair out of her face and sat down next to Paul. He leaned over, kissed her, and whispered in her ear, "You've never looked more beautiful, my dear."

Cindi laughed. "You'd say that no matter what I looked like!" She certainly didn't feel lovely after cooking all morning. Her slacks had food stains on them, and her blouse was untucked. She had long ago tied her hair up on her head and secured it with one of Kaitlyn's clips. Blond strands dangled loosely around her face.

"I think I'm too tired to eat!" said Cindi, sipping her wine.

"Nonsense!" said Anne. "You're going to feast along with the rest of us on this beautiful meal you prepared!"

"You two ladies outdid yourself," said Trevor.

Anne noticed that he had warm caramel-brown eyes that crinkled when he smiled. *Mmmm*, she thought. "Why, thank you, sir. I hope all of you are hungry!"

Anne was seated across from Trevor and next to Cindi and Paul at one end of the table. The children were at the other end.

Paul carved the turkey and said, "Now, I think each of us should take a turn and say what we're most thankful for this year."

"That's a great idea! Why don't you start?" said Cindi.

"I'm grateful for my beautiful new wife, Cinderella, for her daughter, Kaitlyn, and my children, Daniel and Isabella, and I'm grateful for our friends, Trevor and Anne, who were able to join us today," said Paul. He raised his wineglass in a toast, and everyone followed suit.

"I'm grateful for being invited to this Thanksgiving dinner," said Trevor. "And I'm grateful for the opportunity to meet a lovely new woman." He looked directly at Anne, and everyone laughed. Anne blushed.

"I'm thankful for my best friend—Cindi! Here's to you!" she said. She raised her wineglass and then continued, "And Paul, I'm grateful that you came along and have made her a very happy woman. And I'm happy for my life, my work, for new friends, and for the new year that's waiting for us around the corner." Again, everyone raised their glasses and took a sip.

Kaitlyn said, "Me, me! Let me go next!"

"What are you grateful for, Kater-tater?" asked Cindi.

"I'm grateful for my mommy and for my best friend, Arielle ... and for Paul," said Kaitlyn, looking up at Paul with a beaming smile. "And I'm happy that he married my mom and that I have a new stepsister and a stepbrother.

Now, you go next, Isabella." "I'm grateful for my new stepsister, too," said Isabella. "I like you, Katy. You're nice."

Kaitlyn smiled as she looked at Isabella. Cindi sighed. This warmed her heart. Perhaps there was hope that they would be a real family, after all.

"What about you, Daniel? What are you thankful for this year?" asked Paul.

"I don't know," he said. "This is stupid."

Cindi flinched. Everything had been going so well.

"No, it's not stupid. You have a lot of things to be thankful for, young man. Now, come on. Think of one thing," said Paul.

"I don't know," he said and shrugged his shoulders.

"Don't you like staying with us and having me as a stepsister?" asked Kaitlyn.

"No." Daniel rolled his eyes. "You're not my real family. Mama said so."

"Daniel. Don't use that tone of voice. This is your family, too," Paul said.

"I don't want to play this stupid game. And I'm not hungry. I don't see anything here that I like. Can I just go and watch television?"

"No, you cannot. Please tell us something that you're grateful for. Cindi has been graciously preparing this meal all day," Paul said.

Cindi could see that Anne was biting her lip. She knew Anne was annoyed and wanted to say something but was struggling not to.

"Daniel, aren't you thankful for all your toys and friends, your mother, and family?" said Cindi, thinking that she could smooth the tension that had befallen the room.

"Well ... I guess so," he said, reluctantly.

"There, that wasn't so bad, was it?" said Paul.

Daniel shook his head.

"Well, I think that calls for another toast!" said Trevor, who seemed determined to recapture the jovial mood everyone had been in a moment before.

Anne said, "I agree! Here's a toast to all of us! To new friends and extended families and new stepsisters and stepbrothers!"

After they all took a sip, Kaitlyn said, "Mommy, you didn't tell us what you're thankful for this year."

"Oh, I didn't, did I? Well, it's easy. I'm grateful for you, Kater-tater ... for my wonderful friend, Anne, who helps me and is always there for me ... for our guest, Trevor ... for Daniel and Isabella ... and, of course, for my very own Prince Charming, along with our romantic wedding and honeymoon," said Cindi, blushing slightly as she raised her wineglass in a toast.

"You're forgetting something really important, Mom," said Kaitlyn.

"What do you mean, honey?" said Cindi.

"How about being grateful for our new castle that we get to move into real soon!" Kaitlyn said.

Oh, crap! Cindi thought to herself. *Anne doesn't know about the house.*

Her best friend shot her a look that was filled with shock, and Cindi nearly choked on her wine. Cinderella intended to disclose this information to Anne—just not yet. Cindi held her breath.

"Well, that's news to me!" said Anne, setting down her glass of wine.

Paul came to the rescue. "We hadn't planned on telling anyone until we actually closed escrow and were ready to move in. Once we're settled in, we'll have everyone over to celebrate."

"Wait, you're buying a house? I thought you were moving into *your* house, Paul," said Anne. She looked at him, her eyes wide as saucers. "What happened to those plans?"

"Paul found us this beautiful home. It will save us money in the long run, I believe, and ... and ... Can we talk about this later, Anne?"

"Sure," said Anne, determined not to ruin the day. "Sure. Let's toast to Paul and Cindi's new house."

"Buying in this market can be a good investment. I've flipped several properties here in Florida over the last few years. You can find some good deals," piped in Trevor.

"The house is magnificent," said Paul, beaming. "It's a bona fide mansion. Expensive, but it's worth every penny. We were lucky to find it."

Cindi cringed. *Why, oh why, did he have to talk about this?* She didn't like to discuss money or the price of things with her friends. She thought it was very tacky to flaunt one's wealth. She and Anne had talked about this many times when they watched rich men in fancy bars and restaurants. And now her husband was one of those rich guys. She knew exactly what Anne was thinking.

"It's in one of the best neighborhoods in the area," said Paul, proudly.

"It's close to Mommy's house," said Isabella.

"Is that so?" said Anne, bracing herself after hearing yet another appalling bit of information. She flashed a shocked look at her best friend, but Cindi avoided her eyes.

"I think *fairly* close is a better way to describe it," said Cindi. "The plus is that it will make it easier on the children to be near their mom."

"And Mommy says it has a pool," said Kaitlyn. "And we'll get to go swimming every day."

"That will be fun. I can't wait till we can go swimming," Isabella said.

"You can't even swim good," said Daniel, still sullen.

"I can, too!" said Isabella. "Daddy, tell him I can swim."

"Yes, you can swim very well, honey. Danny, quit picking on your sister."

"Why do you always take her side?" asked Daniel.

"Okay, everyone," said Cindi. "Enough talk about our new house. Let's eat. I'm starving all of a sudden, and this food is getting cold."

Anne couldn't wait to hear what Cindi had to say about the new mansion. And Cindi knew she had some post-Thanksgiving explaining to do. In the meantime, Anne hoped that the newlyweds had worked out their household budget and financial details. She was now worried about the consequences of her best friend's very poor financial decision. It was impulsive and so sudden to be buying a mansion. A series of questions flooded her mind: *Hadn't they just started talking about renovating Paul's house? Why the sudden change of heart? How long had they been planning this? Why hadn't Cindi told me?*

At that moment, all Cindi wanted to do was crawl underneath the table and hide.

Chapter 18

After dinner, dessert, coffee, and everyone feeling stuffed to the brim, Anne decided it was time to go home. "Call me and let's set up a lunch date," she told her best friend as she made her way out the door. But before she left, Trevor asked Anne for her phone number. She obliged and received his number in return. He even walked her to her car. Cindi couldn't help but smile as she watched them from her front window. *Maybe this is the beginning of a romance*, she hoped. Paul felt the same way and was very pleased with his attempt at matchmaking.

The celebration had mostly been a success, despite the fact that Paul's boasting of the expensive house and Anne learning they were buying it had embarrassed Cindi. With the exception of that brief moment of Daniel's rudeness, the children had gotten along fairly well.

That night, Mal contacted Paul and demanded that the children come back home instead of spending the weekend with him, which had been the original plan. Mal insisted that both children had prior plans with their school friends that could not be canceled and that she had forgotten to mention it earlier. "Besides, Daniel called me, asking if he could come home tonight," Mal told him. Paul didn't object. He was always trying to please Mal so they could just get along. But Cindi didn't like it. It was obvious that Mal was just manipulating the situation to disrupt their plans, and it irritated her that Paul allowed himself to be controlled by her. Plus, Kaitlyn had been looking forward to Daniel and Isabella spending the weekend with her so they could tour the new mansion together. She was disappointed to hear about their departure.

When Cindi tucked Kaitlyn into bed that night, she told her, "It's okay, Kater-tater. We'll just call Arielle, and you two can visit our new home together, and then we'll take you to a movie or something. If Paul and I go out to dinner, Jacquie will take you to a movie, or you can rent one and watch it here."

"Okay, Mommy. That will be fun. I just wish Danny and Bella liked me," Kaitlyn said.

"Oh, honey, they do like you. They're just upset because their lives are going to be a bit different now that Paul and I are married. And they don't know what to expect. But how could anyone *not* love you, Kater-tater?"

With that, Kaitlyn smiled. Cindi kissed her goodnight, and Kaitlyn cuddled with her stuffed animals. She fell asleep with all the hopes and dreams of a seven-year-old.

When Cindi finally joined Paul in bed, he was loving and tender and seemed to not be able to get enough of her. Just when Cindi thought sex couldn't get any better, it did.

On Friday morning, Paul and Cindi met their banker, and Cindi co-signed the mortgage on the mansion. They decided they would both put their homes on the market right away. But Paul had a sizable mortgage left on his home, which meant there were probably very little or no proceeds available because its value had declined. As a result, he counted on his latest court case to settle quickly.

The plan was that if Cindi's home sold, they would take the proceeds— minus the home equity balance and Paul's settlement money—to provide the down payment. If all went according to plan, they would move in after the new year. But Cindi was very worried. *Two mortgages? And he put an offer on a house without the money for the down payment.* Nevertheless, she decided not to say anything. There would be time to discuss their budgets in depth after the holidays.

And yet, Cindi's stomach was in knots—this was so much money, and she knew it wasn't right. She tried to be positive and upbeat, but deep down inside, she was worried. Then she thought about all the romantic, sexy nights in bed with him and all the thoughtful things he did for her, and she told herself to stop worrying. She knew that this was what Paul wanted, and it made him very happy. When he was happy, she was happy. In fact, when he was happy, everyone was happier—including his children.

On Friday afternoon, she and Paul took Kaitlyn and Arielle on a tour of the new house. Cindi was relieved that Kaitlyn loved it so much and, in fact, nearly did cartwheels when she saw the pool.

"Oh, Mommy! I love it! Look, Arielle, see the pool? We'll be able to swim any time we want."

"I love it, too!" said Arielle. The two little girls ran around it, investigating the pool bathhouse, and surrounding areas.

"See? Isn't this a paradise? This is the perfect solution for our children. Danny and Bella will love it, too," Paul said.

"It's so lovely, Paul. If the children won't be happy here, they won't be happy anywhere!" But deep down, Cindi knew that material things were not likely to change the children's demeanor.

"A castle—our *Castillo de Amor*—for my princess!" he said, twirling Cindi around until she was breathless.

That night, Paul and Cindi stayed in and snuggled on the couch, watching movies and eating popcorn with Kaitlyn and Arielle.

On Saturday, Paul said he had some work to tend to, and Cindi spent the day with Kaitlyn and Arielle. She took them shopping and to an afternoon movie. After the film, Cindi took the girls to Arielle's house to spend the night. That way, she and Paul could have an evening alone. Paul wanted to take her out to a special restaurant as a thank-you and celebration for cosigning the loan. The thought of a night alone with her Prince Charming—the man she loved more than anyone in the world—made her heart beat faster.

Feeling carefree and on top of the world, they walked hand in hand into Paolo's Italiano Rustico, a charming, intimate restaurant that made Cindi feel as though she'd stepped back into an Italian villa in Tuscany. Gleaming, dark hardwood floors, rustic brick walls, lined with bottles of wine, and soft lighting gave the restaurant a romantic, dreamy feel. Frank Sinatra crooned in the background, adding his famous melodies to the ambience.

They were seated in a private area to the side. Paul pulled out her chair, leaned over and kissed her on the cheek, sat down, and immediately ordered a bottle of Dom Perignon. He asked the server to bring ravioli topped with white wine sauce and shaved truffles. Cindi loved it when he ordered for her. They toasted and ate the appetizer, which melted in their mouths. Paul chose veal chops for their *secondi*.

"I love this place," said Cindi. "It reminds me of our wedding and honeymoon. And the food is delicious."

"That's why I brought you here," said Paul, reaching out and taking her hand. "It's romantic, and I knew you'd love it, my dear."

"Paul, do you think we're doing the right thing by buying this very expensive house?" Cindi asked, withdrawing her hand as she carefully cut into the veal chop. It had been braised in red wine and served with puréed root vegetables.

Paul looked at her sharply, and for a brief moment his eyes turned dark. Then, as quick as a flash, his eyes lightened, and he said, "Of course! How could you not think it's the right thing?"

"Oh, I don't know. It's just so expensive. And I'm worried we might be in over our heads a bit."

"Look, I earn a good living as a lawyer," said Paul as he took a bite of veal. "You're doing great with your designs. And I know you're going to hit it big time this year, selling to some celebrities. Your house is paid for, and after we sell it, along with the big settlement coming in any day, we'll have a sizable amount to put down on the new house. Trust me, Cin, it will be fine. We can afford to enjoy our money, and all the children will be much happier."

Cindi nodded, taking a sip of champagne. She still didn't know how much money Paul made or what his complete financial picture looked like. But she didn't want to discuss it now. After all, the restaurant was so romantic, the food so delicious, and she wanted Paul to stay in a loving mood.

They held hands off and on, talking about trivial things and how they hoped Anne and Trevor liked each other and would start dating. Paul leaned over periodically to kiss her on the cheek and tell her how lovely she looked in her little black dress.

Finally, the server brought tiramisu for dessert.

"I know our loan will get approved, and we'll be able to move into our new home within a few months. And, speaking of our new home, I went out to the new house and property today and looked around to see what we need to do—if anything," he said.

"Did you find anything that needs repair? Anything the inspector missed?" she asked.

"I noticed that the property was missing something in the front, and I finally figured it out."

"What was it?" she asked.

"Something that will make the home look even more palatial—a Canary Island date palm!" he exclaimed.

"But the property already has lots of trees and landscaping on it. Besides, there are palm trees on the property already. What's so special about this palm tree?" she asked.

"It's not just any palm tree. A Canary Island date palm is the mac daddy of palm trees. All the expensive homes have one or more. My landscaper specializes in these kinds of trees, and honestly, Cin, it's the perfect palm we need for the front yard. They're tall, thick, and lush, with a full canopy of palm fronds at the top."

"Interesting. I didn't know there were different kinds of palm trees. So how much does this mac daddy tree cost?" she asked. She tried to sound casual, worried that he might get upset if she asked too many questions.

"The one I found and really love is about $15,000, including installation. It's an investment that's worth every penny."

"$15,000?!" she gasped. "Are you serious?" Cindi thought back to when she had landscaped her *entire* yard for less than $5,000.

"You get what you pay for," Paul snapped. "And I don't want something crappy looking in our front yard. Don't you want the house to look good? We'll be the envy of the whole neighborhood."

"It's just that, well ... I think maybe we should save for a while before splurging on trees," said Cindi, avoiding his eyes. "We don't actually *need* a new palm tree at the moment. I think we should get that later." Her hand was trembling.

"Look, let's get this straight right now. I can afford whatever I want!" Paul said with a loud voice and dark eyes. "I work hard for my money—I'm a litigator, for God's sake, and I've given you everything you could ever dream of: an expensive engagement ring, a wedding and honeymoon in Italy, and *even a mansion*. So if I want a damn palm tree, I don't see what the issue is!"

"I ... I ... just thought maybe we should save some money first ...," she said.

Paul was furious. *Furious!* "Dammit, I don't need this s**t! F**k it!" he said.

At that moment, a bulldozer might as well have run over Cindi. Before she could respond, Paul loudly scooted his chair back, stood up, threw his napkin on the table, and bolted out of the restaurant.

Cinderella sat there stunned. Diners who sat nearby looked at her sympathetically and whispered to one another, but Cindi just kept her eyes on her table. *What just happened? We were having such a lovely evening.* She felt as though he had just slapped her. His words were harsh and stinging. Cutting.

The server witnessed the blowup and asked if she needed anything. He had the kindest eyes. She shook her head no and took a sip of her drink. Tears filled her eyes. She did not want to sit there crying like a pitifully rejected woman, so she breathed deeply and sat there, nibbling on dessert and trying to gather her thoughts.

She waited. Surely Paul would come back. He wouldn't just leave her with no way to get home. He just needed to walk around and cool off a bit, she decided. But after thirty minutes, she knew he wasn't coming back. Embarrassed, Cindi asked the server for the check and paid for dinner. She then asked him to call a cab. Although she wanted to, she was simply too horrified and embarrassed to call Anne and tell her what had happened.

When Cindi returned home, she noticed right away that Paul's Range Rover was not in the driveway or garage. She assumed he was at his house and wouldn't be coming home. He had spent a couple of weekends with his children at his house, but he'd never stayed there out of anger. This was unsettling, and she didn't know what to do.

When Cindi went inside, she kicked off her heels, turned on the hall light, and went into the kitchen to make some tea. Her hands were trembling. Paul's words and behavior had shocked her to the core. She could barely breathe. And he had left her there! At the restaurant ... alone! She sat down at the kitchen table in the dark, moonlight streaming through the windows, and she cried. And cried. *What did I do wrong?* she asked herself.

Chapter 19

indi cried for a couple of hours until she was numb. *Paul was acting crazy, right? Why would anyone get so mad because I suggested saving money and not buying a $15,000 palm tree?* she asked herself. Sure, Richard never wanted to spend any money, but he had never done anything like this. Cindi didn't have a lot of men to compare Paul with. *Am I missing something? Why is it so important for Paul to spend so much money and flaunt it? And why does he have tantrums when I question him?*

She went into her sunroom and picked up the messenger bag she had taken to Italy and Paris. She rummaged through it and found the financial planning book Anne had loaned her. She scanned the table of contents and was drawn to a chapter titled "Women and Their Relationship with Money." She read the following:

Even the most sophisticated and successful women are often caught under the spell of believing Prince Charming exists. In fact, 73% of women think that money will buy happiness, and many of these individuals are looking for someone to help them meet their financial needs.

For most people, money is never just about money. Our beliefs about money and our emotional attachments to it strongly influence the way we spend and handle money. So even if you do find your so-called Prince Charming, it is a good idea to be sure that you are both on the same page when it comes to dealing with money. After all, money is one of the top causes of divorce.

The key to creating wealth is living well below your means and saving the rest. Therefore, don't use money to make yourself feel good. Remember, the emotional high that comes from spending is fleeting—just like other vices. So rather than perpetuate unhealthy spending habits, do things that promote self-respect, and don't address those feelings with money. For instance, one step you can take is to delay making large purchases; take a week to think over them before deciding to buy.

If money worries you, try taking control of your fear and using it to motivate you into taking action. This is a great first step. And never be ashamed of consulting with a mental health expert, such as a therapist, in order to deal with any self-sabotaging struggles you have.

If you are a procrastinator—specifically, when it comes to addressing the most important aspects of your financial life—discover the root causes of your tendency to delay making major decisions. Part of this process may entail working on your self-esteem. The good news is that when women boost their self-confidence, oftentimes their attitudes and feelings about money improve as well.

The bottom line is that money is power because it gives you choices. So harness your power by taking charge of your finances right away, which will help increase your financial and emotional independence.

On Sunday morning, Cindi woke up, went to the sink, and splashed water on her face. Her eyes were red and swollen from the night before. She bit her lip. She felt like crying again but knew it would get her nowhere. So, she went into the kitchen to make coffee. She was still numb from the previous night. It all felt so surreal that, for a moment, she wondered if she had dreamed it.

Cindi continued reading Anne's financial planning book, and it felt as though the book was written for her. Every word stung as she realized she had done almost all the book's "don'ts."

There was still no word from Paul. Cindi drank two cups of coffee and called Anne.

"Morning, Cin. Isn't it a little early for you?"

"Yes ... I guess so. Can you meet me for lunch at the Bistro Provence?" Cindi asked.

"Sure," Anne said.

"Great, see you there at 11:00."

Anne didn't like the sound of Cindi's voice. She knew something was wrong. When she arrived at the restaurant, Cindi was already there, reading Anne's financial-planning book through big sunglasses.

"I can't believe you beat me here! I think this is a first," Anne said.

"I know. I got up early and needed to get out of the house."

"Okay, now that sounds serious." Anne, sitting down, motioned to the server to take her order. "What's going on, Cindi? You never get up early on Sunday, *especially* since you've been married."

"Oh, Anne. I don't know where to begin." Cindi started to cry.

"Tell me what's wrong, sweetie. I'm here for you." Anne took Cindi's hand and looked at her friend. Cindi's hair was tousled in stringy curls, her skin looked splotchy, and she took her sunglasses off revealing swollen, bloodshot eyes. The sad sight nearly brought her best friend to tears.

Cindi proceeded to tell Anne everything—about Paul's outbursts, reckless spending, roller-coaster-like behavior, angry outbursts, preoccupation with looking young, hair coloring, late nights at the spa, and frequent unexplained absences. And lastly, about the previous evening at the restaurant and his announcement that he wanted to buy a $15,000 palm tree.

"It's like he's having a midlife crisis, Anne. I mean, he's only 45 years old, but you'd think he was 60. And ..."

"Wait. Did you just say that he wanted to buy a $15,000 palm tree?" asked Anne.

"Yes."

"Holy hell! What kind of palm tree costs $15,000?"

"I know. It's some special kind—I can't even remember the name. But what shocked me the most is that he left me there. Walked out on me. And I was left having to pay the bill and call a cab. *He walked out on me, Anne!*"

"His behavior is inexcusable. He clearly sounds like he's having some kind of breakdown. Was he waiting for you when you took the taxi home?"

"No. And I haven't heard a word from him since," Cindi said.

"Cindi, I'm so sorry this has happened. I thought everything was going so well."

"It has been, Anne. Paul can be the most loving, wonderful, and attentive man in the world, a true prince in every way. But then, there are other times—at the drop of the hat—when he can turn on me and get so angry and withdrawn. I don't know where it comes from. And he won't even discuss money," Cindi said.

"I'm no expert, but there is definitely something wrong with him. It's like he's exhibiting traits of a personality disorder. Who knows ... maybe he's a narcissist. I read about narcissism when I went through my divorce. It's when everything a person does is self-serving. Deep down, these people are usually very insecure. Yes, they can blind you with their brilliant bursts of charm, but it's all for their own pleasure—a way for them to seduce and manipulate," Anne said.

"I don't know, maybe it's just the stress of a new marriage and family. It's a lot to take on for anyone. He has a difficult ex-wife—to say the least—two resentful children, a stressful job, and now he has a new wife and step-daughter. That has to be a big burden," Cindi said.

"Cinderella, please stop making excuses for him. He's a grown man, and more importantly, this is not your fault. Paul clearly has serious issues ... not to mention being a spendthrift. And you said yourself that you have no idea how much money he makes or what his debts are. He's fiscally irresponsible. I thought that from day one. Of course, maybe he can afford that house, I don't know. But apparently, you don't know, either. I just hate to see you get roped into something that's not fiscally wise."

"Well, the loan has been signed, and I cosigned it—and everything is in motion for us to move into the new house in January or February. Anne, I meant to tell you about this new house we're buying," said Cindi as she began to cry. "I just didn't want to talk to you about it on Thanksgiving. And then Kaitlyn let it slip, and I ..."

"Don't worry, Cin. I understand. I do. How did he talk you into buying it?"

Cindi explained in detail how Paul had sprung the new house on her and convinced her to contribute to the down payment. Anne shook her head.

"He didn't really give you a choice, did he? Just like he didn't give you much of a choice with the palm tree. He isn't really interested in compromise or making financial decisions *together*. It sounds like he's very selfish."

"I know. He didn't give me a choice, really, or the option to discuss it together. And I was afraid if I refused to cosign for it, he'd get upset and it would ruin our Thanksgiving," Cindi said.

"So, his angry outbursts have been going on for a while?"

"Yes. I didn't really notice them until after we got home from our honeymoon. And it seems to be getting worse. He's also so obsessed with his body that he's taking all these anti-aging meds. Anne, he's much more vain and self-absorbed than I ever imagined. All his body stuff just seems so … so … obsessive!"

"I'll help you with whatever you need. We'll figure this out and get to the bottom of it. I'm here for you and Kaitlyn; you know that," said Anne, while hugging her friend.

"I know. I'm so grateful for your friendship," Cindi said.

Anne held her best friend as she cried. She did not want to hate Paul, but it was difficult not to at this moment. *How in the world could he treat sweet, lovable Cindi like that? How could he walk out on her at the restaurant? What is wrong with him?*

Chapter 20

After returning home from lunch with Anne, Cindi thought that surely Paul would be there waiting for her, ready to apologize profusely for what he had done, but that had not happened. It was 3:00 p.m. when she went to her bedroom and changed into her pjs. The sky was overcast, and the forecast called for rain. She had spent several hours with Anne, discussing Paul's behavior and their financial issues, and trying to figure out what was causing his outbursts of anger—or childish tantrums, as Anne would say. They had come up with several theories, but neither she nor Anne was sure what underlying problems would explain his behavior.

They came up with a list of "initiatives"—ways for Cindi to take responsibility and feel empowered regardless of what Paul did.

"If you protect yourself financially—as much as possible—then no matter what happens between you and Paul, you'll claim your own power and not succumb to being a victim. And the best part is that you can be beautiful, smart, and just as successful as any man," Anne said.

"It feels like I'm sacrificing a lot of my hard-earned money for this new house, and even though I know we're married, I sometimes worry I'll be paying more than my share," Cindi said.

"Money gives you choices. And when you have choices—as long as you're not completely financially or economically dependent on anyone— you at least have the option not to let anyone treat you less than you deserve to be treated. If you allow others to make financial decisions on your behalf without your input, voluntarily hand your power over to them. You become a willing victim."

Cindi nodded. "It feels like that's exactly what I've done."

Anne said, "Let's make a to-do list and come up with some financial goals so you'll feel more empowered."

"I really appreciate your help. But do we really need to do this now?" Cindi asked.

"I promise it will make you feel better. This list will help put things in perspective for you. You'll be able to identify things you already know and things you might want to learn."

Anne composed the following list:

- Educate yourself in money management and investing. Buy the *Wall Street Journal's Guide to Understanding Money and Investing*, or sign up for classes on financial planning and investing.
- Seek professional advice from a reputable CERTIFIED FINANCIAL PLANNER™ professional (CFP®), preferably fee-only. That way, you'll experience greater potential to remove conflicts of interest and allow for independent, unbiased advice.
- Create a budget and itemize your expenses in Quicken, Mint.com, or another personal finance software program of your choice. This will help you stick to a budget.
- Build an emergency/cushion fund.
- Spend responsibly, which means that you spend less than you earn and invest the rest. (It's the secret to creating wealth.)
- Pay off any credit-card debt.
- Contribute to a savings plan, a retirement plan, or both. Maximize the contributions and save at least 10–15 percent of your income.
- Review your insurance coverage. Make sure you have term life insurance for Kaitlyn's sake.

- Make sure you have an updated will and other estate planning documents.
- Keep solid financial records and update them as often as needed.

"Of course, I don't have a magic wand," Anne said. "But these guidelines will empower you, no matter what Paul does or what happens in your marriage. If we take the proper steps—regardless of that mortgage—we can focus getting you back on track to become financially independent."

Anne always felt better when she made to-do lists and organized her finances. Although she was not artistically talented like Cindi, she had other gifts. She was convinced that everyone could benefit from creating a financial plan and organizing their financial life. It truly was one significant way for a woman to feel empowered.

"What about the emotional planning?" asked Cindi, with tears shining in her eyes. "How do I handle all these emotions?"

"Honey, I don't know how to explain all of this, but we can do some research and hopefully find a good therapist who can help," Anne said.

"It's a start," said Cindi. But even though she spoke the words, her heart was not in it. She hadn't hit bottom, but it felt like it. And all the budget planning and psychotherapists or psychiatrists in the world could not change that.

As the afternoon turned into early evening, Cindi lay in bed and forgot about her to-do list and researching mental health experts. She simply wished Paul would come home. She started feeling as though maybe she had blown the whole incident out of proportion and that maybe, just maybe, he had a reason to be frustrated with her. In fact, perhaps he was trying so hard to be the perfect husband and give her everything she could ever dream of. And then when he suggested that they buy a special palm tree for their front yard, she questioned him, which made him defensive. Maybe if she had trusted him more, this would have never happened. Wasn't she undermining his intelligence when she suggested that he couldn't afford that palm tree? He was old enough to know what he could afford.

At the same time, it upset her when she thought about cosigning the loan for a house that was beyond their means. But was she just exaggerating her problems? After all, Paul might have much more money than she suspected. The more she thought about it, the more she realized that perhaps she was wrong and had behaved badly.

Cindi called his cell phone and left a message, "Paul, call me when you can. I ... I ... I'm really sorry about last night." She couldn't stand it when he was angry with her.

The skies became gray, and within minutes, big drops of rain slashed haphazardly against the windows. She went into her studio in the sunroom, which belied its name and looked gloomy and gray. The colors suited her mood. She sat down to work on some sketches while thinking over everything she and Anne had discussed.

Cindi began sketching a long midnight blue—almost Gothic-looking— dress with long, flowing sleeves and an oversized hood. It was nothing like the classic, elegant clothes she usually created.

She looked at the clock. The moments crawled by. One second. Two seconds. Each tick of the clock mimicked her heartbeat.

She had left the message for Paul an hour ago, and still no answer. She became nervous and fidgety. She thought about driving by his house to see if his car was there. But Kaitlyn was supposed to be home anytime, so she couldn't leave. She wanted to talk to him, hear his voice, and smooth things over. She wanted to make this marriage work and create a beautiful family for Kaitlyn, Daniel, and Isabella. She wanted to be the perfect wife, and she hated all this anxiety and stress.

When Kaitlyn came home, she asked, "Mommy, where's Paul?"

"He's busy. He's been working on some cases and may not be home tonight," Cindi said.

"But where will he sleep?"

"Oh, he can sleep at his house since it's so close to his office." Cindi didn't really know what to say to Kaitlyn, but she knew she did not want to alarm her or cause her to worry.

Cindi made mac 'n' cheese for dinner and insisted that Kaitlyn get to bed early for school the next day.

"Are you sure everything's okay?" asked Kaitlyn.

"Why, of course, honey! Why do you ask?"

"Your eyes look puffy," Kaitlyn said.

"It's just the weather, Kater-tater. You know how my sinuses get when it rains. Don't you worry your pretty little head about anything. Everything is perfectly fine."

"Okay, Mommy. If Paul comes home tonight, tell him to give me a kiss goodnight. I miss him!"

"I will, honey," Cindi said, biting her lip. She would not start bawling. She tucked Kaitlyn in, turned the light out, and went back to the kitchen, where she poured herself a glass of wine.

Anne called at 8:30 and asked, "Cin, how are you doing? Any word from Paul?"

"No, I left him a message on his phone around 3:00 but haven't heard anything from him all day. Anne, I don't want him to be mad at me."

"Look. Stop this ridiculousness right now. He should be calling you and apologizing for his immature outbursts. On his knees would be a good start. None of this is your fault, so please stop making excuses for his bad behavior. I don't mean to be tough with you, but believe me, you didn't do anything wrong," Anne said.

"But I can't stand it when we're fighting. It makes me feel sick and horrible inside, and ... well, maybe I blew the whole thing out of proportion," Cindi said.

"No, you didn't. You're a married couple. You're supposed to make joint financial decisions and *compromise*. You need to know about his finances, and you have a right to question big purchases. I think he's used to getting his way because he's so handsome and charming. I imagine women fall all over his feet to do what he wants, but Cin, he's your husband, and you have every right to question him. Remember, you're strong. You're empowered. You have your own financial and career goals. Remember this, okay?"

"It's just that, in the overall scheme of things, careers and finances don't seem that important. Love is what's important, and I want to make this marriage work."

"Being in control of your life—finances and all—makes love better. Going broke will not make your relationship better ... that much I know. Promise me you won't call him again tonight," said Anne.

"I'll try not to," said Cindi.

"It's possible he just needs a night or two to cool off, and then everything will be okay," said Anne, trying her best to reassure Cindi.

"I hope you're right."

"Meanwhile, let's get together tomorrow afternoon. Can you meet for coffee after lunch?" asked Anne.

"Sure. I promised my agent that I'd send over some sketches, but I should be free around 3:30, after I take Kaitlyn to ice-skating practice."

"Sounds good. I have a light day, so let's meet. Meanwhile, before we get together, I want to do some research. I have some ideas about what could be triggering Paul's outbursts," Anne said.

"All right, Anne. Thanks for being there for me."

"Sweetie, I will always be here for you. You can always count on me!"

"Love you, Anne," Cindi said.

"Love you, too. Now stop thinking about this and get some rest!"

The rain continued throughout the evening, pooling in large puddles in the yard and on the street. Cindi drank some more wine and worked on her sketches. At 10:00 p.m., she stood up and stretched. She was now really upset that Paul hadn't called. She just wanted him to come home. The house felt empty and lonely without him. *Dammit*, she said to herself. *Why did I have to make such a big deal of things?*

As she stretched her arms above her head, Cindi heard someone open the front door. Her heart lurched a bit, and she walked to the hallway. There stood Paul in the dark, carrying a dozen red roses. Behind him, the rain shimmered like falling icicles in front of the streetlight, casting a halo behind his body. His hair was wet and plastered to his head, and the flowers were a bit droopy from the rain. "Can you forgive me?" he said sheepishly as he stepped inside.

"Oh, Paul!" she cried. "I am so sorry about last night ... for doubting you ... for questioning you," she said.

She ran to him, and he dropped the flowers on the floor as he took her in his arms and said, "I am an idiot. I don't know why I got so upset. I am so sorry ... oh, Cinderella ..."

"I'm so sorry, too. If you want a new palm tree, then we'll get a new palm tree! I don't care!" Cinderella said.

He lifted her, grabbed her buttocks with both his hands, and started carrying her to the living room. But they didn't get very far. One minute they were standing, and the next they were on the floor in the hallway. They tore off each other's clothes, and the next thing Cindi knew, he was on top of her—his body hard and firm against hers. She felt his hot mouth on her skin and his big hands on her shoulders. Then his hands flew all over her body. His mouth, hot and wet, fastened onto her as she moaned in ecstasy. Then he went lower, devouring every inch of her—until she felt the urgency to have him. "Now," she demanded. "*Now!*"

He cried out her name as he finally arched into her, and she felt her own body shuddering in release. *God!*

They lay on the floor in each other's arms for a long while afterward, listening to the rain pound the streets. Finally, the weather calmed, and they went to bed. All was right in Cindi's world as long as her Prince Charming loved her.

Chapter 21

The next day, Paul left early for work while Cindi was still in bed. He told her he would be home at a decent time for dinner. "That was a wonderful night, my Cinderella," he said as he kissed her and headed out. She then helped Kaitlyn prepare for school, assuring her that Paul had come home and all was well.

Cindi was so happy that Paul was back to being his loving, romantic self. This was how she liked him—when he brought her flowers, whispered sweet things in her ear, and made love to her like a feisty pirate who had just come in from a stormy night at sea!

At the same time, she couldn't help but worry about when the next outburst might come. Maybe that was the last one. Or maybe if she were more patient and trusting, they would not have to go through another fight like that ever again. After all, if he wanted to purchase things for their new home, what was the big deal? They were both earning solid incomes, so why would she allow Anne's concerns influence her own sense of what was right? The bottom line was that

Cindi wanted this marriage to work, and she would do whatever was necessary to make it happen.

Now that Paul and Kaitlyn had left, she was finally alone in the house. She tried to work on her sketches, but her mind darted all over the place. She decided that the only way to calm her distracted state would be to figure out the reason behind Paul's erratic mood swings.

Cindi went into the bedroom and opened his closet door. They each had their own closet and separate vanities. Normally, she would never go into his closet—it would be a violation of his privacy, after all. But tough times called for drastic action. Her marriage was at stake, so she needed to investigate. She looked to see if she could find something that might provide answers.

In Paul's bathroom, she opened a drawer and saw bottles of common over-the-counter medications, toothpaste, a bottle of liquid that looked as though it was prescribed, and two used syringes. She looked at the bottle and syringes and saw the word *Testosterone* printed on them. Resting at the bottom of the drawer was a brochure. She thumbed through it and read the following:

Isn't it time to experience a new, younger you? Physician's Advanced Anti-Aging Program *is a proven age-management regimen for men.*

Aging is inevitable, but how you age is not. So take control and start your journey to the Fountain of Youth today. Call for a free consultation or visit us online ...

The brochure showed before and after images of men in their late 50s and 60s. The "before" photos reflected overweight, unhealthy guys who needed to cut back on donuts and beer and would benefit from spending time on a treadmill. The "after" shots revealed strapping, strong, virile men, ready to please their ladies. Their sculpted six-packs and strong arms signaled that this anti-aging protocol could yield amazing results.

The Physician's Advanced Anti-Aging Program claimed to do the following:

- *Increase youthful energy*
- *Boost lean muscle mass*
- *Heighten thinking*
- *Develop healthier bones*
- *Increase libido*

- *Boost the immune system*
- *Develop vitality and a sense of well-being*

It certainly sounds good. Heck, maybe there's a version of this for women, thought Cindi. Underneath the brochure, she found a price sheet. The cost to start the program was $4,000 followed by a Monthly Consultation Fee that comprised blood work and meetings with a team of specialists: doctors, nutritionists, psychologists, and personal trainers. This cost $1,000 per month with a minimum six-month commitment, prepaid upon beginning the program. What followed was a big disclaimer at the bottom that read:

Health insurance does not cover this type of medical treatment.

It shocked Cindi to think that Paul had paid $10,000 to participate in the Physician's Advanced Anti-Aging Program. She knew that, for both men and women, aggressive and expensive anti-aging solutions were becoming more popular. *But Paul is a relatively young 45 years old, while the guys in the photos are a decade or more older than he is!*

In her eyes, 45 was too young to start such drastic and costly treatment. To her dismay, there was a paragraph in fine print that listed possible side effects, which included weakness, dizziness, pain throughout the body, and moderate to severe mood changes, including irritability.

Cindi could not help but wonder if these gels and injections had anything to do with Paul's erratic moods and angry outbursts. She had heard that testosterone could make men more aggressive. If too much male hormone was the problem, it would ease her mind.

Cindi went to her computer and Googled "testosterone side effects." Many sites proclaimed miraculous benefits. A few featured negative side effects, such as increased irritability, anger, and mood swings. She printed out a few pages to take with her so she could show Anne.

Anne and Cindi planned to meet for coffee that afternoon. Anne had done some research of her own and brought that information with her.

Once she arrived at Starbucks, Cindi scanned the room and spotted her best friend. She pulled a chair up to the table where Anne was sitting. "From the look of happiness on your face, I'd say that Paul came home last night," Anne said.

"Yes," said Cindi, blushing. "He was so sweet and apologetic. He brought me a dozen red roses. Honestly, Anne, I was just relieved and happy to see him."

"What's that on your arm?" Anne asked as she stared at the bruise.

"Where?" Cindi scanned her arm. "Oh, that! Um, well, we might have gotten a little ... you know ... on the floor ..."

"Oh, please!" said Anne, laughing. "I don't need to hear about it. It's been quite a long time since I've had to worry about bruises or anything."

"God, he's so sexy and amazing in bed. I mean, Richard and I had okay sex. But it was boring compared to what Paul and I have."

"It's just so strange how he can be so sexy, romantic, and loving one night and then turn around and act like a complete jackass the next."

"I agree, but remember, I was partly to blame because I didn't trust him. I think he's trying hard to impress me and be a true Prince Charming, and it's putting a lot of pressure on him."

"Please stop. We've gone over this already. You were not to blame in any way, so enough of that. Anyway, I wanted to show you something. I've been doing some Internet research, and maybe I'm reaching here, but it's possible that Paul has a personality disorder. In other words, maybe he has a problem that causes him to behave this way. Not that it's an excuse, but it may be an explanation." Anne put her stack of notes on the table.

"I guess that's possible. But, to be honest, I don't know anything about personality disorders. In the meantime, I've been looking through his things, and I found some anti-aging gels in his bathroom," Cindi said.

"Anti-aging gels?" asked Anne.

"It's actually testosterone, and I think Paul's taking large doses of it. I found a bottle of gel and some empty syringes of it. It seems like an awful lot of hormones. In my eyes, he's far too young to be taking such drastic action. But you know how focused he is on his looks. Anyway, I discovered that the side effects include irritability, mood swings, and anger. Look, I printed out some of the reports," Cindi said. She showed them to Anne.

"Good God. This stuff looks expensive!" said Anne.

"Oh, it is," Cindi said. She hadn't planned on telling Anne that he had already amassed invoices for thousands of dollars.

"Do you think the gels could be causing a personality disorder? To be honest, based on what you've shared already, it wouldn't surprise me. Here's some information I found about narcissistic personality disorder." Cindi picked up one of the pages, which read:

People with narcissistic personality disorder may do the following:

- *React to criticism with rage, shame, or humiliation.*
- *Feel deep insecurity about certain aspects of their lives and view criticism as threatening, shameful, or humiliating. They may react with rage to protect themselves.*
- *Overcompensate for, or behave in direct opposition to, an area in which they feel insecure. For example, if they have an insecurity about not having enough money or not being good-looking enough, they may spend too much or excessively focus on physical appearances—these are in an effort to hide what they feel insecure about.*
- *Blame others rather than take responsibility for their actions.*
- *Seek immediate gratification.*
- *Take advantage of others to achieve their own goals.*
- *Have excessive feelings of self-importance.*
- *Exaggerate achievements and talents.*
- *Be preoccupied with fantasies of success, power, beauty, intelligence, or ideal love.*
- *Need constant attention and admiration.*
- *Disregard the feelings of others and have little ability to feel empathy.*
- *Have obsessive self-interest.*
- *Pursue mainly selfish goals.*

"Wow!" said Cindi. "Some of this does sound a *little* like Paul." Her words felt as if she was betraying her husband.

"Yes. But maybe the medicine is causing these traits to be magnified," Anne said.

"It honestly would make me feel a whole lot better if the hormone stuff is the reason for his mood swings and he's not permanently like this. Because that's easier to treat—stop taking the medicine, and the anger outbursts stop. If he has a personality disorder even *without* the extra hormones, I don't know if there's any cure."

"All these hormones have to be adversely affecting him. Maybe you should talk to him about it," Anne said.

"I really hate to bring up anything controversial or stress inducing right now. Christmas is around the corner, there's our new house, and I just don't know if this is a good time."

"You may be right. But if his mood swings continue, you might be forced to discuss this with him. I mean, you can't be afraid to speak with your husband about things. You can't always walk on eggshells!" Anne said.

"I know," said Cindi. Then Cindi realized she'd been totally self-absorbed for quite a while now. She felt as though she had been taking and not giving when it came to Anne for the past few weeks.

"By the way, how are you doing, Anne? We've been so focused on my drama for the past couple of days ... well, ever since my wedding. You haven't told me what's going on in your life," Cindi asked.

"Oh, things are good. Work is very busy—especially now at the end of the year," Anne said.

"Did Trevor call?" Cindi asked.

"As a matter of fact, he did. We're going out for a casual dinner this weekend," Anne said with a big smile.

"That's great! He seems like such a nice guy. Paul has had nothing but great things to say about him," said Cindi.

"We'll see. It's no big deal, of course. Just two adults having dinner," Anne said.

"Well, you never know. You two just might hit it off," Cindi said.

"Mmm, we might. It would be nice," Anne said.

They finished their drinks and talked until it was time for Cindi to pick up Kaitlyn from ice-skating practice.

"Before I head out, I just want to make sure—are you coming to Kaitlyn's ice-skating recital?" asked Cindi.

"This Friday?"

"Yes," said Cindi. "Does it conflict with your date?"

"Oh no, it does! Trevor and I made plans to go out Friday night, but here's what I can do. I'll bring him to the recital first, and then he and I can have a late dinner afterward. I'm sure the recital will only last until about 9:00 p.m., and I don't mind eating later, anyway. Trevor seemed to like Kaitlyn a lot, so I think he'll be game to go," said Anne.

"That's a great idea! She's been planning on Paul coming, so we can all sit together," said Cindi.

"You're welcome to come to dinner with us afterward—Kaitlyn, too," said Anne.

"Anne, I'd *never* show up to any first date of yours. You and Trevor need to get to know one another."

"I guess you're right—we do."

They shared a laugh and then parted company. If only life were simple and fun like this all the time. But that is not the case.

Chapter 22

*P*aul arrived home around 6:00 p.m. with pizza for Cindi and Kaitlyn. He was lighthearted and charming. Although Cindi would have preferred that he brought something healthier to eat, more than anything she was just happy to have him home. And of course, Kaitlyn was delighted with both Paul and the pizza.

Life had seemed to return to normal. Once again, she had her Prince Charming back. Paul was attentive and loving, and she was busy designing new clothes for her agent to show to celebrities. Meanwhile, Kaitlyn was making a list for Santa, and everyone's attention was on Christmas.

Their loan was approved, and they would be able to move into *Castillo de Amor* in a couple of months. They had not decided exactly when to sell their current homes but would address that topic after the holidays.

That week, Paul proceeded to make plans to purchase the expensive palm tree, and all seemed well. He came home late most nights due to massage appointments or working late, but Cindi was too busy to notice. When he did arrive, he was loving and attentive—every bit the Prince Charming she had first met. As a result, his late nights away from home didn't matter to her as much.

It was Friday evening—the night of Kaitlyn's ice-skating recital—and everyone was excited. Paul knew that Trevor and Anne were going to join them at the rink, and he liked the idea. He had even suggested that maybe all of them could go out later for a hot chocolate. To Cindi's surprise, Trevor had agreed. She thought they should leave Trevor and Anne alone so they could have dinner by themselves, but Trevor insisted. "No, I think it will be fun for all of us to go out," he said.

Kaitlyn was beside herself, eager to show off her ice-skating talents as well as her new costume, which Cindi had designed. The children from Kaitlyn's ice-skating studio were performing *The Nutcracker on Ice*—a version of the classic ballet—and there was a definite holiday feeling in the air.

Paul called that afternoon and told Cindi that he would be late to the recital due to a last-minute case he needed to work on. As always, Cindi was understanding. She and Kaitlyn went to the ice-skating rink without him.

When they arrived, Kaitlyn squealed with happiness. Living in tropical Florida, the rink was the closest they would get to a "winter wonderland" for Christmas. The entire space was decorated with snow and twinkling lights. Cindi took her daughter backstage to get dressed for the recital.

"Is Paul really coming?" asked Kaitlyn, her eyes gleaming with anticipation.

"He'll be here as soon as he can. He wouldn't miss your big night. I promise you!" she said.

"I wish Danny and Bella could have come. They don't know how to ice-skate, but I think they'd like it," Kaitlyn said.

"I wish they could be here, too," said Cindi.

"At least Auntie Anne and her new friend, Trevor, are here!" said Kaitlyn.

"Yes, that's true." Cindi laughed. "Now, go get into costume. I'll be out in the audience, cheering you on."

"Okay, Mommy. Love you!" Kaitlyn said.

"Love you, too, Kater-tater."

Cinderella left her daughter and found Anne and Trevor sitting halfway up in the bleachers.

"We don't want to be too close to the floor, or we'll miss the overall spectacle," Anne said.

"I agree. Glad you could make it, Trevor," said Cindi.

"I wouldn't miss it for anything. I don't have any children of my own, and Kaitlyn is really special," he said.

"It's so sweet of you to say that. By the way, did you see Paul at work before you left?" Cindi asked.

"No. He and I are working on different cases. It's been crazy busy around the office the past couple of weeks, though," Trevor said.

"Where is he, by the way?" asked Anne.

"He said he'd be here later," said Cindi.

"Yeah, I'm sure he'll be along any moment," said Trevor.

Cindi pulled her jacket close around her. It was cold inside the rink, and if she didn't know any better, she would have thought snowfall would come down at any moment. They were all dressed in jeans and sweaters, prepared for the winter spectacle. Cindi had brought her video camera and planned on taping the entire show.

The lights dimmed, and the rink was transformed into a winter wonderland. Kaitlyn skated onto the rink and skillfully twirled and danced on the ice with the other skaters. Cindi was so proud of her. Even at seven years old, she was elegant and poised.

As the evening wore on, Cindi looked around expectantly for Paul, but he didn't show up. Cindi texted him, asking where he was, but he didn't respond. It did not make any sense to her. The uncomfortably familiar sick feeling settled in her stomach. *Our week has gone so well—no arguments, and no disagreements over trees or money. Actually, no discussions about either. None of this makes sense,* she thought to herself.

When the show was over, Kaitlyn came running out from backstage after she had changed out of her costume. "Mommy, where's Paul? Did he come?" asked Kaitlyn, looking around the rink.

"Honey, he's still tied up at work or something. He couldn't make it," Cindi said.

Kaitlyn's face fell.

"I'm sure something must have happened at work," Anne assured both Cindi and Kaitlyn. "Paul knows how important this night is."

"Yes, I'm sure he must be delayed. More importantly, you were great, Kaitlyn!" Trevor said.

"Yes, honey, you were wonderful. You were so graceful out there on the ice," Anne said.

"Thank you. I had so much fun," Kaitlyn said.

"Well, let's all go get some hot chocolate. Cindi, why not just text Paul and tell him where we are?" Anne said.

"That sounds good," Cindi said. She texted Paul the name of the bistro where they planned to go. She tried not to show it, but it really upset her that he had missed Kaitlyn's recital. And she knew that Kaitlyn was deeply disappointed, too. But Kaitlyn, like her mom, was trying to act as though it didn't bother her.

They arrived at Bistro Provence, which was known for its exquisite hot chocolate. After a few minutes, Paul came in looking disheveled, nervous, and uptight. He was apologetic and said that he had just wrapped things up at the office. Cindi tried to act nonchalant about it, and even Kaitlyn smiled when she saw him. They all told Paul how wonderful Kaitlyn had performed, and Cindi promised to show him photos. On the outside, Paul and Cindi's relationship appeared to be okay. But deep in Cindi's heart, she knew things were not okay. Not at all.

Chapter 23

After drinking hot chocolate at Bistro Provence, the newlyweds said goodbye to Anne and Trevor, and everyone parted company. Paul and Cindi drove in separate cars, so Cindi did not have a chance to ask him about his night. On their way home, Kaitlyn reflected on her performance and the excitement of the night.

"I'm so happy that Paul could have hot chocolate with us, but I wish he could have seen me ice-skate, Mommy. He would have been proud of me," she said.

"I'm so proud of you, Kater-tater. And yes, Paul missed a wonderful night. But, as he said, he was busy with work. He has an extremely demanding job, honey," Cindi said.

"I know, Mom. It's just that Daddy never comes to any of my shows, and I was hoping Paul would come. He's never seen me ice-skate in a recital."

While they were in the bistro, Paul had avoided eye contact with Cindi and tried hard to be upbeat and charming. But it was an act and an obvious one at that. He had fidgeted and was even short with the server several times. His eyes darted around the room continually, as if he were looking for someone, which didn't make any sense to Cindi.

Anne had looked pointedly at Cindi a few times with raised eyebrows and eyes that asked, "What's up with Paul?" Cindi shrugged a couple of times. She didn't know.

But Cindi knew something was "off" with him. She didn't want to ruin Kaitlyn's evening, so she just stayed neutral and spoke and smiled at the appropriate times. Deep down, she was furious with Paul for missing Kaitlyn's recital.

After they arrived home, Kaitlyn prepared for bed, and Cindi kissed her goodnight. She then started her bedtime routine.

Despite marriage and cohabitation, she still wasn't exactly sure what he did before bed. What she did know was that it consisted of showering, injecting hormones into his body, and slathering prescription gels on his skin. Cindi's nightly routine comprised of taking a hot bath, brushing her teeth, and putting on her PJs. At night, her regimen took about fifteen minutes—unless she wanted to luxuriate in bubbles while sipping a glass of wine or indulging in an occasional visit from Paul in the tub. Tonight, it felt as though she had been waiting for hours for Paul to finish with his nightly routine.

The two went about their evening without saying a word to one another. The silence spoke volumes. Normally, after an evening out with Kaitlyn and friends, she and Paul would return home, maybe have some wine, and talk late into the evening until they collapsed in each other's arms. Tonight, however, Cindi's frustration and Paul's evasiveness stretched before them like an abyss that would swallow them whole if either of them opened up and started sharing thoughts and feelings.

Cindi worked up the courage to break the silence. "I'm sorry you couldn't come to Kaitlyn's recital tonight," she said.

"Well, I have things to do this weekend and won't have time to work on my case, so I had to get it done tonight."

"But you promised Kaitlyn you'd be there, and she was looking forward to you seeing her recital. She was really disappointed," she said.

"Look, I'm doing the best I can. I had to work, and I couldn't get there. I came for hot chocolate, so get off my back," he said.

"I ... I ... I was just saying that Kaitlyn was disappointed, that's all," Cindi said, taken aback by his sudden anger. She tried to smooth things out. "But she was happy you came for hot chocolate. We just wish you could have been at the recital. You promised, after all."

"Everyone is so f**king demanding of my time, and I have mammoth amount of responsibilities at work that you don't understand. How can I be everywhere at once?" he shouted.

"I don't know why you get so angry over my questions. It's not right. I don't think there's anything wrong with me asking these things," she said.

"I'm done talking, so leave me the f**k alone. Since I can't get any peace in here, I'm sleeping in the den," Paul said. He grabbed a pillow and a blanket off the chaise lounge and stormed out of the bedroom.

Cindi sat there, shocked. Once again, Paul had blindsided her with his angry and disrespectful outburst. But this time, it wasn't at a restaurant where he abandoned her. It was in her own house.

On Saturday, Paul had already left by the time Cindi woke up. She hadn't slept much the night before and only fell asleep after deciding that she would empower herself to take charge of her life—whether Paul liked it or not. She continually heard Anne's words of encouragement as she tossed and turned in bed.

Later that day, Anne and Cindi spoke on the phone while Kaitlyn played in her room. "How was your date with Trevor?" Cindi asked.

"It was nice. After the hot chocolate, we had a late dinner and drinks. It was really sweet, and we talked late into the evening. And no, we didn't sleep together. I know that's what you're wondering," Anne said.

"You make a nice couple. And no, I wasn't going to ask if you slept together. Are you going to see each other again?" Cindi asked.

"Yes. I don't know if it will go anywhere. He's shy, and I'm not sure if we'd be compatible in the long term, but for now I'm enjoying his company," Anne said.

"I'm glad," said Cindi.

"How about you? Did Paul explain what took so long at work and why he had to miss the recital?"

"Not really," Cindi said. "He was irritated with me last night because I questioned him. He ended up sleeping on the couch. Then, this morning, he left early for God knows where."

"Cindi, I think you might want to consider seeing a therapist or psychiatrist next week to get some insight. Not that I'm an expert, but I don't think his behavior is appropriate in the least."

"Do you think I should ask Paul to go with me?"

"Do you think he'd go?"

"No. In fact, it might make him even angrier if I suggested it. He thinks everything is my problem, not his. Maybe I should go first and get some guidance about next steps," Cindi said.

"It couldn't hurt. After all, we know he has mood swings and anger issues on top of being a spendthrift. Plus, you're not sure how much money he has or what his budget is, but he has no problem getting you to spend your money for things he wants, like that ridiculous palm tree. And I'm no expert, but from what I've read, his self-centered behaviors make it seem like he has a blend of some personality disorders. Who knows if his anti-aging medicine is causing it or if that just exacerbates whatever struggles he already has. But we do know that the anti-aging medicine can affect a person's moods and personality. There is plenty here that needs to be addressed. A mental-health expert could help you sort through all this, including your emotions. It would be a start, Cin, and a good one."

"Thanks, Anne. I'll do some research and call one next week. What are you doing later?" Cindi asked.

"I have to do some work today. Last-minute, end-of-the-year client issues. I don't know why everyone waits until now to do estate planning and get their affairs in order."

"Procrastination. I get that!" said Cindi, laughing.

"I know, but it's frustrating. Anyway, Trevor and I are going out for a late dinner after I finish," Anne said.

"That's so great. Let me know how it goes, okay?"

"Absolutely! And, Cin, don't worry. Things are going to be all right."

"I hope so," said Cindi.

"Paul is a good man deep down. And if he's willing to work on himself and work through these issues, you'll have a great marriage and the man of your dreams. After all, many people go through a rough transition period during the first year of marriage. You'll find your footing," Anne said.

"I really hope so. There are times when he really is a Prince Charming, and the sex is absolutely wonderful. That's the man I want. But when he disappears into this selfish, sullen, angry, spendthrift child, I can't stand him."

"Well, going to see a therapist would be a good start to addressing the issues."

"Thanks, Anne. I'll talk to you later. Have a great night with Trevor," Cindi said.

"Okay," said Anne.

The day was clear, sunny, breezy, and perfect. The birds sang, and all seemed right with the world. *It's an illusion*, Cindi thought. She resisted the urge to cry. But instead, she kept repeating the same mantra to herself: *I am a strong, independent, financially secure woman, and I can do anything. I will survive.*

Cindi worked on her designs and did laundry. She even visited the attic and pulled out boxes of Christmas decorations. Kaitlyn was begging her to put up the tree and adorn the house for the holidays. She didn't know what to buy for Daniel and Isabella and worried that anything she purchased would not be good enough for them. They were unappreciative of her efforts—not to mention that they expected expensive toys and special treatment. Paul said that Mal had spoiled them, but she wondered if Paul was really the contributor to their feelings of entitlement. Cindi also didn't know what she would buy Paul for Christmas. After all, she was purchasing a $15,000 palm tree for their new house. Did they even need to buy each other anything else?

Cinderella went to Whole Foods Market and bought groceries for the upcoming week. Ever since she and Paul got married, she made an effort to cook healthy meals. They had not been husband and wife for that long, and her cooking skills needed some improvement. She tried her best nonetheless. She wanted to be the perfect wife, mother, and professional. But things weren't moving in the direction that Cindi had hoped.

Paul arrived home on Saturday evening and acted as though nothing had happened. Cindi did not ask him where he had been, and he did not volunteer an explanation. She suspected he had been at the spa because he smelled of mango oil, which they used during salt scrubs and massages.

Paul took Kaitlyn and Cindi to a children's movie. Kaitlyn loved the movie, and Cindi's heart melted at his gesture. Meanwhile, Paul hadn't apologized for the evening before or commented on sleeping on the couch. And he barely talked to Cindi or Kaitlyn. They discussed the movie and superficial matters, such as how they would decorate the house. Kaitlyn was just happy to be with the two of them.

To anyone on the outside, it seemed like the perfect evening. But Cindi knew it wasn't. She felt as though he was alienating her emotionally. His abuse was painful and felt like rejection. It was one thing if a client rejected her designs—she could handle that. But it was another when someone she loved rejected her *emotionally*.

That Saturday evening, she and Paul had sex, but that's all it was—sex. There were no long, loving kisses, no tender lovemaking, no pillow talk, no love poems tucked in unusual places, and no intimate whispers in her ear. The sex didn't mean that things were okay between them, and she knew this. She wondered if

Paul was trying to punish her for questioning him. He knew she cherished their lovemaking and his insatiable appetite when they made love. It was almost as if he was purposefully withholding from her emotionally.

On Sunday, after a quiet breakfast of eggs and toast while Paul read the newspaper and Kaitlyn chatted about her day's plans with Arielle, Paul disappeared again. His parting words were, "I have work to do. I'll be back later." He coldly kissed Cindi on the cheek—the peck was empty and emotionless—and headed out the door.

Kaitlyn went to Arielle's for the day. Since she was restless, Cindi decided to drive to their new house, their *Castillo de Amor*, to see where they might plant the palm tree. While driving, Cindi thought about everything that was happening in her marriage. How could he have changed so completely? *How could he be so charming and wonderful one minute and so cold, distant, and angry the next? What have I done wrong? Is it me, or is it really Paul and all his anti-aging medicines?*

As she drove through her new neighborhood, she passed Mal's house. Cindi had mixed emotions about living this close to Paul's ex-wife. Sure, she understood that it could be good for the children, but was it good for her marriage? She slowed down her car as she approached their new house.

She saw Paul's car, the real estate agent's, and another car she did not recognize, all parked in front of *Castillo de Amor*. Cindi braked hard, and with her heart beating like a galloping horse, she pulled over and parked along the curb. Leaving their new house was Paul, the agent, and a beautiful young woman. Cindi knew immediately who it was: Andrea Parks, the 25-year-old paralegal from Paul's firm.

Cindi's heart dropped into her stomach.

Chapter 24

Cindi sat in her car stunned. *Stunned!* Fortunately, Paul couldn't see her. The real estate agent, Paul, and Andrea stood by their cars, laughing and talking for a few moments. Paul then opened Andrea's door, and she stepped inside. One by one, they all left. Cindi slumped down in her car seat just in case he looked her way as he drove off. He did not.

What the hell? Is he having an affair—and so soon after our wedding? thought Cindi.

Paul had often talked about how cheating was unacceptable. And with the exception of a couple of nights when they were fighting, Cindi and Paul had sex almost every day. She knew there had to be a reasonable explanation. He was probably just bragging and showing off the house to Andrea. He liked to boast about his accomplishments. In fact, Paul had told everyone at the firm about their new house. It would be just like him to bring Andrea to see it. And Cindi had not witnessed them kiss or hug or do anything else that would imply they were more than friends.

Still, it shocked her, and she was jealous. She hated being jealous. It was Sunday, and he could have been home with Cindi, enjoying the day with his wife instead of showing their new house to a coworker! And a young, pretty one at that.

Cindi sat there for a few minutes, trying to decide what to do. Should she call Anne? No, she shouldn't, she decided. They had plans to meet on Monday to recap Anne's latest date with Trevor. Besides, Anne might be with Trevor today, and Cindi didn't want to spoil that. Cindi decided she would call a psychiatrist on Monday.

Cindi drove past *Castillo de Amor* and saw the area where they would plant the palm tree when they finally closed on the house. Cindi would never love it. She continued driving toward home, feeling alone and abandoned. Naturally, Paul wasn't there when she arrived, but Cindi did not want to know where he was. She might not like the answer.

Arielle's mother dropped Kaitlyn off later in the day, and Kaitlyn begged for spaghetti for dinner, so Cindi obliged. It was an easy meal to prepare, and it would take her mind off her worries.

When Paul arrived home, he said, "Something smells good."

"Mommy made spaghetti!" Kaitlyn announced when he came into the kitchen. "And I'm helping make the salad."

"Well, it smells good," he said. He kissed Cindi lightly on the cheek.

Before she could stop herself, she said, "Did you have a good day?"

"Yes. Just work stuff. You know how busy I am these days."

"I know. It's a busy time of the year."

"I'm going to take a quick shower before dinner," he said, heading for the hallway.

"Okay. Dinner will be ready soon."

Once again, Cindi and Paul were acting very normal with one another. But underneath it all, there was discontent. She was dying to ask him why he was with Andrea Parks and the real estate agent at their new house, but she worried that he would think she was spying on him.

Paul was still cool around her—pleasant but detached. He was the perfect actor—he could perform, smile, and charm anyone at any time. But the more she got to know him, the less she saw Prince Charming. If people outside could see the real Paul, they would know that he was not so charming after all. Or, was it only her imagination? Do men act this way after marriage? Could it be the anti-aging medicine? Worse yet, was it her? Was she being paranoid and insecure?

She replayed their courtship over and over in her mind. He had been wonderful *all the time* during that period. Their lovemaking was passionate and exquisite. And hot! He wrote her love notes and poems. He constantly introduced her to new, fun destinations and took her out to dinner. And he doted on Kaitlyn, giving her presents and spending time with her. But when Cindi really thought about it, after about two months he began to disappear during the days and often came home late at night. He always said he was working out or was at the firm. There were nights when he was detached and a bit irritable, but never as he'd been the past few nights. Had she just been blinded by his attention and affection? After all, she had felt starved for love, and maybe she had ignored the red flags.

Sunday night, Paul said goodnight to her in bed, switched off the light on his nightstand, turned his back to her, and went to sleep.

Cindi lay there, wanting him to reach out, caress her, and make wild, passionate love to her. She wanted to say, "I love you, Paul. I love you more than anything in the world." She wanted to have him close so she could be assured that he loved her and wanted her. But she turned her back to him and went to sleep.

The next day, after Paul left for work and Kaitlyn went to school, Cindi called her physician and received a referral to Dr. Philip Thompson, a psychiatrist. When she phoned Dr. Thompson's office, Cindi explained that her situation was urgent and asked if a same-day appointment was an option. His administrative assistant was able to accommodate her last-minute request.

When Cindi arrived and met Dr. Thompson, she noticed that he was an attractive, tall, slender man with brown hair that was short and fashionably styled. He was probably just a few years older than Cindi. His best features were his warm brown eyes that crinkled at the corners and his pleasing smile. Plus, he had a calm and friendly demeanor. His office was comfortably decorated with sofas, plants, and tables, and Cindi immediately felt at home.

"Please, please, come in and make yourself comfortable," said Dr. Thompson. "Would you like a cup of tea or coffee?"

"Coffee would be great, thank you," said Cindi.

Dr. Thompson asked his assistant to bring them their beverages and then turned toward Cindi and asked, "What can I do for you, Mrs. Francis?"

It felt strange to have anyone address her as Mrs. Francis.

"Please call me Cindi," she said.

"What can I do for you, Cindi?" he asked.

Cindi began describing her relationship with Paul. For forty minutes, she talked nonstop. She told the therapist how wonderful Paul had been when they first met—the love notes, the romantic gestures, and the absolute chivalry. He was a true Prince Charming who was romantic and loving in every way. She shared how everyone fell in love with him when they met him and how he was irresistible in every way. Cindi went on to talk about their wedding and honeymoon and Paul's excessive spending. And she told him about the anti-aging medicine and the obsession with his body. She described him as being loving and attentive one minute and, in the next, a cold distant stranger.

Dr. Thompson nodded from time to time and wrote notes as they talked.

Finally, Cindi said, "It might all be my fault, Dr. Thompson."

"Please call me Philip."

"Okay ... Philip ... It might be all my fault, even though my best friend, Anne, says it isn't. But, honestly, maybe I'm just being paranoid and making a mountain out of a molehill. Maybe I'm being selfish and not understanding Paul's needs. I want this marriage to work, and I'm trying to be the best wife I can be, but I don't know if I'm doing the right things or saying the right things."

"Don't be so hard on yourself. This isn't your fault. What kind of anti-aging medicine is Paul taking?"

"From what I can tell, he's injecting testosterone and applying it topically, too," said Cindi.

"These hormones can wreak havoc on a person's personality and health. And I'm not aware of any reason why he would be using gels *and* injections. I highly doubt that any doctor would prescribe both at the same time. In fact, depending upon the dosage, the side effects of these hormones can be so serious that people can have manic episodes, which may intensify bipolar disorder or an underlying personality disorder."

"My friend Anne and I have learned a little about narcissistic personality disorder. But neither one of us knows much about it," said Cindi.

"I'm not saying that your husband has a disorder or that his manic episodes are a result of his anti-aging medicine. I'm just saying that it's a possibility. As I see it, we have several things we need to work on. If Paul is willing, I'd like to see each of you individually once a week and together once a week," said Dr. Thompson.

"What areas do you think are the most important to address?" asked Cindi.

"My preliminary assessment for you is that we need to work on you, your self-esteem and your own empowerment, as your friend Anne suggested. You can't really change anyone else. You can only change yourself and your attitude. If you empower yourself, you'll be better able to manage your martial issues and continue it—if you feel that's what's best for you and your daughter, and only you can decide that. As long as you feel insecure and emotional, you can't make good decisions about yourself and your family."

"So, it does start with me. I figured it was my fault," she said.

"You are not to blame. You just fell in love with a good-looking, charming man, who may have some serious issues. These men can be irresistible. But you're not a victim, either. It's up to you to feel good about yourself and empower yourself—emotionally and financially. It's up to you to be with people who bring out the best in you—not the worst."

"I want to do that. I honestly do."

"The best-case scenario is that Paul will agree to come to therapy with you as well as on his own—if he wants this marriage to work. It sounds as though he has a number of problems to deal with: he's spending beyond his means, he has a little-boy, "Peter Pan" syndrome, which we'll talk about eventually, he has an obsession with anti-aging, and perhaps anti-social and narcissistic tendencies," he said.

"Is there any hope for us?" Cindi asked.

"There's always hope. It all depends on how committed both of you are."

"I'm committed, but I'm not sure about Paul. I mean, one moment he's the most loving, wonderful man in the world, and the next, he's an angry, selfish little boy throwing a temper tantrum."

"Do you think he'll agree to therapy?"

"I don't know," said Cindi. "But I'll ask."

Dr. Thompson glanced at his wristwatch. "I'm afraid that our time is up. It was a pleasure to meet you. I look forward to seeing you next week, and let me know if Paul agrees to attend our next appointment. Before you go, let me give you a recommendation for a book," he said.

Dr. Thompson pulled his business card from his pocket and wrote the following book title on the back: *Emotional Vampires: Dealing with People Who Drain You Dry* by Albert Bernstein.

"It's a powerful book, and I think it will give you some good insight. If you have a Kindle, you can download it right away," he said.

"Thanks, Philip. At this point, I'll read anything I can get my hands on. I'll download it tonight," Cindi said.

They shook hands, and Cindi left Dr. Thompson's office. She then headed to Las Palmas to meet Anne for pomegranate margaritas. She felt somewhat better after seeing Dr. Thompson, and she liked him. *But, damn!* She had a lot to work on, and she wasn't sure Paul would agree to see the therapist. She even feared that he might throw a tantrum if she asked.

She drove silently through the streets. Pewter-gray storm clouds gathered in the sky, and the humidity was thick. Cindi felt suffocated by the enormity of her situation, as if a huge boulder were bearing down heavily on her shoulders—a new, big mortgage and a marriage to a self-absorbed man who may or may not have a personality disorder and who may or may not be having an affair with his paralegal. Even worse, she worried that her husband could be damaging his health with risky anti-aging medicine, and then there was the pressure to fix her own insecurity issues. Meanwhile, she loved him. She was crazy about him. How was she supposed to become more empowered and secure when her husband made her feel completely the opposite? How was she supposed to become financially independent when she had just cosigned a huge mortgage? How were they going to have a fun Christmas with Kaitlyn when all these other problems were weighing heavily on her heart and soul?

Raindrops were beginning to plop noisily onto the windshield as she drove into the parking lot of the bar. She quickly found a spot to park her car and then headed inside to find Anne.

Just as she entered the bar, the skies opened up, and rain beat down hard on the building. It sounded like a machine gun spitting out bullets on the roof. She pasted a smile on her face and looked for Anne.

Chapter 25

Anne had already ordered a pomegranate margarita for Cindi, and it was sitting on the table waiting for her.

"Anne, you're the best!" said Cindi. She sat down to join her.

"It's pouring outside. I barely got inside before all hell broke loose," Cindi said.

"I know. Bad weather coming from the north!" said Anne.

"So tell me, how was your date with Trevor?"

"It was good," said Anne.

"Good?" asked Cindi, inquiring as if she felt there was something more. "Nothing more to report?"

"Honestly, we're just getting to know one another. He's very sweet and a true gentleman, but I'm taking it slow."

"I think it's a good idea to take it slow. Apparently, nine months wasn't slow enough for me. It just goes to show you that you need more than a few months to know a person fully," Cindi said.

"That's true. I've known other women who have learned things about their husbands several *years* after they were married! Seems like some men can maintain a façade for quite a while before their true colors come out," Anne said.

"Well, Paul sure had me fooled. For those first few months and in Europe, he was absolutely the most wonderful man in the world. That's the man I want to be with. Where's *that* Paul?"

"So how did the rest of the weekend go?" Anne asked.

Cindi took a long sip of her margarita. "I didn't see much of him. He was gone all day on Sunday," Cindi said.

"Was it work? I know I've been swamped with year-end stuff," Anne said.

"No, well ... I don't know exactly what it was. He said it was work, but I ..." Cindi paused. "I was restless, so I drove over to the new house Sunday afternoon—you know, just to look around to see where we'll put that damn palm tree—and I saw him there with the real estate agent."

"So? That's okay, isn't it? I mean, it's possible he had some questions, don't you think?" Anne asked.

"Yes ... but that's not all." Cindi slowly took another sip of her drink.

"What do you mean?"

"Do you remember that tall, good-looking woman who's a paralegal at Paul's office? She was at our wedding party. Andrea Parks," said Cindi.

"Yes, I know exactly who you're talking about." Anne said.

"Well, she was at the house with Paul on Sunday!"

"Paul took her to see your new house?" Anne asked.

"Yes—along with the real estate agent. The good news is that they weren't by themselves," Cindi said.

"He was probably just showing off. Seems like him—you've mentioned how he likes to brag about stuff," Anne said.

"Maybe, but I'm upset and can't help but worry," said Cindi.

"Look, Cin, don't jump to conclusions. Paul doesn't strike me as the cheating type. When he's on his best behavior, he seems totally committed to you and only you."

"But as you know, he hasn't been on his best behavior lately. Anyway, I didn't confront him about her, and I'm not going to say anything ... not just yet," Cindi said.

"I understand why you wouldn't want to start an argument over a suspicion. I'm sure there's an innocent explanation," said Anne. Although she was skeptical, she tried to sound convincing because she hoped there was a good reason. For Cindi's sake.

"Anyway, the whole incident unnerved me and prompted me to call a psychiatrist this morning," Cindi said.

"That's wonderful! When is your appointment?"

"I just left his office. I saw him this afternoon, and he was very helpful," said Cindi.

"Who is it? What did he say?" asked Anne.

"His name is Dr. Philip Thompson. He came highly recommended by my general physician. I really like him, Anne. I told him everything about Paul."

"What did he say?"

"I think he hears a lot of similar stories, to be honest. I think men like Paul are more common than we think. Dr. Thompson didn't seem surprised at all. He explained that Paul could have a personality disorder and manic bi-polar-like episodes that could be the result of his anti-aging medicine, but more likely it's a combination of both. He said Paul's personality could be somewhat like that to begin with, and the medicines could just be exaggerating his tendencies. He also said that the side effects of these anti-aging medicines include irritability and aggression. He wants to see both of us, individually and as a couple, and wants me to ask Paul if he'll come," said Cindi.

"Do you think Paul will agree to this?" Anne drained the last sip of her margarita.

"I don't know, Anne. I'm inclined to wait until after the holidays to ask him because I don't want to ruin Christmas or New Year's," said Cindi.

"I understand. At the same time, I'm not sure if I would wait. After all, you're going to close on your home right after the New Year if all goes well, and Paul's willingness to go to therapy—or not—might affect what you want to do in the way of living in the new house. And maybe there's still a way for you to get out of the mortgage," said Anne.

"I think I want to wait. I can't deal with his moods right now, and I don't want to ruin my holiday with Kaitlyn. The thing is, I do love him, and I'm totally dedicated to making this marriage work. Maybe I'm just being paranoid when I think about Andrea Parks. I'm jealous, but that's my own problem. Dr. Thompson said I needed to work on my insecurities," Cindi said.

"This is not your issue; Paul has to *want* to make changes, too—to learn how to control his mood swings, temper, and spending, right?" said Anne.

"Right. Of course. I don't know what's going to happen, but I'm trying to be positive."

"I understand. I hope it all works out for you. What are you doing for Christmas?" asked Anne.

"As far as I know, it's going to be a quiet one. I haven't even done much shopping. Paul's children will be staying with us from Christmas to New Year's, and so far we haven't discussed what we're going to do. We could take them to Disney World. To tell you the truth, I'm dreading the week with his children. There's always so much drama!" Cindi said.

"Maybe they'll be better than they were at Thanksgiving," said Anne.

"I hope so. Isabella usually warms up after a while and plays well with Kaitlyn. But Daniel is a tough one. What about you? What are your plans?" asked Cindi.

"Trevor mentioned a ski trip out West."

"What?" said Cindi. She looked more closely at her best friend. Anne's face was glowing, her eyes were sparkling, and her cheeks were flushed. Oh, thought Cindi. *Anne is falling in love!*

"Have you been holding out on me? A ski trip?" Cindi asked.

"We've discussed it. No definite plans yet, but it might be fun," Anne said.

"Oh, Anne, I'm so excited for you! Keep me posted. I want to know everything about these new plans. I would love for this relationship to work out for you," Cindi said.

"Thanks, Cindi. It would be nice, but like I've said ... we're taking it slow and easy."

"Actually ... it sounds like it's heating up," Cindi said, laughing.

"Yeah ... a little bit," Anne said, blushing. "But, I wouldn't say I've fallen head over heels in love or anything. It's a nice, warm feeling, though. Hey, not to change the subject, but when do you see Dr. Thompson again?"

"Next week. And yes, you're good at changing the subject," Cindi said with a smile. "Since I'm *probably* going to wait until after Christmas to ask Paul to go to the therapist, it will just be me for now. But that's okay. I need to know what I can do to mend this relationship and make it work."

"Oh, Cin, you have to remember, you cannot control Paul's actions. And this relationship will work only if he works as hard as you on mending the broken pieces."

"I know ... I know." Cindi sighed. "But, as you've said, I need to empower myself to be strong and independent, and I think I have a lot to learn."

"You are empowering yourself. By going to the therapist, you've already taken a step forward, and you're working on your new designs, which will help you in your career. You've also begun putting together your financial plan. You're doing the right things," Anne said.

"I hope so. And I hope Paul is as committed as I am to doing whatever it takes to make our marriage work," Cindi said.

They laughed and talked about Christmas shopping and New Year's resolutions and then headed home. Cindi had to pick up Kaitlyn from her ballet lesson at school and felt much better after talking with Anne. She wondered why her mood had improved, and then she realized what it was. *Hope.* She felt hopeful—and maybe it was just the effect of the margarita—that she and Paul would be all right and would recapture the wonder and magic of the relationship, that he would return to being the Prince Charming she was so crazy about. And she felt determined that she was going to empower herself and realize her own dreams, with or without Paul. She had to.

As for Anne, she was encouraged that Cindi was seeing an expert to help her understand and navigate her marriage problems. Anne would help her with her financial plan, but she didn't feel equipped to help her with all the other issues— the anti-aging medicines, personality disorders, or spendthrift behavior. So far, Trevor didn't exhibit any alarming traits, and she hoped he never would. *He might just be a keeper*, she thought to herself. *Time will tell.*

Meanwhile, both friends were hopeful that the new year would bring wonderful things into their lives. Happiness. Good fortune. Lasting love.

Chapter 26

*A*fter Cindi picked up Kaitlyn from her ballet lesson, she stopped at a Chinese restaurant for takeout. When they arrived home, Paul wasn't there, which came as no surprise because she'd grown used to his late nights at the office.

Cindi leaned against the kitchen counter as she looked through the day's mail. She saw a Christmas card addressed to Kaitlyn. She knew it was Richard's obligatory holiday card, which usually contained money. He rarely sent her a gift that required any consideration of Kaitlyn's preferences and personality.

"I think this is for you," said Cindi. She handed the envelope to Kaitlyn.

"Yay! This is from Daddy!" Kaitlyn opened the letter and took out the one hundred dollar bill that was folded inside the card. "Look, Mommy! It's a hundred-dollar bill!"

"That's very generous of your father. What are you going to do with it?" Cindi asked.

"I could go Christmas shopping. Or get a new pair of ice skates. Mommy, can you take me to the mall this week?"

"Honey, let's think about this. This is a lot of money." Cindi had already bought Kaitlyn a new pair of skates for Christmas. They were from "Santa," and she did not want to divulge that information.

"I know! I'm rich!" Kaitlyn twirled around the room, laughing. "This is the most money I've ever had!"

"I have an idea. You want to be a smart and successful woman when you grow up, don't you?" Cindi asked.

"Yes, Mommy. I want to be either an ice-skater for Disney or a ballerina ... or I might want to make jewelry for your pretty dresses ... There are so many things I love to do!"

"All those things are wonderful ideas. And you have plenty of time to decide. If I were you—and I wish someone had given me this advice when I was your age—I'd start a savings account right now and put some of your Christmas money into it. Start saving now, and by the time you get out of college, you'll have a nice big account. It will help give you choices, no matter what career you choose."

"Mom, I already have a piggy bank full of money," Kaitlyn said.

"But that's not as much as you have right now," Cindi said.

"Did Auntie Anne tell you I should save money?"

"No, not exactly. But it's something she would say if she were here. She's smart when it comes to money. What do you think, Kater-tater? Want to start a big-girl savings account now?" Cindi asked.

"I *am* a big girl, Mommy," said Kaitlyn.

"I know you are, honey," said Cindi.

"How much do I have to put in the bank?" asked Kaitlyn.

"How about $75.00? That way, you'll still have $25.00 to spend on Christmas gifts for yourself and your friends."

"Okay.

I'll still have a lot of money to spend," Kaitlyn said.

"Wonderful! I'm so proud of you, Kater-tater. We'll go to the bank this week and open a savings account for you. Then I'll take you to the mall."

Cindi didn't tell her that she would add money to Kaitlyn's savings account. Or that she had already started a college fund for her. She wanted her daughter to grow up strong, independent, and secure. This little lesson on savings would have a great impact over the years.

They sat down at the kitchen table to eat moo shu chicken and vegetables. Kaitlyn couldn't stop talking about her new savings account and the toys she wanted to buy at the mall. At seven years old, life was so simple.

Finally, the rain stopped, but when Cindi looked outside to see if Paul had come home, she noticed that the whole world still felt dreary.

"I'm so excited that I don't have to go back to school for a while! And Christmas is going to be soooo much fun with Danny and Bella this year. It's our first Christmas together, and I can't wait!" Kaitlyn said.

Cindi thought it interesting how children remained hopeful and optimistic, no matter what. They saw the good in people. Even though Daniel and Isabella were often unfriendly to Kaitlyn, she never gave up hope that they could all get along and love one another.

They had exactly one week before Christmas, and Cindi was beginning to feel stressed about the Christmas shopping she still needed to do.

"We'll plan some fun things for you kids to do. Like maybe go to Disney World or something," she told Kaitlyn.

"Oooooh, that would be fun! I know what else I want for Christmas," Kaitlyn said.

"Oh? What's that, Kater-tater?" asked Cindi.

"I know I'm rich, but what I want more than anything is for us to be a big, happy family in our new house. I want Danny and Bella to like me and to want to be my brother and sister," said Kaitlyn.

Cindi felt a pang in her heart. "Oh, honey, that's going to happen. We're going to be one big, happy family, and Danny and Bella are going to love you," Cindi said.

"Sometimes they act like they love me, and sometimes they don't," Kaitlyn said.

"As they get to know you more and more, they won't be able to keep themselves from loving you. You're just too lovable!" said Cindi.

Kaitlyn smiled big and said, "What do you want for Christmas, Mommy?"

"I want the same thing, sweetie. I want us to be one big, happy family together," Cindi said.

After dinner, Cindi helped Kaitlyn get ready for bed, turned on the night-light, and said goodnight. She then went into her studio and looked at her new designs. Several of them were stunning, and she was thrilled.

Around 10:00 p.m., Paul arrived. "I'm home!" he said.

"In here," she called out to him.

"Sorry I was late," he said.

"Did you eat dinner? Kaitlyn and I had moo shu chicken, and there's some left over," she said.

"I've already eaten, but thanks. By the way, we're having our firm's Christmas party Wednesday night," Paul said.

"Are spouses invited?" asked Cindi.

"Yes," Paul said. "Do you want to go?"

"Sure!" said Cindi.

"Great. It starts at 8:00, and it's semiformal," Paul said.

They then talked about the rain and work. Cindi told him that she had margaritas with Anne earlier and that Anne and Trevor might be going away on a ski trip for Christmas.

"I think he really likes her, from what he's said," Paul said.

"Like what?" asked Cindi.

"Oh, not much. Just that she is super smart and really fun to be with," Paul said.

"I'm glad they're getting along. She deserves someone nice, someone special," Cindi said.

That night, Cindi and Paul made love, and he was sweeter to her than he had been in a while. He kissed her neck, nuzzled his head in her hair, and said, "I love you, Mrs. Paul Francis, my one and only Cinderella."

"I love you, too, Paul," she said. She held him close, feeling his muscles against her body and his heartbeat against her heart and wishing that things were all right between them. But she felt as though she was keeping things from him. Secrets. She did not tell him that she went to see a therapist. Not yet. And she did not tell him that she had seen him at their new house with Andrea Parks. She didn't like him keeping secrets either and would soon discuss all this with him. But for now, she wanted to enjoy being in his arms.

Deep down she knew, however, that secrets would not make a happy marriage.

Chapter 27

C indi was excited about attending Paul's Christmas party and happy that Anne would be there with Trevor. But she was also nervous and anxious. She wanted to look stunning. She didn't have time to design and sew something new, so she looked in her closet and found a beautiful cocktail dress the color of stone that glimmered in candlelight. The color reminded Cindi of the stone walls that shimmered in the twilight at the Castello di Barone Ricasoli in Italy.

The dress was short enough that it showed off Cindi's slender legs. It had one luxurious silk chiffon shoulder strap as well as ruched chiffon straps around the front bodice. The dress hugged her in all the right places. Champagne-colored paillettes were layered one on top of another over the whole dress.

Kaitlyn bounced in the room, and Cindi kissed her precious daughter once on each cheek and then three times on the tip of the nose. Cindi had been so distracted lately that she had not done that in a long while.

"Mommy, are you going to another ball?" asked Kaitlyn.

"No, honey, this is just a Christmas party for Paul's firm. Nothing as fancy as a ball," said Cindi.

"But you look like a princess tonight!" said Kaitlyn.

"Do you want to help me with my hair, Kater-tater?"

"Yes!"

Kaitlyn ran to her room to retrieve her jewelry box of special combs and hair clips. When she returned, she helped Cindi swoop her hair up on one side, letting it fall in soft curls on her shoulder on the other side.

"I love it! You really are an artist when it comes to hair," Cindi said.

"You look so beautiful! Just like a real princess," said Kaitlyn.

Just then, Paul emerged from the bathroom wearing slacks and carrying his shirt in one hand. His chest was bare. Cindi couldn't help but admire his broad physique. How did he always make her melt like that?

"Look how pretty Mommy is. I combed her hair for her," Kaitlyn said.

"Looks like you helped turn your mother into a real Cinderella tonight, Kaitlyn!" said Paul.

"She's very talented. Now Kaitlyn, scoot on out of here and go see what your babysitter is up to. She's going to feel neglected if you leave her all alone."

"Okay, Mom," she said as she twirled out of the room.

"You do look lovely. Is that dress one of your designs?" he asked.

"No, it's something I've had in my closet for a while. You like it?"

"It's really beautiful," Paul said.

Cindi's heart warmed. He always gave her that butterfly feeling in her belly. It seemed as though all was okay, but there were still so many unresolved issues. *After Christmas*, she kept telling herself. *After Christmas ...*

The firm's Christmas party was held in the banquet hall of one of the area's largest hotels. It felt like a ball but on a lesser scale—the venue was smaller, and the guest list was as well. The lights were soft and low, and a six-piece band played jazz on a stage. Buffet tables situated at one end of the room were piled high with hors d'oeuvres. About a hundred people mingled with one another throughout the room, champagne or cocktails in hand. A waiter approached Cindi and Paul, carrying a tray of champagne. Cindi took one and gulped it down.

"Pace yourself. The night has just begun," Paul said.

"I'm a little nervous to be here with all your coworkers. I don't really know anyone," Cindi said.

"Relax, honey. You already met a few of them at our wedding party. And Anne and Trevor are here somewhere," Paul said.

"Can we look for them?" Cindi asked.

"Why don't you stay here and hold a table for us, and I'll go and see if I can find them," Paul said.

She sat down at one of the tables and looked around the room. Paul's male associates appeared affluent and quite polished in their designer suits. The women were just as elegant—some wearing long gowns and others in sexy cocktail dresses similar to Cindi's. They were beautiful people. It was as if they had stepped out of a fashion magazine.

Cindi scanned the room, looking for Andrea Parks, but she did not see her anywhere. Cindi began to relax. She was relieved at the thought that Andrea wouldn't be here. After all, she was 25 years old, and most people her age would probably be out clubbing instead of attending a stuffy office party.

"There you are!" said Anne. Cindi had never been so happy to see someone.

"I'm saving a table for us. Paul went to look for you," Cindi said.

Anne laughed. "Trevor went to look for you and Paul."

"Anne, you look absolutely gorgeous," said Cindi.

"Thank you. You look beautiful yourself," Anne said.

Anne wore a Carolina Herrera crimson, draped-waist long dress that complemented her dark brown hair. The gown fit her waist and hips, which perfectly showed off her figure.

"I can barely sit down, this dress is so tight," said Anne, laughing.

"Mine is short, so I worry about sitting down at all," Cindi said.

"Thank heavens for long tablecloths!" Anne laughed and then turned more serious. "How are things going, by the way?"

"Good. Paul has been sweet, and so far everything is good. No fights or angry outbursts. Of course, I haven't said anything to him about *things* ..." Cindi said.

"After Christmas, right?" Anne asked.

"Right," Cindi said.

"Well, here's to a wonderful evening," said Anne, holding up her champagne glass.

"I agree! Here's to a wonderful Christmas and New Year's!"

The two sat and chatted. They commented on the people at the party. Trevor joined them with a plate piled high with food. "I brought this for everyone," he said.

"Trevor, did you happen to see Paul? He went looking for you," said Cindi.

"He was at the bar the last time we spoke. He sounded like he was coming back to the table at any moment," Trevor said.

"There are so many people here. He's probably having a difficult time working his way back to the table," Anne said.

"You're probably right," said Cindi.

By now, more than two hundred people filled the event space. The guests comprised members of the firm, their spouses, and select clients. Some attendees were dancing, others were at the buffet tables filling plates with food, and the rest mingled or sat at tables.

Anne and Trevor decided to hit the dance floor, and Cindi excused herself to visit the ladies room. She walked carefully through the crowd and made her way to the hallway. It felt good to leave the main event for a moment and breathe fresh air.

As she walked down the hall, she heard voices in one of the sitting areas off the main reception area. It sounded like Paul's voice. *So that's where he is!* She bounded around the corner.

"Paul, I wondered where you were!" Cindi said.

She froze.

Paul sat on the sofa, laughing and talking to Andrea Parks.

"Oh, I'm sorry," said Cindi quickly. "I didn't mean to interrupt ... I ... I ..."

"You're not interrupting. Cindi. You remember Andrea, don't you? She was at our wedding party," he said.

"Yes," said Cindi, coldly. "I remember her. Nice to see you, Andrea."

"Likewise," said Andrea. She stood up and turned to Paul. "Thanks for your help. I'll talk to you later."

She nodded at Cindi and then walked away. She was dressed in a revealing French Connection sequin sheath mini-dress that shimmered like black diamonds. She was so tall, thin, and willowy that it seemed as though a slight breeze could blow her over.

"Andrea had some questions about law school," said Paul. He was smooth and collected, but Cindi could detect a hint of nervousness on his part.

"Law school?" asked Cindi with a bit of sarcasm.

"Yeah, she thinks she wants to be a lawyer, which would be a natural fit for her, given her experience as a paralegal."

Cindi did not buy his explanation, but she did not want him to know that she felt jealous and insecure.

"Were you checking up on me?" Paul asked in a slightly sarcastic tone.

"No, not at all. Trevor, Anne, and I—we all wondered where you were, but I was looking for the ladies room when I saw you," she said. Now she was miffed.

"It's down the hall," he said.

"Thanks. I'll meet you back at the table," she said curtly.

Cindi entered the restroom. She was angry and shaking. Did she interrupt something? Or was Andrea simply getting advice from Paul? They were friends, obviously, and it would be natural for her to seek his advice. But at a Christmas party? It sounded ridiculous, and yet there was no proof that it was anything other than what Paul had told her. She hated feeling jealous. She hated that he made her feel this way.

When she returned to their table, Paul was sitting with Trevor and Anne. He was laughing and talking as if nothing had happened. Cindi joined them and did her best to act as though everything was okay. And maybe everything *was* okay. But she was secretly angry and worried all at once. There was no mistaking the look on Paul's face when she caught him and Andrea talking in the lounge area; it was one of guilt.

Cindi didn't see Andrea for the rest of the evening. When Cindi and Paul left the event, they departed arm in arm, appearing as if they were the quintessential happy couple. In fact, Cindi was beginning to feel adept at creating an illusion for the world to see. And she was also beginning to become fed up with Paul's unpredictable behavior.

Chapter 28

On the drive home, Cindi watched as the full moon followed alongside the car. It was pale and solemn, as if it carried the weight of the world on its shoulders, and it mirrored Cindi's mood perfectly.

When Paul and Cindi arrived home, he headed into the kitchen, and Cindi asked the babysitter if everything was all right.

"Oh, yes," said Jacquie. "Kaitlyn and I had a great night. She gave me several different hairstyles!" Her hair was in curls, so Cindi suspected they had been using the hot rollers.

"Is she asleep?" asked Cindi.

"Yes, she's been in bed for about an hour," said Jacquie.

"It's always comforting to know I can depend on you. Here's a little something for Christmas," said Cindi. She gave her an extra $100.

"Thank you, Cindi! That's so generous," said Jacquie. "And I love staying with Kaitlyn. She's like a little sister to me. I hope you guys have a Merry Christmas!"

And with that, she went out the door into the starry night. Cindi then joined Paul in the kitchen.

"We have some Cakebread wine in the fridge. Want a nightcap?" Paul asked.

"Sure," she said, kicking off her stiletto heels. "But let me go and check on Kaitlyn first."

She entered Kaitlyn's bedroom and saw that her daughter was sound asleep. With her soft, blond curls tousled over her head, she was snuggled up with her stuffed animals, looking serene and peaceful. Cindi smiled and kissed her lightly on the cheek.

She then went to the den and sat down on the sofa. Cinderella still felt depressed because there were so many unanswered questions. She was conflicted about seeing Paul talking privately with Andrea at the Christmas party. *What were they* really *talking about?* She remembered how Richard had cheated on her and, as a result, she was wary of any odd behavior between her husband and a younger, beautiful woman.

There was a chasm between Cindi and Paul, and it seemed to be growing wider and deeper every day. She sighed, not knowing what the new year had in store for the newlyweds.

Paul brought the wine and sat down opposite her. He took off his suit jacket and undid his tie. "That feels better," he said. "It was good to see Trevor and Anne getting along so well."

"I know. He seems like a nice guy, and I'm happy for Anne," she said.

"You were quiet all night, though. You didn't mingle very much," he said.

Cindi took a sip of wine. "I didn't feel much like socializing," she said.

"But you're usually very social," said Paul.

"I have a lot of things on my mind. Paul, I think we need to talk."

"Sure, honey. What about?"

"Why were you *really* talking to Andrea tonight? Is there anything going on between you two?" Cindi asked.

He looked at her hard. Suddenly, the chiseled cheekbones on his face became rigid and turned to stone.

"What are you talking about?" asked Paul after a pause. He shook his head. "I already told you; she wanted to get my advice on going to law school. She's a paralegal, a smart woman, and it would be a natural for her. That's all. You're just being paranoid ... and *jealous*. I can't believe you're jealous of my paralegal!"

"I ... I ... guess you're right. I'm sorry. I just found it odd that you'd be sitting out in the hallway having a private conversation with Andrea while your firm was having a party. I mean, she can talk to you at work anytime," Cindi said.

"Since when am I not allowed to have a private conversation with my paralegal? Do I now need your permission to talk to other women?"

Cindi tried to change the subject to calm him down. Perhaps she was being paranoid. The pain of her ex-husband's infidelity made her leery of that happening again.

"I'm sorry. But I know how drawn you are to young people—and she *is* young and beautiful, you can't deny that. And I know how you want to be younger, too. You're taking all this anti-aging medicine and ..."

"What?! Good God, Cindi, where is this interrogation coming from?"

"Don't turn this around, Paul. You seem secretive and ... I found the anti-aging stuff. I was cleaning your bathroom and saw it and found some needles and a bottle of gel ... and ... it's so expensive ... and ...," Cindi hurriedly said. She hadn't intended to bring this up now—it had just slipped out.

"What were you doing snooping in my bathroom?" He set his wineglass down and anxiously ran his hands through his hair.

"I didn't mean to pry—I was just cleaning things ... and ... you never told me ... and ..."

"For one thing, it's none of your business what medicines I take or don't take. I was taking them long before I met you. And another thing, my doctor prescribed the testosterone injections to help with my low hormone levels. I started with the gel, but I didn't notice any improvement, so my doctor prescribed the injections. God, Cindi, what's wrong with me trying to stay young and healthy? I would think that you'd want that," Paul said.

"That's just it. I do want what's best for you. But, as for those medicines, there are side effects—dangerous ones. They can be toxic to the liver and heart, and you're using the gel *and* the injections ... and you're still a young man! I'm honestly worried about your health. These things can be so dangerous," Cindi said.

"I know what I'm doing. Don't you think I have any damn sense?"

"Please don't get angry. I just want you to be careful with that medicine. I don't want anything to happen to you."

"Look, if it'll please you, I'll stop using the gel. But I'm going to continue with the injections. I'll talk to my doctor at my next visit, and if he thinks it's a risk, I'll reconsider," Paul said.

"And what about Andrea Parks?" Cindi asked.

"What about her? I told you, she's just a friend, and there's nothing else going on between us, so get off my damn back!"

"I ... I'm sorry. Honestly, I'm sorry, but I saw you with her and our real estate agent at the new house," she said.

"You *what?*" He stood up and raised his hands in the air, his voice growing louder and louder. "Were you following me?"

"I drove there the other day to see where we'd put the new palm tree—the day you were supposedly at the office—and I saw you there at the house with her and our agent. I just wondered why you'd take her out there ... and—."

"What the f**k is wrong with you?!" he exploded. His beautiful blue-green eyes turned dark and menacing. "Are you f**king wacko? I think you need help. You are so damn paranoid and jealous. Christ! First, you're on my back about my medicine—*prescribed by my own doctor*—and now you're accusing me of an affair. I can't stay here tonight. I don't need this crap! F**k this!"

Paul grabbed his car keys and stormed out the door. Cindi sat there, feeling numb. She assumed that he was on his way to his house. Once they closed on their new house, sold their respective homes and moved, where would he then escape? Would he continue to run away when they had a disagreement? And why couldn't she ask him questions and receive a calm answer? Would uncontrolled tantrums always be his reaction to any questions that made him uncomfortable? Why did he always seem to turn things around and make her feel bad?

She had not planned on saying anything to him about Andrea or the prescription drugs, but after seeing him talking to the young paralegal that evening, she couldn't help herself. She was fed up with suppressing her emotions, and she was ready to address the problems in their relationship.

Cinderella entered her bathroom, set her wine on the edge of the tub, and ran a hot bath. Tears rolled down her cheeks as she poured in lavender bath salts and undressed. She twisted her hair up on her head and then gently sank into the hot water, letting the warm liquid soothe her.

Am I the one with the problem? Why am I doubting Paul so much? Is something wrong with me, or is it him? The tears flowed freely. She wanted this marriage to work, and right now it wasn't.

Cinderella had been buying presents for Daniel, Isabella, and Kaitlyn all week long. She had decorated the house with a beautiful Christmas tree that she, Kaitlyn, and Paul had bought a couple of days before. She'd worked hard to make sure that her home was perfectly adorned for the holidays. She also wanted to make things right between Paul and her. But tonight, she felt that all her efforts were for naught. How would everyone have a great Christmas when things seemed to be rapidly falling apart?

Chapter 29

The next day, despite the fact that it was Christmas Eve, Cindi called Dr. Thompson to see if she could arrange an emergency appointment. Fortunately, he told her he could see her after lunch. Kaitlyn went to Arielle's for the afternoon so Cindi was able to see the therapist.

"Hello, Cindi," Dr. Thompson said, as he ushered her into his office. "How are you doing?"

"Not so good, Philip," she said as she sank into his overstuffed sofa and rubbed her eyes. "Thanks so much for seeing me on Christmas Eve. I ... well ... I had a bad night last night."

"What happened?" he asked.

Cindi proceeded to tell Dr. Thompson about her jealousy and suspicions, and her fight with Paul. She also shared that Paul, once again, left the house and spent the night somewhere else.

"Do you think Paul is having an affair?" asked Dr. Thompson.

"No ... I don't really think so. I just feel threatened because this woman is younger, beautiful, he loves the attention, and things have been rocky between Paul and me lately. I just don't get why I can't talk to him about it. I don't understand why he turns so angry and defensive any time I try to ask him even simple questions. He always somehow manages to turn things around and make it seem like my fault."

"You have every right to ask him questions. And it's possible that Paul is deeply insecure about himself: his looks, his money, and more. He might be trying to mask his raging insecurities by taking anti-aging medicine. And it's possible that this woman really did need his advice and that he craves the ego boost. His overspending could be a way for him to create a false 'house of cards.' In other words, it's a wealthy persona to make him look and feel richer than he is. It does seem that he has a lot of issues," the doctor said.

Cindi nodded. Dr. Thompson made her feel sane.

"Both narcissists' and anti-socials' motivation is self-interest. They often have a high need for stimulation, are impulsive, and use emotional explosions—like tantrums—to manipulate others. They can also be very insecure. In fact, the greater Paul's insecurities, the more vivid is his image of himself and the stronger his need to project perfection. This makes him look and feel like a young, successful litigator who has the world at his fingertips. In reality, he's more like a little boy with huge insecurities who hasn't grown up," he said.

"That all sounds like him, but what about me? Is any of this my fault? I feel responsible for him getting so angry. And I'm fed up with his behavior, but at the same time I don't want to be the one who ruins our marriage."

"It is not your fault that he's taking anti-aging medicine that could be dangerous to his health and is exacerbating his short temper. And it is not your fault that he overspends or gets angry when you ask him questions that center on his time and health. You're doing the right thing by seeing me. If I can work with you to feel more empowered and secure, that's a worthwhile goal," he said.

"I don't want to burden my friend Anne with my problems. She's such a good person, and I feel like I'm just bringing her down when I tell her what's going on with Paul and me."

"You're living with inner pain and emotional insecurity right now, which is understandable. The way you manage it makes the difference. There are those who wear a mask and suffer in silence because they don't want to burden others. Then there are those who take off the mask to look introspectively and take responsibility for their emotions and empower themselves to work it out. You're doing that. You're doing the right things, Cindi. You're a lot stronger than you're giving yourself credit for," Dr. Thompson said.

"I don't feel very strong sometimes."

"But you are. It takes a lot of courage to *come* to a psychiatrist when things get bumpy—even to admit there's a problem."

"Do you think there's hope for Paul and me? I really do love him, despite all of his issues."

"There's always hope. I can't say for certain that things will work out. You can't heal the relationship by yourself. He has to make a commitment to change in order for it to work. He has to be willing to seek outside support and focus on his own issues," Dr. Thompson said.

"I want to get through Christmas. Then I'll ask him if he'll come and see you."

"Meanwhile, remember that it might take time. Although some of Paul's behavior could stem from those hormones he's taking, it's possible that he already had a personality disorder and these anti-aging medicines are simply magnifying what was there all along. But we won't know for sure what his underlying issue is until I work with him. The hormones may have just triggered some deeper problem," he said.

They continued to talk until Dr. Thompson glanced at his wristwatch and told her that an hour had passed.

"Thanks so much for seeing me on Christmas Eve," said Cindi.

"Of course. Have a Merry Christmas, Cindi, and let's see if we can get your husband in here after the first of the year."

Cindi smiled and felt hopeful again. "Merry Christmas to you, too, Philip."

As she drove home, the sun was shining, and her heart was lighter. As she pulled into the driveway, she saw Paul's car and was relieved.

The moment she walked in the door, Paul greeted her, "Hello, Cinderella. Where were you?"

"Oh, out and about," said Cindi. She was determined not to mention the therapist until after Christmas. "I suppose you stayed at your house last night."

He nodded and then sheepishly said, "Look, I'm sorry about last night. I was a jerk. I've been edgy lately with my caseload and ..."

"I understand," said Cindi, unconvincingly. "I'm sorry, too. I'm sorry that my questions make you so angry."

"Look, if you're really worried, I'm going to stop taking the anti-aging medicine. For a while, anyway, to see if I feel any different," he said.

"Really?"

"Yes."

"Thank you. I'll feel better since I've read so many negative things about it," she said.

"Look, I want us to have a good Christmas, too. I'm going to pick up Danny and Bella in a few minutes, and I think we should open some of the gifts tonight," Paul said.

"Tonight? But don't you think we should wait until Santa comes in the morning?" asked Cindi.

"I'm going to tell them Santa dropped off an early present. Trust me, you'll understand after you see what I got them ... got *us* ..."

"Okay," said Cindi. "If you think it's a good idea."

"I'll get my kids, and we can start Christmas tonight!" he said.

Paul swooped Cindi up in his arms and kissed her. He giggled and acted like a little boy who couldn't keep a secret. Cindi actually liked him when he was like this. "Be back in a few!" he said, laughing as he went out the door.

Cindi stood there wondering, *What is going on?*

On the night of Christmas Eve, just as the stars began to shine around the pale, silver moon and families were dressing to go to church or have an evening dinner, Paul asked his family to gather in the den around the Christmas tree.

Daniel, Isabella, Kaitlyn, and Cindi spread themselves out on the sofa and floor, patiently waiting for their big Christmas surprise. The children sipped mugs of hot chocolate, and Paul kept running to the bedroom to wrap "secret" presents. He had put on a Christmas CD of Michael Buble and lit the fire in the gas fireplace, which gave the room a cozy, Christmas feeling—never mind that it was 80 degrees outside.

Cindi had no idea what Paul was up to. She was relieved that he didn't seem to be harboring any ill feelings about her questions or their fight the previous night. That was the thing about him: One minute he could be angry and screaming, and the next moment he could be all smiles and loving. She was truly beginning to wonder if he did have some kind of personality disorder.

But for the sake of the children and Christmas, Cinderella was happy that Paul was being his old charming self this evening.

"Does anyone know what's going on? Kaitlyn, do you know?" Bella asked.

"Nope, but I can't wait," Kaitlyn said.

"Your dad has a big surprise for all of us, I'm told," Cindi said.

From the bedroom, Paul brought in a stack of small, impeccably wrapped boxes that were generally used for neckties.

"Kids, Santa stopped by our house this afternoon and left some presents for all of us. He said he would be back later with other gifts, but he felt like we needed these tonight because they're very special," Paul said.

"Daddy, what is it?" asked Isabella. She had her father's blue-green eyes and dark hair along with the cutest dimples Cindi had ever seen. Daniel was more fair-skinned with lighter brown hair and blue eyes. *He probably looks like Mal,* Cindi realized.

"It's a surprise. A huge surprise. But Santa said that each of you had been so good this year, you deserved a special *big* surprise," Paul said.

Even Daniel seemed interested. "Did he stop at everyone's house with these gifts? Will my friend William get the same gift?" Daniel asked.

"Oh, no! He just came to our house early. I know that for a fact. He said it was because you're special children who deserve a special Christmas," Paul said.

Cindi had to admit that Paul's Christmas spirit was touching, and it warmed her heart.

"How did he know Danny and Bella would be here with me?" asked Kaitlyn.

"Yeah," Daniel said. "What if we had stayed at Mom's tonight? Would we have gotten this special gift?"

"Santa knows everything. He knows exactly where you are at every moment," Paul said.

"Daddy, can we open our gifts now?" asked Isabella.

"Absolutely!" he said.

Paul gave a gift to each child and one to Cindi. The kids tore off the wrapping paper as quickly as they could.

Cindi untied the bow and then gently unwrapped the paper around the box, opening her gift with care. *What could he have bought everyone?* On the top of the tissue was a Christmas card, and inside was a poem written in Paul's handwriting.

My Dearest Cindi,

The greatest gift of all is being blessed to be given the opportunity to experience true love.

I have spent a lifetime hoping and praying that I would meet someone who would make my spirit soar and my heart sing.

In fact, I reached a point in my life where I was not sure whether I'd ever find that special someone that God created especially for me.

Lightning struck me, and you entered my life on that magical night at the ball.

I quickly found my heart unfolding and found the "wonder that keeps the stars apart." That wonder is you—my love— my Cinderella.

I also found something else—the magic of love—the type of love that warms your soul and gives you eternal happiness here on Earth. The love that gives you a glimpse of heaven.

You are a breath of heaven to me.

I am so lucky to get more than a glimpse, but rather a cup that never runs dry.

I feel like the little kid for whom Santa saved the best gift for last—that gift is your love.

I am honored to be your prince, and I would like you to be my princess, Cinderella.

Merry Christmas!

All my love,

Paul

Tears filled Cindi's eyes. Then she looked underneath the tissue paper and saw a first class round-trip ticket to the Vail Airport in Colorado, leaving Christmas Day and returning New Year's Day. She looked up at Paul with wide eyes and asked, "Paul? We're going to Colorado?" He never ceased to amaze her.

"Yes, I'm taking all of you on a ski trip. I came up with the idea when you told me that Trevor and Anne were going away on a ski trip for the holidays. It sounded like so much fun!" he said.

The children were all holding up their tickets in delight. "I can't wait!" said Isabella.

"I love to ski!"

Kaitlyn jumped up and down, and even Daniel was smiling.

"Mommy, Mommy! We're going skiing!" said Kaitlyn. They had been snow skiing only once and were not that skilled, but Cindi had to admit it was fun.

"It ... it ... sounds so expensive!" said Cindi.

"Our firm gets special rates at the Ritz-Carlton in Beaver Creek, and honestly, Cindi, this is just what we need. And that's why we had to open these gifts tonight so we could pack and get ready to leave tomorrow," he said.

While the children were dancing around the den, laughing and talking about the ski trip and everything they needed to pack, Paul came over and hugged Cindi.

"I know I haven't been the easiest person to live with lately, but honestly, Cindi, I'm committed to you. I love you and want us to have the best Christmas and New Year's possible," he said.

"I want that, too, Paul." She relaxed into his arms, and he kissed her deeply.

Was it possible that he could change back into the Prince Charming she first met? She wanted to believe it with all her heart.

Chapter 30

The next few hours were a blur as they drank eggnog, listened to Christmas music, and started packing for their trip to Beaver Creek. Paul had already told Mal that he was taking Daniel and Isabella. He had secretly packed their ski gear beforehand. Cindi was surprised that Mal didn't object.

"As long as I don't take them out of the country, I don't really need her permission. But she didn't argue, which was a nice change not to have drama," he said.

Cindi was suspicious about Mal being so cooperative; *perhaps Mal had a new boyfriend and wanted some alone time.* Nevertheless, she couldn't help but look at this ski trip as a way to rekindle the romance in their marriage and to forge a strong bond with Daniel and Isabella. And if Mal had a new boyfriend, that might just make things even better.

None of them slept much that night because they were excited about their grand adventure. The next morning, much to the children's excitement, Santa had left a room full of presents for them. Each child received a ski mask, goggles, boots, and a new ski jacket, along with toys. *Lavish! And probably way too much money,* Cindi thought. She could not help but tally up the cost of all the gifts in her mind. *Yes, way too much!* But she vowed not to say a word. There was no way she was going to spoil this Christmas for her family.

Paul had given her a blue Bogner Kea-D down ski jacket, which cost over $1,000. Despite feeling uncomfortable about its hefty price tag, she accepted it graciously. She gave him a beautiful Lotuff leather briefcase from Barney's New York. She had purchased it wholesale because her agent, Max Harper, had recommended a place where she could buy it at a huge discount.

Cindi then opened a gift from Anne. Inside the box was a periwinkle cashmere sweater. No doubt, Anne knew she and Paul were going skiing. "What a thoughtful gift," she told Paul. Cindi laughed when she realized she had bought Anne the very same cashmere sweater, only in red instead of periwinkle.

Anne and Trevor were going skiing in Park City, Utah, and for a moment Cindi wished they were going to be in Colorado. It would have been fun to ski with them.

It was a cozy Christmas morning in Florida with a temperature of 80 degrees. The children were looking forward to the snow and a colder climate and were eager to wear their ski outfits.

Paul cooked pancakes for breakfast. Meanwhile, Cindi drank her first cup of coffee and stood in her pajamas, gazing at him. *What happened to the angry, tantrum-throwing little boy of late? Am I dreaming?* She wanted this Paul to stay around forever. She knew to be cautious because, in the blink of an eye, his mood could change. But for now, this was really nice.

Their plane was scheduled to depart that afternoon, so they had to quickly clean up the kitchen and prepare to leave for the airport.

As their plane took off from Miami International, Paul held Cinderella's hand and smiled sweetly at her. He seemed to be very happy. *If only he was like this every day,* she thought.

The children sat across the aisle and were busy laughing and talking about their plans for the week. Cindi smiled. There was no better feeling in the world than to have her family happy and enjoying one another.

After they arrived at the Eagle County Regional Airport in Vail, Paul rented a Mercedes G-Class SUV and they headed to Beaver Creek. Snow fell in huge flakes, and the children squealed. The entire ski area bore the influence of renowned resorts, such as Switzerland's St. Moritz, Italy's Cortina, and Spain's Val d'Aran.

Naturally, Paul would want to go somewhere that looked European, thought Cindi. She loved it.

Paul was excited about introducing his wife to this resort. During their time on the plane, he had explained to her that at the heart of the resort were quaint European-style shops, art galleries, bistros, bars, and restaurants—all conveniently connected by heated walkways and escalators. Paul's warmth and generosity reminded Cindi of the way he'd been when he took her to Italy for their wedding. She began to wonder if all their problems had really stemmed from her own insecurities—ones she'd developed while married to Richard. After all, the therapist had told her that she needed to work on her own struggles and find ways to become more empowered. She also reminded herself that she had not told him about seeing a psychiatrist. She was keeping it a secret from him, and it created turmoil in her mind. One moment, she would be upset over the things he had done, and the next moment, she'd be feeling as though it was her fault.

She had brought her messenger bag, which was filled to the brim with her camera, a couple of lenses, a sketch pad, her laptop, and design software. She knew the mountains would inspire her—just as Europe had—and she wanted to be prepared.

Lately, Cinderella had been creating stunning clothes—both day wear and evening wear—and her agent, Max, had been impressed. "Wow! They are truly inspirational! You're on your way. Your trip to Italy and France is certainly influencing your work. These clothes are stunning. I suspect we're going to see one of your creations on the red carpet soon," he said.

This had encouraged Cindi more than she could express. When she told Anne about it, Anne said, "You go, girl! I always knew you had it in you and that someday I'd be able to say, '*I knew her when she was just starting out! She is my best friend.*'"

Cindi blushed. She wasn't interested in being famous. She simply wanted to design beautiful clothes for celebrities who would pay her what she deserved. Some of her dresses took hours and hours to design and execute. At the same time, she wanted to create flattering looks for the everyday woman who couldn't afford haute couture.

Cindi briefly thought about the financial guidebook Anne had given her. Cindi didn't bring it this time, but she hadn't forgotten Anne's advice regarding her budget and financial responsibilities. Cindi was determined to get all this straightened out after the first of the year.

They arrived at dusk. It had stopped snowing, and the stars were already sparkling in the sky as a silvery moon hung low and lopsided. Hundreds of windows glowed with diffused light, soft as butter, offsetting the building's regal structure. The Ritz-Carlton looked like a European king's estate set against majestic tree-lined mountains that rose up to heaven. Cindi could hardly speak, it was so magnificent.

The children, their eyes as big as saucers, were full of "ooohs" and "ahhhs" as they approached the valet at the front door.

"This really looks like a castle made for a queen, a king, and a princess. I love it here," said Kaitlyn.

"Me, too," said Isabella. "Katy, we're going to be princesses this week! And Daddy and Cindi will be our king and queen!"

"You girls are silly," said Daniel, through a supportive smile. He acted as if he was many years older than the girls, even though he was only eleven years old. It was one of the first times Cindi had ever seen the boy appear genuinely happy. She and Paul exchanged looks, and she knew that he was relieved to see the children getting along so well.

Paul checked them into the Ritz, and the concierge brought their luggage to their two-bedroom suite, which was larger than Cindi's first apartment. "Oh, my goodness!" exclaimed Cindi. The children, who were equally astonished, immediately ran to their bedroom at the far end of the suite.

The spacious living room was designed with red, green, and brown plaid sofas, leather accent chairs, a flat-screen TV, rustic hardwood floors, and a massive stone fireplace, where a fire was already blazing and waiting for them. The entire suite was rustic yet rich with modern elements. Overall, it could be described as "Wild West Chic." There were floor-to-ceiling windows with panoramic mountain views, a large living room, a second bedroom and bathroom, a dining room, a kitchen, a master bedroom with a fireplace, a marble Jacuzzi in the bathroom, and a balcony. It was breathtaking.

Cindi and Paul unpacked their luggage in the master bedroom and prepared for their evening dinner.

"Paul, it's all so lovely. This was the nicest, most thoughtful Christmas present ever," Cindi said.

"Do you like it?" he asked. "I know I sprang it on you without warning, but I didn't think you'd be able to resist."

"You're right. It was without warning, and I *wouldn't* resist! It was such a nice surprise and honestly, it's just breathtaking. I can't wait to ski and take pictures. I know I'll feel inspired while I'm here," Cindi said.

"You'll have to create a collection and call it *Snow.* I can just imagine how beautiful the designs will be," Paul said.

"*Snow*—I love it! What a great name for my next line," she said.

"Honey, I know things have been bumpy lately, and I've been an ass at times, but I've had a lot of pressure and responsibilities at work, and ..."

"It's okay. That's all in the past now. Let's just concentrate on our new beginning. We have so much to be grateful for," she said.

"I like that," he said, reaching out to hug her. "Here's to a new beginning. This whole week will be a celebration."

"I agree." Cindi simply would not let herself bring up money or anti-aging medicine. Or Andrea Parks. Or his obsession with himself and his body. Nothing. They were there on a beautiful snowy, romantic adventure, and that was that. She knew they could discuss any of these topics at a later date, and besides, maybe Paul was all right now. Maybe his behavior was a result of the anti-aging medicine and work problems. After all, he had promised to stop taking the hormones, and it was possible that his bad temper and unpredictable moods had been a result of the injections. And she had to confront her own issues as well. *Maybe I was just paranoid and had been partially at fault.*

She put her arms around him. "I love you and appreciate you, my darling. I know you work very hard to give me, Kaitlyn, Daniel, and Isabella everything. I love you, Paul. I just want you to know that," Cindi said.

"I love you too, baby." He kissed her and held her tight. The passion she felt for him stirred in her body.

"Mmm, we'd better get dressed for dinner," said Cindi, giggling and pulling away slightly. "Or we're not going to make it out of here ..."

"I want you right now," Paul said, nuzzling his face in her hair. "But I guess I'll have to wait. We have children to attend to." They both laughed and prepared for dinner.

Paul watched his wife as she put on a pair of gray wool slacks and a white pullover turtleneck sweater. As she bent over to slip on a pair of boots, her long blond hair fell forward and curled around her shoulders. *God, with those huge blue eyes, slender figure, and soft, luminous skin, she is so beautiful!*

She could easily be mistaken for a 25-year-old. And she could have been a model herself, but she would never think that. She was usually self-deprecating or overly modest. That was one reason he loved her so much. She was down-to-earth and had no idea how beautiful she really was. When she was out in public, men and women both noticed her striking appearance. Cinderella was an all-American natural beauty, and she wasn't aware of it.

Paul still found it impossible to believe she had ever looked at him twice, let alone married him. After all, he was in his forties, not exactly young, and recently began carrying quite a bit of extra weight, although his natural physique hid it pretty well. She would empathize more about the anti-aging medicine when she was his age. Right now, she couldn't understand. He winced inwardly when he thought of how angry and dismissive he was with her at times. It wasn't something he was proud of, and he didn't know why he behaved the way he did. Paul vowed to take it easy this week and not let things bother him so much.

Cindi looked up at him. "Do you know where we should eat tonight, Paul?"

"Shall we go to Spago's?" asked Paul. It was the flagship restaurant of Master Chef Wolfgang Puck.

"I'm not sure the children would appreciate it. They won't want anything fancy tonight. Is there a restaurant in the hotel that's more casual? Remember, they're tired after the long flight," she said.

"You're right. Let's go to Daniel's Ski Bar. It's right here in our hotel. It's a very lively place for kids. And Daniel will get a kick out of it having his name."

"That's perfect," she said.

It was settled. Paul and Cindi took the children to Daniel's Ski Bar. When they arrived, the dining room was already filling up with guests. Everyone was dressed casually in fleeces and jeans. There was a crackling blaze in the stone fire pit in the center of the room. A massive Christmas tree stood in the corner, decorated in shimmering icicles, red velvet ribbons, and golden ornaments. The smell of fresh pine wafted throughout the room. Red and white gingham tablecloths covered the tables, and the massive cathedral windows looked out onto the mountains, where evening skiers had already taken to the slopes.

Paul and the children enjoyed hamburgers, fries, and milkshakes. Meanwhile, Cindi ordered a light salad since she wasn't very hungry. She had too many butterflies in her stomach. *So much depends on this trip*, she thought to herself. She hoped the children would bond more and become a real family. And she and Paul would feel a renewed commitment to one another and perhaps even experience a second honeymoon.

They were seated close to the big fire pit and felt warm and toasty. It looked as though they were going to have an amazing week on the slopes, but for now, they were all tired from the flight and needed to go to bed early in order to be prepared for the next day's skiing.

"Paul, thank you so much for bringing us here," said Kaitlyn as she nibbled on a French fry. "This is the best Christmas present ever!"

"Thank you, sweetheart. I want us to have lots of fun! Are you a good skier?" he asked. Cindi loved it when Paul was affectionate toward Kaitlyn. It showed his loving side and indicated that he was really trying to make everyone feel comfortable.

"I've only been once," said Kaitlyn. "I skied the bunny slope, but I was really good, wasn't I, Mommy?"

"Yes, Kater-tater, you were great," said Cindi.

"I've only been one other time, too," said Isabella. "I'm not very good yet."

"What about you, Danny?" asked Cindi. "Do you know how to ski?"

"Yes," he said. "I've been a couple of times, but never to this place."

"Danny's a good skier because he's older than Bella and Kaitlyn, and he's been more times. I'm sure the girls will catch up with him on this trip," said Paul.

"Yeah, Danny, I'll be as good as you when the week is over," said Isabella, scrunching her nose up at him.

"There's no way. I'm bigger and older," Daniel said.

The children began teasing each other about who would be the best skier, but it was lighthearted and harmless. Cindi smiled. She never dreamed that she would be sitting in a restaurant in a lavish ski resort in Colorado with a husband and three children! Miracles really did exist.

After they finished dinner and retired to their suite, the children quickly took baths and went to bed. They fell asleep in minutes. Paul and Cindi retired to the master bedroom and slipped into luxurious, white, plush robes furnished by the hotel. The concierge also left them a few bottles of Chianti Classico and an assortment of European cheeses.

"Oh, my goodness! I can't believe you remembered the Castello di Brolio Chianti Classico from Ricassoli! Oh, Paul, this is so sweet," she said. This brought back memories of their sexy and wonderful wedding and honeymoon. How could she resist Paul when those memories were the most romantic in the world? She could not.

"I wanted to celebrate our first Christmas together, our new life together, and our new home, which we'll be moving into after the first of the year," Paul said.

"Tuscany seems like so long ago, but it's one of my best memories of us together," she said.

"Me, too," Paul said. He turned the lights down and poured each of them a glass of wine. Then they sank into the sofa in front of the fire. The flames danced in the hearth, casting long shadows across the room.

Paul and Cindi felt close—closer than they had in a long while. Perhaps it was the Christmas spirit that compelled them to talk about their loved ones. Cindi shared how much she missed her mother. "I still find it hard to believe she's gone, even after all these years. I miss her every day," she said.

"I miss my mother, too. After my father passed, she depended on me for everything. I was only twelve years old when he died of a heart attack, and I had to take on a lot of responsibilities. I even got a newspaper route to try to help with the bills. She was a great mom, but I had a lot to take on at a very young age," he said.

Cindi was surprised to hear this. Paul had never really discussed his childhood, and she didn't like to pry. From everything Paul had said prior to their conversation tonight, his mother had spoiled and pampered him. Cindi could now understand why he liked to pamper himself, whether or not he could afford it.

Paul went on to explain, "Sometimes I don't feel good enough for you, Cinderella, so I try to be better, give you more, and work harder."

"Oh, Paul, you don't have to give me material things. You should know that. I just want you," she said.

"I know. But I also know that beautiful women love beautiful things. And often, clients don't pay on time or at all, and then their cases drag on and on ..."

"Look, you have nothing to prove to me. I love you whether or not you're rich. You could be as poor as a pauper, and I'd still love you. I just want you to be happy and to treat me with love and respect," she said.

"I love you, Cinderella, and I will—I promise," he said. He set the wineglass down, pulled Cindi to him, and kissed her. He opened his robe and then hers and ran his hands over her body. Then he pressed himself to her. "You are so beautiful, my Cinderella. Your skin is so soft," he said.

"Paul," she said, but he quickly covered her mouth with his, kissing her so deeply she felt as though she had melded into his body. Every inch of her was on fire. No one had ever, ever, made her feel so on fire ... so alive ... so in love. He pulled her to the floor, set her on the thick rug in front of the fire, and lay on top of her. He kissed her throat and her shoulders. His tongue was gently exploring... slowly, he devoured her. Cindi moaned, *"Please ... Paul ... now ..."* They lay there naked in each other's arms until the early hours of the morning before drifting off to sleep.

She woke up the next morning. *Oh, yes! This is going to be a magical week.*

Chapter 31

They started the next day early. Through the hotel concierge, Paul had not only scheduled ski lessons for the children, but he had also hired a private instructor to stay with them throughout the day. In fact, the children had activities lined up every day of their trip, including skiing, ice-skating, treasure hunts, arts and crafts, scavenger hunts, and festivals.

Cindi was pleasantly surprised at everything the resort offered for the children. She and Paul would be able to ski the more advanced slopes and feel secure in knowing their children were being entertained and looked after.

It was a bright, sunny day, and fluffy, new snow covered the slopes. Cindi had skied enough to know that fresh snow was far better—from a skiing perspective—than its hardened counterpart. She loved the feeling of floating on it as if on a cushion of powder.

The first night after everyone had skied all day, the entire family collapsed in the hotel suite, too tired to clean up and dress for dinner. The children opted for room service, hot baths, and early bed.

After the children went to sleep, Paul and Cindi soaked in the Jacuzzi together. They drank wine and relaxed as jets of water soothed and massaged their sore muscles. Before going to bed, they made love slowly and tenderly, and fell asleep to sweet dreams.

There were several days that Cindi spent alone while Paul went to the spa or chatted with other professionals in the bar. She didn't mind, as she appreciated the private time to sketch designs that were inspired by the majestic mountains and snow.

Most of the time, though, they were together on the slopes skiing. Some days, they went skiing with the children to see how they were progressing. They were pleased at how the children's skills had improved over such a short span of time.

At night, the family visited some of the famous restaurants in the area and attended family events. There were only a few times when the children argued, but their squabbles were over trivial things, such as where they should eat or what activity they should do next. The family enjoyed the elite restaurants, where they dined on signature dishes, such as lobster mascarpone at the Grouse Mountain Grill.

On New Year's Eve, the family attended a party in one of the hotel's massive banquet halls. Their night ended with adults toasting each other with champagne while children sipped apple cider. Paul kissed Cindi passionately and told her she was the most beautiful woman in the world. Cindi was delighted to feel adored by the love of her life. She had forgotten about her emergency meetings with Dr. Thompson, personal pledges to discuss budgets, or concerns about Paul's anti-aging medicine. She was totally and completely in love with him—just as she had been on their wedding night.

On New Year's Day, they relaxed and started packing for their return to Florida. Everyone agreed that it had been the very best Christmas present in the whole world.

The next day, as they were checking out, the front desk clerk handed them their bill. Paul looked at it and—for just a moment—seemed stressed. Then, nonchalantly and in a quiet voice, he said, "Cin, I hate to ask you this, but could you split this bill with me? I don't want to put all of it on my American Express."

She thought this was strange, but when she looked at the bill, she nearly fainted. "Wasn't there a discount?" she asked.

"It's already been included," said Paul in an abrupt tone. "I'll take care of it when we get home. Remember, I'm due a huge fee any day since my case is almost over. Don't worry, everything will be fine."

The bill was more than $10,000, and the bottom line shocked her. *Well, yes, of course I can help out,* she thought. As she perused the bill, she saw exorbitant charges for the spa, which Paul had used more times than she had known about. In addition, she was astonished at how much the additional activities and supervision for the children cost. She thought they were included in the weeklong package.

Cindi took a deep breath and tried not to overreact so she would sound as nonchalant as Paul. "Sure. Here's my card," she said. Reality set in. *I am definitely going to have a talk with him about our spending after we return to Florida. I have to plan a budget for us.*

"Thanks, love," he said. He gave the two credit cards to the front desk clerk. After paying their bill, they departed for the airport.

The children slept through most of the flight. Meanwhile, Cindi remained awake and quiet. Paul held her hand and kissed her several times. He did not seem to notice her silence.

Damn! The week was nearly perfect, she thought to herself.

Chapter 32

Paul gently shook her. "Wake up, Cindi! You're having another nightmare," he said.

Cindi opened her eyes. *Where am I?* Her recurring dream of standing on a precipice always seemed so real. Her heart was pounding hard.

"You were screaming," said Paul, kissing her lightly on the cheek.

"Wow! I was about to fall off a cliff," she said.

"Well, good thing it was only a dream. Now, get up, sleepyhead," Paul said, good-naturedly. "We're closing on our house today!"

The two weeks after they arrived home from their ski trip had been hectic. The idyllic memories of the snow-covered mountains in Colorado quickly faded into the past as life in Florida charged forward at a frenetic pace. Once they moved, Kaitlyn would be going to the same school as Daniel and Isabella. Cindi hoped that would make the children even closer.

Paul sold his house to an associate at his firm for much less than he'd paid for it. As for work, Paul persuaded one of his major clients to settle his case quickly in order for Paul to collect his much-needed fee, which he used for the down payment on their new house.

Meanwhile, Cindi's house was on the market but had not sold. She had mixed feelings about selling it and would miss her old house when the time came to leave. It had been Kaitlyn's and her refuge after she divorced Richard. But eventually she would want to sell it because she intuitively knew that she and Paul would need the money.

After the sale of Paul's house, they quickly closed on their new home. Cindi matched the amount of Paul's down payment by using her savings and some of the line of credit on her current home. She also used the line of credit to buy the palm tree Paul was so adamant about having. She reasoned with herself that it was worth it if it would help maintain Paul's good mood. And as long as Cindi didn't ask him questions about money or his anti-aging medicine—and, for that matter, as long as she didn't question him about anything—he seemed to stay in a good mood.

In fact, Paul was so excited and happy that he took her, Kaitlyn, Daniel, and Isabella out to dinner to celebrate their new home. He ordered a bottle of champagne and toasted, "To our new home, *Castillo de Amor*."

"Thank you, Daddy, for buying a house with a swimming pool. I'll become the best swimmer ever!" Isabella said.

"Yeah, me, too," Kaitlyn chimed in. She and Isabella had grown much closer since the ski trip, and Cindi loved that they were acting like real sisters. Daniel was still moody but had more moments of good behavior than before.

"You children deserve a home with a pool. You deserve anything money can buy, and I intend to make sure you have everything you want and need!" Paul said.

The children were excited about the new house, and Cindi tried to rationalize that maybe it was a good thing they were buying it. But she would talk to Paul later about giving the children everything they wanted. Isabella and Daniel were already spoiled and had an air of entitlement, and she didn't want that to rub off on Kaitlyn.

After they closed on the new house, Cindi and Paul went over to their property to discuss the new furniture and decorations they needed. Paul said that some of their old furniture wouldn't work very well in the new house and that they would have to buy certain pieces to match the interior. Cindi repeatedly asked herself, *How much can we stretch our budget? Is this a good decision?* Everything was moving so overwhelmingly fast that she did not have time to make objective decisions.

At the same time, she thought about Anne and her financial advice. And she still had not had a chance to schedule an appointment with Dr. Thompson or even see Anne, for that matter.

A few days after Paul and Cindi closed on their new home, Anne called.

"Hello, stranger! Where have you been, Cin?" Anne said.

"Oh, Anne, I've been planning to call. So much has happened. Can you meet this afternoon?" Cindi asked.

"Absolutely! I'll meet you at Las Palmas," Anne said.

That afternoon, Anne was waiting with two pomegranate margaritas and a basket of chips and salsa when Cindi arrived. Anne's long brown hair glistened on her shoulders, and her almond-shaped brown eyes twinkled. She looked happy and relaxed. They hugged each other.

"I'm so sorry I didn't call as soon as we got home from our trip. We've been so busy with the kids and the houses," Cindi said.

"Well, it's a good thing you emailed me and told me you were away, or I would have been worried about your whereabouts!" Anne laughed.

"I know, it was a big surprise for all of us. I honestly didn't know we were going until Christmas Eve, and I have to admit, it was a great trip. But how about you? How was Park City?" Cindi asked.

"It was the best ski trip ever. We had so much fun. It was the softest powder you can imagine—perfect for skiing. I didn't realize how nice Park City was. You can be sure I'll be going back there, even though it takes longer to get there than Colorado. We had to change planes, which made for a long day of travel."

"And what about Trevor? How are things with you two?" she asked.

"Perfect. I like him a lot, Cin—I really do."

"Do I hear wedding bells?" asked Cindi, licking off the salt around the rim of her glass.

"No, no, nothing like that. Trust me, I'm going to take my time when it comes to getting married again. But for now, I couldn't ask for a better friend and companion," Anne said.

"And what about the ...?" Cindi asked.

"Yes, the sex is great," Anne blushed. "But I do want to take my time. Hey! Enough about me."

"I'm thrilled that you've met someone you enjoy being with. He seems like such a nice guy," Cindi said.

"He is. By the way, thanks, Cin, for that beautiful sweater. I love it and Trevor loves it, too. He said I look good in red," Anne said.

"You do! It's your color ... and thank *you* for the sweater you gave *me*," said Cindi. The two women laughed. "I couldn't believe we bought the same sweater for each other. I thought for sure that you knew about Paul's plans for the ski trip because you bought me that sweater," Cindi said.

"No, I didn't, but we definitely have the same taste in clothes," said Anne.

They both took a sip of their margaritas.

"Hey, you haven't said anything about Paul. How are things?" Anne asked.

"He was every bit the Prince Charming on our trip," said Cindi, reaching for a tortilla chip. She dipped it in the salsa and took a bite.

"Oh, Cin, I'm so glad. Maybe he's going to be okay, and maybe those angry outbursts are over. Maybe it was just stress, after all," Anne said.

"Uh, well, things were *almost* perfect—until we got our hotel bill," said Cindi.

"Let me guess. It was way more expensive than you expected," Anne said.

"Right. Anne, we're talking in the *ten thousand* range!"

Cindi's best friend gasped. "What did you do?" she asked.

"I paid half the bill with my credit card. He told me that once he was paid his fee for the big settlement he was working on, he'd pay me back. And his client did settle last week, and Paul was paid. But we had to close on our new house, so I used my savings and some of the line of credit on my home to pay the down payment and buy that palm tree. Things are moving very quickly," said Cindi.

"Oh, Cin. It sounds like his spending is out of control again. And now you're being dragged into making poor decisions because of it. I ... I ... well, I guess I simply don't understand his financial irresponsibility. Have you talked to him about a budget yet?" Anne asked.

"Not yet, but I'm going to ... as soon as we get through the house stuff. I mean, I think we'll be all right. Paul has some other big cases that should settle soon. He spends the money before he has it, but he does finally get it, and then it seems like he's always trying to catch up. It's like a pattern for him. It stresses me out."

"And the new house? You said you closed this week?" Anne didn't want to sound bossy or judgmental, but it sounded as though Paul was quickly sucking her into his overspending habits and his financially impulsive way of living. Anne was worried about how the stress was affecting her best friend. Cindi had dark circles under those gorgeous blue eyes.

"Yes, we did. We're ready to move in, and Paul is talking about buying new furniture to match the *personality* of this new house. What guy even thinks of those things, Anne? Most guys just want a man cave with a big flat-screen TV where they can watch football. And while I agree that each house has its own personality, I also believe we should wait until we've caught up on our bills. We can always buy new furniture later, and between the two of us, we *already* have a lot of furniture," Cindi said.

"It's typical of him, isn't it?" said Anne, trying to be understanding, but in her mind she couldn't help but tally up all the bills they were accruing.

"Yes. This overspending is an obsession of his. I think it's because he's trying to project an image he wants others to believe. And maybe his childhood stuff causes him to self-indulge and treat himself with new toys and gifts."

"What did your therapist say about this?"

"Dr. Thompson explained that his behaviors are symptoms of a personality disorder. For instance, selfish behavior, immediate gratification without considering consequences, having delusions about money, and overspending are common characteristics. But Paul did stop taking his anti-aging medicine ... or at least he told me he did," Cindi said.

"That's great. But how can you be sure?" asked Anne.

"He said that he stopped the injections, but he's still using the gels. He said he wanted to finish off the prescription he already paid for—otherwise, it would be a waste of expensive medication," Cindi said.

"I don't know much about this stuff, but it sounds suspicious," said Anne.

"I know. I'm going to ask Dr. Thompson about it. He might be able to give me additional information."

"Have you been back to see him lately?" Anne asked.

"No, I honestly haven't had time to even think about it. But I do need to make another appointment," Cindi said.

"I think that's a great idea. He's a physician, so maybe he can provide more insight into the side effects of the medication. In addition, you and Paul absolutely need to sit down and discuss your finances and agree to a reasonable spending budget," Anne said.

"You're right. Hey, not to change the subject, but did I tell you that my agent wants me to go to New York to meet some bigwigs in the industry and discuss some of my new designs?" Cindi asked.

"That's amazing news! I'm thrilled for you! When are you going?"

"This weekend. Kaitlyn is staying with Arielle, and Paul said he has a lot of work, so I'll go on my own. Do you want to come? We could have a fun girls' weekend!"

"Oh, hon, I'd love to, but Trevor and I have plans to go hear the Miami Symphony Orchestra. Maybe another time," said Anne.

"Sure. No problem. I'm really happy that you and Trevor are getting along so well," Cindi said.

"Me, too. But I want to take it slow—take my time to really get to know him. Trevor is one of the good guys."

"I think he is, too," said Cindi. She still hoped that Paul was one of the good guys—but deep down, she wasn't sure anymore.

Chapter 33

*C*indi started packing for her weekend trip to New York, despite the fact that some of their luggage was still half-packed from the Colorado trip. Life had been busy for the newlyweds since they had returned from skiing.

As Cindi emptied the rest of the things from Paul's luggage, she discovered testosterone syringes and a bottle of gel among his belongings. *He lied to me!* He was still using the gels and injections. Her heart sank as she realized that she couldn't trust him. This was one example among many half-truths. *Maybe he took the syringes to Colorado but stopped the injections during the trip*, she thought. But she couldn't be sure, and she was tired of making excuses for him.

Unfortunately, she did not have time to discuss this with him. She was in the midst of preparing for one of the most important events of her career. New York was waiting for her, as were Max and design industry power brokers—all of whom could take her career to the next level. Paul had acted rather jealous when she told him she had to go to New York to meet with Max. She invited him to accompany her, but work deadlines meant that he had to decline.

When Paul returned home from work the night before her trip, he pouted. "Can't you reschedule so I can come, too?" he asked. It was a request he had previously made and one that she could not fulfill because Max had already lined up important meetings for her. Although she wanted to broach the subject of the syringes in his suitcase, she knew his sullenness over her trip could escalate into a temper tantrum. As a result, she remained sweet and pampered him to raise his spirits. Later, it horrified her to think that she was trying to placate him just so he would feel better. He had lied to her, after all. She remembered that his mother had treated him the same way, and it made her cringe. *I will not become his mother!*

By the time Friday arrived, he seemed to have put his disappointment over Cindi's travels behind him. He took her to the airport and was in a better mood. He even became slightly giddy when they talked about *Castillo de Amor* and how it was in the perfect neighborhood. And even though he remained jealous about her important meeting with top designers, he tried to be supportive. She thought, *Well, I'll applaud him for that.* But she stopped herself and asked, *Why am I always making excuses and changing who I am to try to get his behavior to improve?* She began to feel as though her whole life revolved around him and his needs.

"Just think, Cinderella. You'll be able to design for some of the top celebrities, and we can invite them to our home someday. *Castillo de Amor* is so impressive, even celebrities would feel at home there. And you never know, some of them might need a lawyer down the road," he said.

"I think we're getting ahead of ourselves. I'm a nobody in the design world, and I'm not sure any celebrity will ever come and visit," she said. *Paul really does have delusions of grandeur,* she thought. She could not let herself become upset right now, though. This wasn't the time.

"You just wait. Our house will be the envy of the entire neighborhood," Paul said.

"I don't care if it's the envy or not. I just want to sell my designs, and I want us to be a happy family," Cindi said.

"You'll sell your designs. You're incredibly talented. And we are a happy family," he said.

Paul kissed her goodbye and told her to have a wonderful time. *God, life was beginning to feel like a roller-coaster ride with him!* she thought to herself.

The flight to New York went by quickly. In fact, before she knew it, she was one cab away from the Hilton in Manhattan. It had snowed the past couple of days, and the trees were still lined with snow and ice. The entire city looked like a winter wonderland—unlike anything she had ever seen in Florida. It occurred to her that this was her second winter trip with lots of snow. Maybe it was a sign that her new design collection, *Snow*, would be more successful than she had imagined.

Although Paul suggested that she book a room at the world-class New York Palace, she insisted on staying at the modest Hilton located in the Fashion District on 152 West 26th Street. Cindi searched for a good deal online and found a hotel offering a special post-holiday rate.

Just off Seventh Avenue, the Hilton in the Fashion District was exactly what Cindi was looking for. It was just steps away from the Empire State Building, Macy's at Herald Square, Madison Square Garden, and Chelsea Piers, and just fifteen blocks—an easy taxi ride—from Times Square and the Theatre District.

Cindi felt very much at home, and she kicked off her shoes while texting Paul to let him know she had checked in. He responded by texting back:

Have a successful weekend. I love you!

She wanted to text the following:

Oh, Paul, you act as though nothing is wrong in our relationship, and as much as I wish you were right, I know it isn't true. We'll have to deal with our issues soon if we're going to make it.

But she sent him an "*XOXO*" instead.

Next, Cindi checked her iPad and emailed Kaitlyn. Cindi wrote, "I miss you, sweetie, and love you very much, Kater-tater." Then she emailed Anne and told her she had arrived. Anne immediately emailed her back: "Knock 'em dead with your designs, Cindi! I believe in you and love you!"

Cindi felt the warmth radiate around her from the love and support from her best friend, and she was grateful. *What would I do without her?* thought Cindi. Anne had been there through thick and thin. She was her rock, and Cindi loved her like a sister. In fact, they were closer than most sisters.

On Saturday evening, Cindi and Max were meeting the influential designers and financiers in New York. But tonight, just Max and Cindi were meeting for dinner, which made her happy.

Max told her to wear something casual, so Cindi put on a pair of Diesel jeans and a chocolate brown leather jacket over her periwinkle sweater. She then slipped on her favorite leather boots. Richard had bought her the designer jeans and calfskin jacket the first year they were married. She remembered opening his gift and being impressed that he had such good taste in clothes. Unfortunately, his generosity didn't last long. He was exactly the opposite of Paul when it came to money and generosity.

Cindi applied her favorite Bobbi Brown mascara, added a bit of blush and lip gloss, and then brushed her long blond hair and let it fall in natural waves and curls on her shoulders. She was ready. She seldom wore much makeup, and in New York she felt a freedom that she didn't always feel in Florida. It was hard to explain, but she felt younger and more like the designer she wanted to be. Maybe it had something to do with being in the Fashion District.

At 7:00, Cindi grabbed her messenger bag and took a taxi to Gramercy Tavern at 42 East 20th Street. She paid the fare, then went inside, and asked to be seated in the Tavern Room, next to the bar, where Max would be waiting for her. The wood floors and tables were rustic, warm, and inviting. The place was already bustling with activity.

"Cinderella," Max said, waving at her. He stood up and gave her a hug when she approached him. "It's so good to see you, my dear."

"And you, as well," said Cinderella, taking off her jacket and draping it on the back of her chair.

"Please, please, sit. It's been a while since I've seen you. I want to hear about your new designs and everything that's been going on in your life," Max said.

He was in his fifties, single, with salt-and-pepper hair, bushy eyebrows, warm blue eyes, and a thin build. He wore glasses that always sat low on the bridge of his nose, and overall, he was a very handsome man. Max was born and raised in Brooklyn and had been in the design industry for thirty years. Once a designer himself, he segued into managing others because he had a good eye for what was marketable and had access to high-profile Hollywood celebrities. He had been Cindi's agent for many years after discovering her in a talent design contest when she was just starting out.

After small talk about her plane ride, hotel, and the weather, Max said, "I've ordered some wine for us, my dear." He motioned for the server to bring over a bottle of wine.

Cindi felt like a new person in New York. Its fast pace was invigorating. And *inspiring*! Even though her heart was full of worries about Paul and their problems, she began to relax and enjoy the evening. Max was like a father to her, and she took comfort in his presence.

After looking at both the "tasting" and "regular" menus, Cindi asked, "What do you recommend, Max? Everything looks so delicious."

Max said, "You must try the burger. It's actually not listed on the menus— only regular guests even know about it," he said.

His suggestion intrigued Cindi, and she decided to order the secret menu item even though she didn't eat much meat. When it arrived, it looked like the most appetizing hamburger she'd ever seen. Cindi devoured the entire burger.

While they dined, Cindi told Max about her marriage to Paul, their fairy-tale wedding, and the recent ski trip to Colorado. She did not mention any of their problems because they embarrassed her, and he really did not need to know about her marital issues.

She turned on her iPad and showed him photos of some of her designs. She'd brought him sketches of several that she was currently working on. This included the *Snow* collection, which he suggested she rename *Winter Wonderland* to more clearly reflect a fantasy world, the Italy and France collections, and the *Vampire Gray Gothic* collections, which Max thought would attract young adult consumers. The *Vampire Gray Gothic* collections were inspired by rainy days and her melancholy moods whenever she felt sad and abandoned by Paul, which seemed to be much more frequent these days. Those designs comprised various shades of gray with splashes of red, as well as cerulean, and black hooded pieces, all of which had an aura of otherworldly mystique. Max loved the *Winter Wonderland* collection the most.

"*Très jolie*! These are magnificent. Cinderella, it's clear that you've been inspired by your prince of a husband and these trips to Italy and Colorado," Max said.

"Thank you, Max. For a long time, I couldn't create anything beautiful. It was like I had died inside. But now, after meeting Paul and all the travel, the ideas are coming to me faster than I can sketch them," she said.

"People underestimate the importance of new scenery when it comes to creating. You have to take yourself out of your normal environment when things get dull and stagnant. Traveling to new places and having new experiences and adventures releases the creative flow of the mind. Everyone has to jump-start their batteries from time to time."

"I'm beginning to understand that," said Cindi.

"It's like that for most creative people, whether you're a designer, musician, or writer," he said.

"Who are we meeting tomorrow night?" asked Cindi.

"It's a surprise. But remember, these people want to meet you. I've shown them a few samples of your work, and they think you have great promise," Max said.

"Do you think any of the design houses will want to produce my work?" Cindi asked.

"We shall see. Right now, it's important for you to meet them—to get on their radar, so to speak. To network."

"I'm nervous, but I can't wait!" said Cindi.

Cindi and Max spent the rest of the evening discussing her career goals. "One day, I'd love to be able to show my designs at the Mercedes-Benz Fashion Week at Lincoln Center," she said.

"I'll do whatever I can to make that dream come true," Max said, trying to assure her.

"I hope so. But I know it's up to me to do the best work I can," she said.

"Then you must keep on dreaming and being inspired," said Max as he raised his glass to hers. "Cheers! Here's to you, my dear Cinderella!"

Once Cindi returned to her hotel, she checked her iPhone and saw that she had three missed calls from Paul. She phoned him, and he asked about the evening. She shared that everything was going great. Meanwhile, he talked about his stressful day at work, his subsequent evening visit to the spa, and how he missed her terribly.

She had an email from Kaitlyn, which she replied to immediately. "I hope you're in bed right now, behaving, and not staying up too late. XOXO! Love you very much, Kater-tater," she wrote.

She then took a hot bath and luxuriated in the bubbles and quietness of her hotel room, which contrasted with the hustle and bustle taking place on the snow-covered New York streets below.

The next day, Max arrived early, and they spent a few hours walking around the city. The cold air was invigorating.

Max took her to Lincoln Center. Then he told her to start dreaming about her designs resting on the slender figures of top models walking down the runway. Next, he took her to Saks Fifth Avenue, where she was tempted to buy a cute little dress that was on sale but couldn't justify spending the money after splurging on *Castillo de Amor*.

In the late afternoon, she returned to her hotel room in order to prepare for the evening. She tried calling Paul, but he did not answer, so she left a message for him to have a lovely evening. She then called Kaitlyn, and they talked awhile. Her daughter was having a wonderful time at Arielle's, playing new Wii games and dressing up like models. Cindi smiled. She didn't have to worry about

Kaitlyn. Her daughter was always happy, creative, and resourceful when it came to enjoying herself.

Cindi showered and then slipped into a simple, off-the-shoulder cocktail dress she had designed. The black dress was straight but accentuated her figure, and it was simple yet elegant. On her wrist, she wore Kaitlyn's silver charm bracelet, which always made her feel at home no matter where she was.

Max arrived by cab, and they headed to a multimillion-dollar home in Tribeca, one of New York's most expensive areas, according to Max. Tribeca, short for "triangle below Canal Street," was southwest of SoHo. The posh neighborhood was replete with high-end restaurants, trendy bars located in old warehouses, and upscale high-rise apartments that housed celebrities and the wealthy alike.

When Max and Cindi arrived, they went to the penthouse. Cindi nearly gasped when she walked inside and saw the soaring eighteen-foot ceilings, rich Brazilian walnut floors, and floor-to-ceiling windows. A massive stone fireplace covered the length of one wall.

A tall, elegant man approached them. "Cindi, I'd like you to meet Tim Gunn, mentor to the designers on the hit TV show *Project Runway*," Max said.

"Good evening, Cindi," said Tim, offering his hand. "Welcome to my home. Max has told me many great things about your designs."

"It's so nice to meet you, Mr. Gunn," said Cindi.

"Please, call me Tim. I feel like an old man when people call me Mr. Gunn," he said.

Cindi and Max laughed. He was so down-to-earth! Just as he appeared to be on the TV show. She could not believe she was meeting *the famous Mr. Tim Gunn*. She had watched *Project Runway* since it premiered on TV. She had always dreamed of competing on the reality show because it was a gateway to becoming famous and successful as a designer. The finalists always showed their clothes at Mercedes-Benz Fashion Week.

They talked awhile with Tim, and then he excused himself to take care of other guests. She and Max mingled throughout the room. She met Donna Karan, Michael Kors, Georgina Marchesa, and several other famous designers as well as financiers who often backed newcomers. She was in a daze. Cindi could barely believe she was meeting these people. She kept repeating, "Hello, I'm Cinderella Francis from Florida. So nice to meet you."

After an hour of mingling, Cinderella slipped away to the guest bathroom. She looked at herself in the mirror. The wine had flushed her cheeks. She silently asked herself, *Do I belong here? Is my work good enough even to be mentioned in the same breath along with these other designers?*

She remembered Anne telling her to value herself and not to settle for anything less than her dream. She remembered how Max had told her that her new designs were completely original. She also remembered that Paul said she was very talented. She held onto those words of encouragement. *I deserve to be here!* she told herself.

When Cindi entered the main party area, she leaned on the sleek white marble countertops in the kitchen and watched everyone for a few moments. Some of the guests had gone out on the expansive roof deck, where there was an outdoor gas fireplace and hot tub. They did not stay out long, however, because it was quite cold outside.

A young man, about five feet ten inches with long brown hair tied back in a sleek ponytail, approached her and said, "Do you mind if I stand here with you for a little while?"

"Oh, no, I don't mind at all," Cindi said. She noticed that he had a thick accent and looked to be about 30 years old.

"Are you French?" she asked.

"*Oui,*" he said and smiled. "My name is Stefan." He held out his hand, and she shook it. He was dressed impeccably in a Canali suit, and he smelled divine. She wasn't sure what cologne he was wearing, but it was intoxicating.

"Hi, Stefan. I'm Cinderella ... Cindi for short."

"Ah, like the fairy tale," he said.

"Yes, like the fairy tale." She laughed. "I think my mother was setting me up for some disappointments because my life is nothing like the fairy tale."

"Life is what we make it. You could certainly be in a fairy tale if you choose."

"Are you a designer?" asked Cindi.

"No, but my mother is. I'm a photographer. I moved to New York a couple of years ago to do fashion shoots. It keeps me busy and pays the bills," he said.

"That's wonderful. I'm a designer. I'm here tonight with my agent," she said.

The two talked about life in New York, the fashion industry, and France. She told him that she and Paul had honeymooned there.

"Oh, so you're married?" he asked.

She noticed a disappointed look on his face. "Yes—recently. We were married in Italy and then honeymooned there and in Paris," she said.

His disappointment regarding her married state amused her. She wasn't used to men flirting with her these days, and after meeting Paul, she had all but ignored single men.

Stefan didn't stay around long after that. He excused himself and circulated through the room. He was extremely handsome, and it gave Cindi a boost of confidence that he had been attracted to her.

As the party was wrapping up, Max and Cindi decided it was time to leave. They said goodnight to their handsome host and headed back to her hotel. "I gave Tim your portfolio," said Max, beaming like a proud father.

"What do you mean?" Cindi asked with excitement and anticipation.

"In order to appear on *Project Runway*, you have to submit your designs, so I handed him your portfolio. This is the first step. If he likes them, he'll want to see some of the pieces actually made, so we'll need to hire a model and do a photo shoot. If he likes them, he'll pass them on to a panel of judges, and if they agree, you'll be on the next *Project Runway*," Max said.

Chapter 34

After the soiree at Tim Gunn's house, Cindi took a taxi back to her hotel room. Tonight she felt as if she were living in a fairy tale. The snow was still floating down like feathers and piling on the sidewalks, and the city was aglow with excitement and buzzing with energy—Cindi felt Manhattan in her bones.

She had thanked Max over and over again for inviting her to the networking party. She couldn't believe that Tim Gunn had agreed to look at her design portfolio. *What a wonderful start to the new year!* She was finally beginning to believe in herself again. She was passionate about fashion and design and wanted to be an integral part of the couture world. For the first time in a long time, she was beginning to feel as though she had talent and deserved to have good fortune come her way.

Full of hope and excitement, Cindi emailed Kaitlyn and Anne about her wonderful night. When she checked her phone, she was surprised that Paul hadn't called her. But she knew he had a lot of work to do. She texted him that the evening had been successful and that she loved him. Then, like the previous night, she luxuriated in a bubble bath. This time, however, she treated herself to some champagne and sipped it while floating in the bubbles and reflecting on the enchanted evening. It had been a huge success, and she wanted to hold onto those feelings forever.

When Cinderella went to sleep that night, she dreamed of snow, winter wonderlands, high-end fashion, and New York's beautiful people. She imagined a thrilling world that seemed just at the tips of her fingers ... if she could only get there.

On Sunday, Cindi went to a gift shop near the Hilton and bought Kaitlyn a silver charm of the Empire State Building and a poster of *The Nutcracker*, which she knew her daughter would love. She also bought an Empire State Building silver charm for Isabella since she'd noticed that Isabella also had a charm bracelet. It was more challenging, however, to find something that Daniel would like. She finally settled on a puzzle that was a map of New York. She wasn't sure if he liked puzzles, but she thought they were great for children. Then she bought Paul a leather case for his iPad.

After Cindi finished shopping, she met Max at a nearby deli for brunch, and they discussed the success of the prior evening. She nibbled on eggs Benedict and thanked Max again for all his help and support. He told her that her *Winter Wonderland* collection was one of the most beautiful he had ever seen and that he hoped Tim Gunn would like her work as much as he did.

"You've grown so much, my dear Cinderella," said Max, in between sips of coffee. He pushed his eyeglasses back up on his nose. "I'm so proud of you, darling."

"Max, you've been such a good friend and so encouraging. I can't thank you enough for your help. And that party last night—meeting Tim Gunn and all those designers—it was the perfect way to start the new year!" she said.

"Don't forget. You must get started on sewing some of those beautiful pieces!" he said.

"Oh, I will. I can hardly wait!" she said.

They hugged goodbye, and Max promised to let her know as soon as possible about Tim Gunn's review of her designs. Cindi then took a taxi to LaGuardia Airport. The flight was fast and uneventful. After she landed at Miami International, she walked into the terminal and looked for Paul but didn't see him anywhere.

She texted, *Where are you?* But he didn't respond. *That's odd*, she thought. She knew that she had texted her time and flight number to him. In fact, he confirmed her time of arrival. *He's probably just held up at the office*, she told herself. After they returned from Colorado, he'd been consumed with work, closing on their new house, and selling his old one, after all.

At the same time, Cindi was not happy that he wasn't there. She retrieved her luggage at baggage claim, hailed a cab, and headed home. As she watched the palm trees whiz by and people out in shorts and flip-flops walk along the sidewalks, she felt glad to be home. The snow was wonderful and she loved it, but she also loved Florida's warm winter weather.

It would be so good to be home, to see Kaitlyn and Paul, she thought to herself. She had missed her Kater-tater so much! No one else in the world could make her smile the way Kaitlyn could. She missed Anne and couldn't wait to talk to her best friend. She wondered how Anne's weekend with Trevor had been. She was extremely happy that Anne had found someone she enjoyed being with. And she had missed sleeping next to Paul, curled in his arms, and making love with him. Even though it had only been a couple of days since they'd shared an evening together, it seemed as though much more time had passed. *Ah, yes, life was great! And the new year was so promising!*

Despite her optimism, there was a dark cloud hanging over her when she thought about Paul and the talk they needed to have about their budget and their overspending. And she planned to ask him to see Dr. Thompson with her, too. The thought of broaching the subject of couple's therapy caused her stomach to clench. She didn't like confrontation and was worried that Paul would become angry and accuse her of thinking he was crazy and needed psychological help. She remembered the book's advice: "Couples polarize themselves around money. Partners tend to assume defense mechanisms or personalities that are direct opposites of each other."

As far as her career was concerned, events were progressing nicely, and she was hopeful about her designs. She realized, however, that she still had a long way to go before she could consider herself successful. Thus she determined that *mostly*, things were great in her life. And *mostly*, things were good with Paul.

Things had been romantic and wonderful in Colorado, but then there was the huge hotel bill that he asked her to split with him. *I'm his wife, right? Aren't we supposed to share expenses?* She just hadn't realized how exorbitant the bill would be. Yes, things seemed to be *mostly* all right between them, but there were major stumbling blocks on their path—colossal problems concerning money, responsibility, accountability, and health. If they didn't address these issues *now*, she knew that things would just continue to get worse.

She thought back to when she first suspected that her ex, Richard, was having an affair. Cindi tended to provide people many chances. She did not want to give up on someone she loved. But she realized that maybe that was a weakness of hers. For instance, initially she would not allow herself to believe that Richard would cheat on her—that is, until she hired a private detective. It was only then—with indisputable evidence—that she filed for divorce.

Anne was more direct and tended to drop people from her life when they hurt her, whereas Cindi held on, always trying to make things work.

Cindi arrived at her house and paid the cab driver. The sidewalks were wet and shiny, and silence surrounded her, as if the energy and life of her house were fading. *It seems to be that way whenever I decide to move out of one house and into another. It's as if the house is preparing to live without me and getting ready to say goodbye,* she thought.

Cindi noticed that Paul's car was gone. She assumed he was at work or at the new house, and his absence disappointed her. She'd been so excited to share her news with him and was upset when he was not at the airport to pick her up. She had been so inspired and energetic while in New York—it was as if the world was hers and she was on her way! Returning to an empty house with no sign of Paul had totally deflated her effervescent mood.

When she entered her cozy home, she felt nostalgic pangs. She and Kaitlyn would soon be moving out of it and into their new mansion, their *Castillo de Amor*. While she was excited about the new home—a palatial one at that—and building a new life and family with Paul and their three children, she couldn't help but feel melancholy about leaving this house.

Cindi walked into the kitchen and saw a couple of coffee cups in the sink. Other than that, it didn't look as though Paul had been around much.

She phoned Kaitlyn and told her she would pick her up in an hour. Then she called Paul again, but there was still no answer. She texted him and told him she was home.

Cindi then put her luggage in the bedroom and changed clothes. She took off her thick wool sweater and leather jacket and put on a lighter knit top. The afternoon air was a mild 78 degrees outside, but it would get cooler as dusk settled in.

The bed was still made as she had left it, so it was obvious Paul hadn't slept there. Feeling a little unsettled, Cindi headed over to the new house. She was eager to see Paul and check out what he had done regarding the furniture and decorations. She couldn't wait to tell him about meeting Tim Gunn and all the other influential people in New York.

When she pulled into the driveway, the first thing she saw was the palm tree. *He sure didn't waste any time getting it planted,* she thought. It was impossible not to notice the massive tree. While it was pretty, it was so costly that it was hard for her to love it. She would never understand how a palm tree could cost $15,000—even a fancy Canary Island date palm.

She also noticed that Paul's car wasn't there. She parked, walked to the front door, unlocked it with her key, and entered. Directly in front of her, she saw the long, winding staircase in the entryway. It was grand. Palatial. So different from her current house. She almost felt like an intruder. *Could this really be my new home?*

She observed that Paul had moved almost all his furnishings into the house, and there were a few new pieces as well. A Persian rug with soft blues, browns, and reds was in the den. It looked rich underneath the leather sofa and on the gleaming dark hardwood floor. Cindi was positive it was new and expensive. She sighed. *Good heavens! I've been gone only two days.*

She entered the kitchen and saw several used wineglasses on the kitchen counter by the sink. One of them had a lipstick mark. *Hmmm,* she thought. There were empty bottles of Cakebread in the trashcan. Obviously, Paul's associates had been over to look at the house, and she couldn't blame him for that. She knew how proud he was of their new house. But still ...

Cindi wandered around the large home for a while, trying to imagine what it was going to feel like when they all lived here. The children had their own rooms, and she and Paul had a master suite with walk-in closets that were big enough to seem like sitting rooms, and the master bath had a Jacuzzi and a glass-walled shower that was massive and elegant. With the marble floors and arched doorways, it really did feel lavish. *It will be wonderful living here together*, she convinced herself.

Cindi imagined the children laughing and splashing in the pool, delicious aromas wafting from the kitchen, Paul hugging her from behind and happily nibbling on her neck while she cooked, and an expansive studio brimming over with new designs—it would be so wonderful. They could be happy—so happy.

She sighed. Everywhere she looked, she couldn't help but think about all the debts that were piling up. *I'll take care of it. Paul and I will have that talk. And when I sell my house, I can pay off a lot of our bills,* she told herself.

Right now, however, she had a home equity loan, and she had no idea just how huge Paul's bills were. She was almost afraid to find out. She was reminded of Anne's advice, which she clearly wished she had adhered to: "Discuss money issues before buying assets together ... It's important that you have the same money values."

And here she was, stuck with a new mortgage and splitting the bills on a very expensive house—that in addition to her normal, everyday expenses. *What a mess!* she thought. When it had been just Kaitlyn and Cindi, life had been so much easier. *But lonelier, too*, she reminded herself. She had spent many nights longing for someone to hold her, to kiss her, to make love to her, to cuddle with her, and to talk to long into the night. She now had Paul. No, he wasn't perfect. But in many ways, he was her Prince Charming, and she was crazy about him.

Cindi walked back through the house and out the front door. She locked it and then drove to Arielle's house to pick up Kaitlyn. On the way home, they talked about Cindi's adventures. Kaitlyn was very excited for her. Cindi was sure of one thing: Kaitlyn was definitely a believer in her talents. Her adorable Kater-tater never let her down. Cindi knew she was blessed to have her daughter in her life.

When they arrived back at Cindi's house, Paul was there. He appeared a bit disheveled in jeans and a T-shirt, and she wondered if he'd just returned from the spa. He ran to meet her. "Cindi! Kaitlyn! Oh my God, Cindi! I'm so sorry! I know I was supposed to pick you up, but I was with a client and turned off my phone. Then I had an appointment at the spa. I thought I'd be finished in plenty of time, and the next thing I knew, it was too late. I'm so sorry!" he said.

"It's okay, Paul. I just took a cab. I figured you were working. I didn't know you were going to the spa today." *At least he apologized,* she thought. *But a spa appointment? Really?* Now she was angry.

He grabbed her and hugged her. "I missed you so much!"

"Me, too," said Cindi. It felt so good to be in his arms—even though he forgot to pick her up.

He turned to Kaitlyn. "I missed you, too, honey!" He gave her a big hug, which tickled her.

"Mommy has some exciting news about New York," Kaitlyn said, beaming proudly at Cindi. "She met Mr. Gunn. He lives in a big, beautiful pen-house."

"It's *penthouse*, sweetie, not pen-house," Cindi said.

"Penthouse!" said Kaitlyn, giggling.

"What happened?" Paul asked as they walked into the house. "And who's Mr. Gunn?"

"Oh, Paul. It was great. The whole weekend couldn't have gone better if I had planned it. Tim Gunn is the mentor on the hit TV show *Project Runway*. He's a really big deal in the fashion world," Cindi said.

She proceeded to tell him about meeting Tim Gunn and numerous other famous designers and financial backers. Paul seemed impressed, but he also seemed distracted. *Or was it disinterest? Or jealousy?* Cindi wondered. He believed in her and had always told her how wonderful her designs were. And he knew that if she became successful, he could possibly end up with some high-end celebrities as clients. *He wants me to do well ... doesn't he?* And yet, he seemed a bit impatient when she talked about New York.

"Sweetheart, I told you that your designs were wonderful. I've always known you'd be successful someday. I'm very proud of you," he said.

She struggled to believe that he was being completely sincere considering that Paul had no idea who Tim Gunn was, or *Project Runway*, for that matter.

Cindi gave Kaitlyn her gifts. "Oh, I love them!" Kaitlyn squealed. "Thank you so much!"

"Honey, why don't you grab your suitcase and start unpacking," Cindi said.

"Sure, Mommy!" Kaitlyn said. She gave her mom a kiss and went to her room, which left the newlyweds alone.

Cinderella gave Paul his leather iPad case, and he was touched. "This is beautiful. I've been wanting one of these. It's perfect," he said.

"I got a couple of things for Daniel and Isabella, too. I'll give them their gifts when they come," she said.

"That was thoughtful of you. I'm sure they'll love them," he said.

"What about you? What did you do this weekend?" she asked.

"Mostly, I was moving," said Paul, pushing his hair back from his forehead. Cindi noticed that he looked tired and stressed. "I got a lot of things done at the house—the movers were able get everything in the house while you were away, but things were very busy."

"I hope you were able to relax some," she said.

"Um ... yes ... I went to the spa, but mostly, I've been moving things over to the new house. And last night, a few people from work came over to see our new home," he said.

"I drove over there looking for you today and noticed a few wine bottles in the trash. I suppose you had your own party!" She laughed lightly ... *nervously.* She didn't know why she felt left out or why it bothered her. After all, she was at a party last night, as well. But it was truly a business party and was important for her career. For some reason, the fact that Paul had a little get-together at their new house before she even moved in—*without her*—did not seem right.

"Yeah, I had a few people over, and we had some wine. Everyone loved the house, Cin," Paul said.

"I'm glad. But I thought we were going to have a housewarming party after we all moved in. I ... I ... don't even have my furniture moved yet."

"We are. I had an impromptu get-together last night. No big deal, Cinderella. Folks from the firm wanted to see the house, so I invited them over. And hey, I tried to get you to reschedule your New York meeting, so you could have been there if you had been home. You can't complain."

"But New York was already planned. I couldn't change the date. You know that," she said.

"I know," Paul said, flatly, avoiding her eyes.

Cindi could sense that Paul was getting edgy. She could tell when he was tired of being questioned. His eyes quickly flashed from blue-green to dark, and he clenched his jaw. She decided to change the subject.

"Hey, why don't we go out tonight and celebrate our new house and my weekend in New York. I can tell you all about the party last night and what my agent said about my designs," said Cindi.

"That would be great," said Paul.

The three went to Bistro Provence. Cindi liked its casual atmosphere. Meanwhile, Paul always preferred more expensive establishments where they could sit and dine with a bottle of wine.

Cinderella shared her Manhattan weekend, and Kaitlyn was excited to hear every detail. Paul, however, just seemed bored, and even though he made statements like, "I'm so proud of you, love," Cindi didn't think he was paying attention or engaged in the conversation. She tried not to worry about it, though. After all, he was a guy, and most men were not interested in fashion.

Later during their meal, Cindi and Paul discussed the new house and the fact that Kaitlyn would have to switch schools once she and Cindi moved out of their old house. Kaitlyn didn't like the idea of attending a different school from Arielle, but Cindi promised that she would be able to see Arielle at their ice-skating lessons and dance classes as well as on weekends. "It really won't be that different. You'll be with Arielle as much as you want," said Cindi.

When they arrived home, Cindi insisted that Kaitlyn go to bed early because of school the next day. Kaitlyn kissed Paul and Cindi goodnight. She was bubbling with excitement because the following weekend, she, Daniel, and Isabella would all stay in their new home together.

Afterward, Cindi and Paul retired to the den. Paul opened a bottle of Brunello wine, and they sank down in Cindi's overstuffed white sofa in front of the TV. *Life can feel so complete and simple at times,* thought Cindi.

"I really did miss you, love. And I'm sorry I wasn't at the airport to pick you up. Time just got away from me," he said.

"It's really no big deal. I missed you, too, and couldn't wait to get home and tell you and Kaitlyn about everything. I wish you could have been in New York with me. But I'm home now, and we can get started packing some of my things to move to the new house. Kaitlyn's really looking forward to all of us staying there next weekend," she said.

"Love, I think I forgot to tell you. I have to go to Los Angeles on Tuesday to meet a new client. I'll be out there until Friday. So, I ... well ... I won't be able to help you much this week. Sorry, hon," he said.

"No, you didn't tell me. Wow, that's great—a new client. But darn, I wish you didn't have to go this week. I just got home!" she said.

"I know. Bad timing for us, but very good for business. And hey, we don't have to move all your furniture right away. Your house hasn't sold yet, so there's no rush as far as I see it," he said.

"You're right. It takes pressure off me, I suppose, since I need to do some sewing," she said.

Although Cindi wanted to have a serious talk with Paul this week, she now realized that she would have to postpone it ... again.

"I really am proud of you, honey," Paul said. He took the wineglass from her hand, set it on the coffee table, and moved closer.

"You are? I know all this talk about the fashion industry must be boring for you, but it means so much to me," she said.

"I know, babe, I know," he said quietly, almost breathlessly. "Now, let's not talk about work anymore. I have much more interesting things to do with you."

Paul pushed her back on the sofa and lay on top of her, kissing her hard on the mouth. He put his hand up her sweater, unclasped her bra, and began to massage her breasts. *Good Lord*, she moaned inwardly. She wanted him and couldn't wait to have him, was totally addicted to his touch, and couldn't resist him nor deny him anything when he was this way with her. Any serious discussions would just have to wait.

Chapter 35

On Tuesday, Cindi and Paul raced to the airport. As they neared the parking structure, Paul reminded her of his return flight. His prompting made her think about how he hadn't been there when she returned from New York. Remembering his selfishness irritated her, but she didn't want to have a fight before he left for Los Angeles.

On her way home, she drove to *Castillo de Amor*. She planned to walk through the house to determine what they really needed and measure for window treatments.

She entered the house and perused the rooms while taking notes regarding what to add to her to-do list. In their master suite, she noticed that Paul's clothes and shoes were in the closet. The bed was rumpled, and it was clear that he had slept there while she was gone.

In his bathroom, he had already filled his vanity with his personal belongings. She looked through his drawers and saw his testosterone gels and syringes. She wasn't surprised. As far as she could tell, he had not changed his anti-aging routine at all and was still spending money as though they were Rockefellers. *Later*, she reminded herself. *I'll discuss all of this with him later.*

After she completed her list of items they would need to buy, Cindi drove back home feeling very productive. She had some interesting decorating ideas for their *Castillo de Amor*, and she would work on them right away. For her, this was the best way to avoid thinking about Paul's health protocols and his spending. Shortly after returning home, Anne called and asked if Cindi would like to meet for happy hour.

"Yes, sure! Kaitlyn has ice-skating lessons after school, so I'm free. I can't wait to see you!" Cindi said.

"Me, too," Anne said.

It felt good not to worry about anything for the moment. *Am I in denial? Probably.* Last night with Paul had been so intoxicating and sensual that she didn't want to think about anything else. Whenever they had a romantic evening, the afterglow stayed with her throughout the next day, and she felt energized and inspired all over again. Physical intimacy with her Prince Charming temporarily erased her disappointment about him not calling her on Saturday evening and neglecting to pick her up at the airport. She knew she had to deal with the anti-aging medicine, his behavior, and creating a budget—and she would. She also knew she needed to make an appointment with Dr. Thompson. In the meantime, she hadn't said a word to Paul about couple's therapy.

Before meeting Anne at Las Palmas, Cindi headed to Fabric Superstore to look for material for her *Winter Wonderland* collection. As she went through the aisles, she pulled out bolts of fabric and ran her fingers lightly across the textures. She had to have just the right blend of light, airy material that looked ethereal and icy, and at the same time, she wanted white knits and faux furs that were soft, like powdery snow. Just being in the fabric store thrilled her and sent her imagination into overdrive. After she finished shopping, she went to meet Anne.

Once at Las Palmas she spotted her best friend.

"Sweetie, you look fabulous. You must have had a great weekend," said Anne.

"You, too. How was the weekend with Trevor?" Cindi asked.

"Great. We went to hear the Miami Symphony Orchestra. Before that, we went bike riding through the park," Anne said.

"So you like him? I mean, do you, like, really, *really* like him?" asked Cindi.

Anne blushed several shades of red. She was such a strong, confident woman she seldom got embarrassed about anything. *Anne, Tough as Nails* was what some of their friends called her.

"If I'm not careful, I'm going to fall in love with him and have to deal with having my own Prince Charming," she said.

"Anne, I'm so happy about this. Who would have ever thought that in a year's time, you and I both would be with someone we loved?" Cindi said.

"I know. Miracles do happen. So ... things are good with you and Paul? And you had a fabulous, successful weekend in New York?" Anne asked.

"Yes and yes. Things are good with Paul and me, even though there are some issues we need to talk about. And New York was the best! I took Paul to the airport this morning," Cindi said.

"The airport?" asked Anne.

"Yes, he had to go to LA to meet a new client and won't be back until Friday. Can you believe that? I'm gone a couple of nights, and then he has to leave as soon as I get back," Cindi said.

"When married couples have busy careers, like the two of you, it can get complicated," said Anne.

"I know. Actually, it'll give me time to get started on my designs. But I'll miss him like crazy. And honestly, Anne, things couldn't have gone better in New York," Cindi said.

Cindi proceeded to tell her about Max, the party at Tim Gunn's house, how Max gave Tim her portfolio, and the fact that she might have a shot at getting on *Project Runway*.

"You go, girl! God, you deserve this. I can't believe you met Tim Gunn! Was Heidi Klum there, as well?" Anne asked.

"No, Tim said she was traveling with her children in Europe. I was just so excited to meet him!" she said.

"Is he as down-to-earth as he seems on the show?" Anne asked.

"Absolutely," said Cindi.

They ate chips and salsa and sipped their margaritas. The bar was beginning to fill as people arrived after work.

"Okay, you have to tell me. Have you talked to Paul about going to see Dr. Thompson with you or about your finances?"

"I was going to. But there wasn't really time. I do know one thing—he's still taking what seems like excessively high doses of testosterone," Cindi said.

"So, nothing's changed?" asked Anne.

"I don't think so. He moved his things into the new house. As you know, he sold his house pretty quickly and was anxious to get his things out. He's already bought a new Persian rug for the den. At least, I think it's new," Cindi said.

"Good heavens! You were only gone one weekend!" Anne said.

"I know. And, to top it all off, he had a little party at the new house on Saturday evening while I was gone. And, then he forgot to pick me up at the airport," Cindi said.

"I hope he had a good excuse!"

"He told me that he was with a client and lost track of time," Cindi said. She deliberately left out the fact that Paul had gone to the spa after his meeting.

"I thought you were going to have a housewarming party after you moved."

"We were. But Paul is so unpredictable at times and does impulsive things. Most of the time, though, he's great."

"I do think a lot of his crazy behavior is related to his injections. Of course, I'm not a doctor, but he also seems so immature and irresponsible at times," Anne said.

"No doubt, he does seem manic off and on. At the same time, he hasn't lost his temper lately, but it's most likely because I sidestep things and try to dodge the bullets. I've figured out what makes him mad, and I avoid bringing up topics that upset him," Cindi said.

"But not everything about him is bad, right?"

"For sure, the sex is wonderful. I think I'm totally addicted to him. He *is* Prince Charming, for the most part, which makes me feel like his princess," said Cindi.

"Are you going to see Dr. Thompson again this week?" Anne asked.

"If I have time. I want to make this marriage work. Despite his crazy behavior, I love him. And this weekend, all of us—including his two children and Kaitlyn—are planning to stay at our new house for our first big weekend. Kaitlyn is really looking forward to it. But this week, I've also got to work on my designs and, well, I just have a lot to do."

"Staying at the new house together will be symbolic of starting your new life together. I think it's wonderful. Meanwhile, I think it's great that you're focusing on your career. This is a big step in self-empowerment and in taking control of your life. I'm proud of you, Cinderella. But you also need to take control of your fear and use it to get to the root of why you're procrastinating with your financial future. It's important not to wait for a crisis to appear before you take action," Anne said.

"I promise ... I will, and it means a lot, coming from you."

"Honey, ever since we've known each other, you've always underestimated your abilities, and now you're getting a chance to show people what you can do. Paul is supportive, isn't he?"

"For the most part, yes. He tells me he's proud of me, but honestly, sometimes he acts like he's jealous, or maybe he feels like he isn't the center of my attention anymore ... or maybe it's just my imagination. I'm not sure. He just seems distracted," Cindi said.

"Maybe he's just a bit insecure. I'm sure he's proud of you and will love it when you succeed big time," Anne said.

They continued to catch up with each other's lives until Cindi had to pick up Kaitlyn from ice-skating lessons. Cindi planned to order Chinese takeout for dinner. Then, after Kaitlyn went to bed, she would start working on her designs in her studio.

Paul texted that he had landed safely and would call her later. She smiled, remembering last night: the kisses, the passion, and his body. Tonight she would feel lonely without her Prince Charming beside her.

Chapter 36

As promised, Paul called Cindi after he settled in his room at the Century Plaza Hotel. He told her that he loved her and promised that they would all have a wonderful weekend together in their new home. Cindi was relieved that he called. When he was busy with clients or at work, she often did not hear from him.

Since their holiday ski trip, the five of them had not been together as a family, and Cindi felt that it was important for them to be together as often as possible. Luckily, Mal had not been a problem lately, and Cindi was relieved, although something seemed suspicious.

The next morning, the air was fresh and clean after the evening storm. Cindi planned on moving a few things to the new house that week, and she really wanted to work out at the gym, but today she had to concentrate on her work.

Max called her in the afternoon. "How are you doing, Cinderella, my dear?" he asked.

"I'm great! Oh, Max, I'm so excited about my designs after being in New York. Have you heard back from Tim Gunn about my portfolio?" she asked.

"Yes, my dear, which is why I'm calling. He was very impressed with your sketches and asked if you would submit a portfolio of photographs of some of the pieces you've sewn," he said.

"He likes them?" asked Cinderella, taking a deep breath. *Oh my God!*

"My dear, he loves them. He's going to give your portfolio to the judges for consideration for *Project Runway*."

"Oh, Max! I'm so excited. That means I'd better hurry and sew some of the pieces," she said.

"You will need at least six in your collection. You want to show your vision, craftsmanship, and design skills, and these clothes should be put together with the utmost care and attention to detail," he said.

"I understand. I'm a perfectionist—you know that. I'll work hard to make each piece outstanding and beautiful," she said.

"Once you have the pieces sewn, Stefan and I will come to Florida and photograph them for you. I don't want to take any chances with an unknown photographer," he said.

"Perfect! I've got so much to do!" said Cindi.

"Yes, but I know you can do it. And Cinderella, don't forget to name your label," Max said.

"I've been thinking about that. How about just my name, *Cinderella*? And this particular collection could even be *Cinderella Couture*," said Cindi.

"Perfect. It conjures up fantasy and fairy tales. I know you'd love to see some celebrities wear your gowns on the red carpet. Maybe we can make that happen," said Max.

"I know you're my agent and you have to say these things, but your support means everything to me," she said.

After they ended their phone conversation, Cindi could hardly breathe. *Time is running out! Six designs sewn and photographed! A chance to be on the hit TV show* Project Runway! Her head was spinning.

She credited Paul for much of the good fortune she had experienced lately. From the moment she had met him and looked into his mesmerizing blue-green eyes, he had inspired her. Then there was the European wedding followed by the ski trip to Colorado. Being with him had unlocked creativity that had been buried for too long. Yes, there were problems in their marriage—serious ones. But they would survive, wouldn't they?

She took a sip of coffee and thought, *Where do I start with this project?* Fortunately, she had purchased the materials she needed at Fabric Superstore.

Without wasting another moment, Cindi began creating her *Winter Wonderland* pieces. She used ordinary muslin to mock up the designs on a mannequin she had purchased from a seamstress several years ago. Once the fabric was draped and fitted the way she wanted, she would cut out the actual material and sew the clothes. She considered Anne's frame as she trimmed the pieces of muslin and draped them over the mannequin. Thankfully, Anne volunteered to be her live model. Before she went too far into the sewing, she would have Anne come over for a fitting. Cindi worked on her designs late into the evening, listening to the storm rage outside. When she finally went to bed, there was still no word from Paul.

The next day, the rain stopped, and the Florida sun emerged. She texted Paul to ask how his week was going, but he didn't respond. *Mmm, is he really that busy? Forgetful or distracted?* she wondered. She knew his behavior was up and down. One minute, he seemed to be the most attentive, loving husband in the world, and the next minute, he was absent.

That afternoon, when she picked up Kaitlyn from school, they took a few boxes over to the new house. Kaitlyn had already picked out her room and wanted to start decorating it as soon as possible. When they entered *Castillo de Amor*, it felt quiet and lonely. And huge. Kaitlyn immediately ran up the long, spiral staircase in the entryway to the second floor with her box of stuffed animals.

The home's first floor was devoted mostly to a home theater, a living room that opened onto a sunroom, a dining room, and a sprawling kitchen with a breakfast nook. Cindi's studio would be at the side of the house in another charming sunroom, and Paul's office would be on the second floor, which also included the master suite and the other bedrooms. Cindi adored the wide plank oak floors in the kitchen and dining area. And she loved that the entire first floor was filled with natural light. The interiors blended traditional with contemporary along with a touch of old-world Spanish accents.

Cindi noticed that before he left on his business trip, Paul had cleaned up the kitchen and taken out the trash. Either that, or he had hired someone to do it. She was glad because she didn't feel like picking up after him.

While Kaitlyn was playing in her new bedroom, Cindi entered the bathroom in the master suite and looked through the drawers next to Paul's sink. She wanted to take a closer look at all the supplements he was taking so she could discuss them with Dr. Thompson the next time she saw him.

"Mommy, where are you?" Kaitlyn asked.

"I'm in here, Kater-tater," Cindi called out.

"Mom, can we get a puppy once we all move in?" Kaitlyn asked as she popped in, interrupting her mother's thoughts.

"Oh, honey, I don't know. A pet is a big responsibility, and I'm not sure we're ready for that."

"But Bella and Danny will help me. I know they will. Oh, Mommy, it will be so much fun!"

"We'll have to talk to Paul about it this weekend and see what he thinks," said Cindi.

"Okay, Mommy. I bet Paul will want a puppy, too."

I highly doubt it, thought Cinderella. *He's too busy taking care of himself.*

"I wish we could go and get Danny and Bella to come over right now," said Kaitlyn. "They live so close to this house!"

"I know. But when they have visitation with their mother, we need to respect that," Cindi said.

Cindi often wondered why divorced couples had so much trouble maintaining custody agreements. Of course, she wished Richard paid more attention to Kaitlyn than he did, but they didn't really fight about it, and he dutifully abided by their custody arrangement. Cindi was now concerned that the move closer to Mal might be worse for her and Paul's relationship with his kids.

The next evening, there was still no word from Paul, and she was becoming worried. Cindi worked on her designs for a while and then went to the kitchen and made some tea. *Was he in an accident, or did he get sick or something?* She called Anne.

Her best friend was hesitant to reveal that Trevor was Facebook friends with Andrea. Trevor had seen pictures Andrea had posted of her LA travels. One image depicted Paul's arm wrapped around Andrea's shoulder at the Mondrian Hotel's Skybar. Cindi's heart raced.

"I didn't want to say anything. But I knew you needed to know," Anne said.

"Absolutely. Thank you for telling me. I know you always have my back," Cindi said in shock.

"You can count on that," said Anne.

The next day, Cindi was determined to see the photos for herself. From Trevor's iPad, she saw Andrea's page. Posted yesterday were several pictures of Paul and a couple of men she didn't know—probably the new clients—laughing and drinking at the Skybar located on the Sunset Strip. Standing next to Paul, with her hand on his arm, wearing a very short mini, was none other than Andrea Parks. All of them looked as though they were having the time of their lives.

Cindi's heart fell to the floor. Paul hadn't told her that Andrea was traveling with him to Los Angeles. *No, this picture didn't mean that he was having an affair.* But, it did not feel right to Cinderella. He hadn't called her, and she had assumed it was because he was busy. *He was busy, all right!* Cindi was furious. She was fed up with her prince.

Chapter 37

On Friday, Cindi drove to the airport to pick up Paul as they had planned. He had texted her early Friday morning, *I've missed you sooo much. Can't wait to see you! XOXO.*

Their plan was to pick up Daniel and Isabella on Saturday and then head over to the new house for the weekend. Cinderella had barely slept the previous evening. She had been on such an endorphin high with her new designs, and now she felt sick to her stomach and angry at the same time. She couldn't help feeling confused, jealous, and furious. She had no idea how she would bring up her discovery to Paul.

The bottom line was that she didn't know if Paul had done anything wrong other than be an absentee, selfish husband. Andrea had every right to accompany him on this trip as his paralegal. But, deep down, Cindi knew she was making excuses for him—and she could not shake the feeling that his relationship with Andrea Banks was more than just business.

Cindi arrived at the airport and watched for Paul. She saw him burst through the door with his luggage, his hair a little disheveled, wearing jeans and a casual jacket. She waved at him, and he waved back, grinning. Her heart lifted just a little. He seemed happy and boyish, as if all was right with the world. *Oh, how I wish it were!*

"So good to see you, Cinderella," said Paul, rushing up to her and hugging her. He kissed her lightly on the lips before putting his luggage in the trunk of the car.

"You, too," said Cindi, coolly. "How was your flight?"

"Wonderful. No problems," he said.

"And your week? How did it go?"

"Oh, busy as hell!" Paul said. "Sorry I wasn't able to call more often with the time zone difference and the new clients, who took all my time."

"So they hired you?" asked Cindi, reminding herself to be cool.

"Oh, yeah. And it's going to bring the firm a lot of money. I can't really say anything more about it—client confidentiality, you know."

"Sure," said Cindi, smugly. "Client confidentiality."

"How was your week, love?" said Paul, leaning back on the seat and stretching his legs out in front of him in the car. "Did I mention it's great to be home?"

"My week was very busy, too. I'm sewing some pieces for my new collection to be presented for *Project Runway* ... and—"

"That's great!" said Paul, interrupting her. "Hey, how about I take you and Kaitlyn out tonight to celebrate getting some new clients?"

"Well ... I thought we'd move some more things into the new house tonight," said Cindi. "Since we're all going to be going over there tomorrow—"

"That can wait! We don't need to take over a lot of stuff for the weekend. Tonight I feel like celebrating with my two favorite girls," he said.

She couldn't believe he didn't ask her anything more about her designs for *Project Runway*. In fact, she felt as though he dismissed her news as trivial. At the same time, he was in a delightful mood.

They stopped on the way from the airport to pick up Kaitlyn from school. Paul hugged her and told her he had missed her and that he was taking her and Cindi out for a special dinner tonight.

"I can't wait until the weekend to stay in our new home with Bella and Danny! I've been decorating my bedroom, and Mommy says we might get a puppy ... and ...," Kaitlyn said.

"We'll have a great weekend, and we'll talk about the puppy later," Paul said.

He turned to Cindi. "That reminds me. I have to call Mal tonight to make sure everything is okay for the weekend," he said.

"Why wouldn't it be? It's your weekend to have the kids, and she knows we're planning to all stay together at the new house, right? It's kind of a big deal ...," Cindi said. She couldn't help but feel that Paul regularly put Mal's feelings ahead of her own. It was always, "Let me check with Mal" and "I'm not sure what Mal will say"—as if she was his boss.

Once inside Cindi's house, Kaitlyn raced to her room to change, excited that they were going out for dinner. Paul took his luggage to the bedroom and took a quick shower.

Cindi changed clothes. She put on some black knit slacks and the periwinkle sweater that Anne had given her for Christmas. The slacks were loose on her. She realized she'd lost a few pounds recently. She loved feeling skinny, even though Anne constantly told her she looked better with a few extra pounds, which made her look more "voluptuous." Paul seemed to like her with or without a few extra pounds.

Cindi was still upset with Paul because he hadn't called her and, instead, had partied with Andrea Parks. She brushed her hair, letting it fall naturally around her shoulders, and dabbed on her favorite Dior lip gloss. Then she entered the kitchen and poured a glass of wine. As she waited for Kaitlyn and Paul, Cindi sat at the kitchen table and watched the dark rain clouds that were fast approaching. It had been a very rainy few weeks in Florida.

Paul came into the kitchen and poured some wine, then sat down at the kitchen table with Cindi.

"It already feels like we've moved out of this house. It feels strange being here. And this house is so small compared to the new one ...," he said.

"I know. And I didn't get much moved this week. I've been too busy," Cindi said.

"It won't take long to get your things moved. We can hire someone to help. I won't be able to help much at all the next couple of weeks because I'm going to be extra busy with my new clients. But you and some movers should be able to handle it. And we have plenty of time," he said.

Paul didn't even consider that she might be busy, as well, getting her clothes ready to be presented to the *Project Runway* judges. *I don't think he's heard a single thing I've told him about* Project Runway *or my work. Everything is always all about him! It's so frustrating*, she thought to herself.

"About those clients," said Cindi. "Um ... did you go to LA by yourself, or did Trevor or anyone else go with you?"

"Just me. Trevor has some other big cases he's working on, so he stayed behind," Paul said.

"So, no one went with you?" asked Cindi, her heart pounding hard.

"No. These two clients are just mine," he said, taking a big gulp of the wine.

"That's interesting," said Cindi. She could not help herself. "Trevor showed Anne his Facebook page this week, and wouldn't you know it, on Andrea's timeline, there were a couple of pictures of you and your new clients ...," she said.

"What!? Are you Facebook stalking me?" Paul asked. "Can't I even go on a damn business trip without you being controlling? I'm busting my ass trying to make a life for us, and what do I get in return? You've really got some problems. You're f**king paranoid."

"First, stop disrespecting me, and further, let me remind you that it was you who hadn't called for days. You didn't even have the decency to respond to any of my texts. Second, I'm not controlling. I have every right to ask questions— I'm your wife! What am I supposed to think when you have a beer in one hand and your arm wrapped around Andrea's waist?" she asked.

"You f**king bitch!" he said. He stood up and slammed his fist on the table, causing the wineglass to fly to the floor and shatter.

She was speechless at his complete disrespect. It was if someone had thrown a dagger straight into the middle of her heart.

"And your obsession with my meds is insane! You've ruined everything! There's no way I'm going to let some crazy jealous bitch and her daughter step foot in *my* house. And besides, my kids hate you and Kaitlyn. And who'd blame them? Who could stand being around a controlling nutcase and her daughter?" he said.

Just then, Cindi heard a gasp from the doorway. There stood Kaitlyn, beginning to sob. She had heard everything. It was one thing for him to yell at Cindi and call her names, but when he verbally assaulted her in front of Kaitlyn, she knew it had to stop. A surge of maternal instinct kicked in, and her inner lioness roared to life.

"Get out of this house!" Cindi screamed at Paul. "Get out NOW!"

"Once I walk out this door, we're through!" yelled Paul as he grabbed his car keys and bolted out the door.

Cindi ran over to Kaitlyn and took her in her arms. She heard Paul's tires squeal as he pulled out of the driveway.

"Mommy," sobbed Kaitlyn, "Paul said that they ... they ... hate me ... *they hate us ...*"

"Oh, sweetie, he didn't mean that." She tried her best to hold back her tears. "He just got angry about something I did and was trying to hurt my feelings. He honestly didn't mean any of that."

Kaitlyn cried herself to sleep with Cindi holding her in her arms. Her precious daughter shouldn't have been exposed to Paul's abusive behavior. Cindi vowed that she would never, ever let Paul hurt Kaitlyn or her again.

Early Saturday morning, Cindi called Margaret, Arielle's mother, and asked if it would be okay for Kaitlyn to spend the day with Arielle.

"Your timing's perfect. We have tickets to go see the Cirque du Soleil show. Arielle wanted Kaitlyn to go, but Kaitlyn told her that you all had family plans. We still have an extra ticket," Margaret said.

"Well, our plans have been canceled. So if you still have an extra ticket, I know Kaitlyn would love to go," Cindi said.

"That would be perfect. We'll pick her up at 10:00," Margaret said.

Cindi roused Kaitlyn out of bed and told her the good news.

"Thank you, Mommy. You're the best mommy in the whole world," Kaitlyn said.

"And you, my darling, are the best daughter in the whole world," Cindi said.

"Will Paul come back this weekend?" asked Kaitlyn, her large blue eyes on the brink of tears.

"I don't know, pumpkin. Paul has some problems with his temper, and sometimes he just needs to cool off for a while. But I want you to remember this: Paul loves you. And Daniel and Isabella love you. The things he said last night were just a result of him working too hard and getting angry. Adults sometimes say things they don't mean. Paul didn't mean any of it," Cindi said.

"But you never say those kinds of things," said Kaitlyn.

"Some people have more trouble with their temper than others. I want you to forget about last night and go have a fun day with Arielle, okay?" she asked.

"I will, Mommy," said Kaitlyn.

While Kaitlyn dressed, Cindi prepared her favorite blueberry pancakes. When Kaitlyn sat down to eat, her smile was back, and she seemed like her old self again.

After Kaitlyn left with Arielle and her parents, Cindi felt like crying. She was still shaking from what Paul had said and especially from Kaitlyn hearing it all. Although she had cried most of the night, today she was determined to pull herself together and focus on her blossoming career. Cindi straightened up the kitchen and then called Anne.

"Hey there. So, did you bring up the Facebook pictures to Paul?" Anne asked.

"If it's okay, can we talk about it later?" Cindi asked, choking back tears. "What I will tell you now is that we're definitely not spending the weekend together. He blames me for everything. It's all for the best since I'm not feeling hopeful about our future. Besides, right now I need to focus on my designs," Cindi said.

"Honey, can I come over?" asked Anne. She knew something was wrong. *Very* wrong.

"I'd love that. And I'd love for you to be my model for some of the stuff I've worked on," said Cindi.

Cindi had some important decisions to make. When she thought about the pain in Kaitlyn's eyes after hearing Paul's words, she could not accept his behavior. Not anymore. Not unless he would agree to make some serious changes. Meanwhile, she had to create beautiful clothes for the judges on *Project Runway*. She drank her coffee and waited for Anne. She couldn't help notice—but was not surprised—that there was no word from Paul.

Chapter 38

fter Kaitlyn left, Cindi unraveled. Her hands shook, and her heart broke as she realized that she was in love with a serial abuser—someone who treated her like a princess one moment and then like dirt the next.

I've had it! I've had it! I've had it! Cindi thought as she paced from room to room while waiting for Anne. *I can't take this anymore! I won't take this anymore!*

Anne arrived as storm clouds that looked bruised, gray, and swollen gathered in the sky. A cool breeze ruffled through the trees.

"Okay," said Anne, hugging Cindi when she came through the door. "What happened?"

"Would you like some tea?" asked Cindi. Anne followed her into the kitchen. They sat down at the table.

"What happened, sweetie?" Anne asked again. Her best friend had dark circles under her eyes, and she looked crestfallen and gaunt. This was not the bouncy, happy Cinderella she knew. This was a woman in crisis.

"I've had it," said Cindi, as she began to wail, tears falling onto the table's surface. "I've simply had it with Paul. You won't believe what happened last night."

Cindi recounted the previous evening's events. She had to stop several times as she choked on her tears. She took deep breaths and sips of tea to calm her nerves.

"And Anne, Kaitlyn heard everything!" she cried.

"Oh my God! Please tell me she didn't hear what he said about his kids hating you or her!" Anne said.

"She heard *everything*, which breaks my heart. Hopefully, today will help her forget about it. She's with her friend Arielle at the Cirque du Soleil show," Cindi said.

"Children have an amazing ability to forgive and forget. Their little hearts are big. They haven't learned how to close off to the world yet," Anne said.

"I hope you're right. She's a sensitive child, though, and I worry about her," Cindi said.

"She has you, and that's all that matters," said Anne.

"I just can't believe it. It's like we move two steps forward in our relationship, then five steps back. And the way Paul gets angry and just leaves and then turns it all around to be my fault when he's the guilty party ... I just can't take it anymore," Cindi said.

"So, he left, and you haven't heard from him since?"

"Right. I'm sure he's at the new house—*our house*—with his kids. The way he's excluding Kaitlyn and me, it's like he's punishing me because I dared question him! I've had it, Anne. He immediately got defensive when I asked him about those photos Andrea posted on her Facebook page. When a guy does that, he's obviously hiding something, right? And, he lied about it to my face. How can he treat me this way? I mean, I own half the house, I'm paying half the mortgage and half the bills, and he tells me I can't go there with Kaitlyn this weekend because his kids don't like us? Something else must be going on. It doesn't make sense," Cindi said.

"Maybe I shouldn't have told you ...," Anne said.

"No! You absolutely needed to tell me, Anne. You and I made a pact long ago to tell each other anything we knew about our spouses or boyfriends, even if it was going to hurt. Full disclosure. And I appreciate it. Clearly, Paul wasn't going to tell me Andrea was with him on the trip. I have to wonder what else he's lied to me about," Cindi said.

"Some men lie because—to them—it's easier than telling the truth and then having to answer your questions about whatever it is you asked. They don't like having to be accountable to begin with, and they want to do whatever they want, whenever they want, and not have to deal with the consequences," Anne said.

"I've never in my life dealt with someone who has so many problems. Sure, Richard had his issues, but Paul is a complete roller coaster," Cindi said.

"Do you think his swings into anger are only because of the testosterone he's taking?" asked Anne.

"I honestly think he has some major problems to begin with and injections might make them worse, but I've come to accept that the testosterone can't be the only reason for his erratic behavior," Cindi said.

"I can't get over the way he talks to you and then just walks out—instead of staying and trying to work on your marriage," said Anne.

"I know! Instead of facing the problem, he hurls insults then just runs away like a child blaming me for everything. And then he usually comes back all sweet and apologetic, and woos me and seduces me with his charms and sex. But you know what? He's not nearly as appealing after all of these anger episodes. It's exhausting. I'm losing my attraction to him," Cindi said.

"A real relationship should move beyond sexual desire and toward emotional intimacy," Anne said. "I know that from dating a few master seducers myself. Some men are master manipulators when it comes to the art of sex but severely lacking when it comes to genuine love. They can't sustain a committed love relationship because they don't know what love is to begin with. They mistakenly believe infatuation is love."

"I've always heard that men see a beautiful woman who attracts them and they think it's love. It's very visual for them. Meanwhile, women have to get to know a man and then fall in love. I'm sure there are exceptions, of course," Cindi said.

"My mother used to say that men are very visual, but creative women are, too. And you're so artistic, Cindi, that I'm sure you were attracted to Paul's good looks right away," Anne said.

"Anne, it was more than that. He had this charisma and charm and affection that I was starved for ... he just blinded me with the superficial trappings."

"Bottom line, he's an immature coward who has real problems, Cin. He's one big show on the outside with very little substance on the inside. And no matter how beautiful and alluring those trappings are, it's not worth it if it hurts you over and over again. Cin ... I don't know how you've put up with it this long."

"I know," said Cindi. "I've been trying to hold onto the dream—that dream of him being my Prince Charming. And he was at first. And, he is at times. I should have known he was too good to be true, that *all of it* was too good to be true. He just swept me off my feet, Anne. I nearly lost myself because of him."

"Look, at least you can get a handle on the spending right now. Let's go through your budget and figure out a way to unravel this mess. The really positive thing is that, despite his roller coaster, you've managed to advance your career with your new designs and opportunities in the midst of all this. You're becoming stronger each day, Cindi. Don't forget that. I think it's what you do with your problems that makes a difference—how you solve them. It's about empowering yourself to take charge emotionally and financially. When you're financially independent, you automatically have more power to not let anyone treat you worse than you deserve," Anne said.

"I absolutely need to solve some problems—I feel like such a failure. How could I fall for a man like this? And this is my second marriage!"

"It doesn't matter if it's your second, third, fourth, or fifth marriage. The important thing is to know when to get out," Anne said.

"What he did last night was the last straw," said Cindi.

"As I mentioned before, some men are master con artists. They've done this their entire adult lives and are experts when it comes to sweeping women off their feet. They love the conquest. I'll bet anything Paul cheated on his first wife and had similar problems with her. She probably stayed with him as long as she did because of the children or because she was financially dependent on him. I've known of a lot of women who do that," Anne said.

"I wish I had spoken with his ex-wife. I'm beginning to understand why she's so angry with Paul—I can't imagine what she must have experienced. I should have asked him more questions, but it doesn't matter anymore. What matters now is what I do about this."

"What do you *want* to do?" asked Anne.

"Well, I plan to talk to Dr. Thompson on Monday. I feel so angry, hurt, and betrayed; I never want to see Paul again. I need to calm down, focus on what's important right now, fit you in the new clothes I've designed, and make a plan. I can't afford to fall into a depression—I have to focus on my daughter and my career," said Cindi.

"There's no shame in divorcing him, Cindi. You don't deserve the emotional and verbal abuse. If you get out now, he won't take you down with him financially," said Anne.

"I know, but at the same time, I've always had this thing about trying harder—sacrificing myself to help others, hoping I can fix their problems and make things better. I've given men way too many chances in the past. But I'm tired of it, and I'm beginning to feel like a doormat. Paul thinks he can just walk all over me any time he wants. I'm tired of trying to smooth things over with him when it's clear that he is the one with real problems—problems he won't face and work through. And as you and I both know, you can't change others—you can only change yourself."

"You have the biggest heart in the world, and sure, manipulative, selfish people sometimes take advantage of your kindness. But you certainly aren't a doormat. I know you're a strong, independent, determined woman who is already achieving great things in her life. Yes, you love with all your heart and soul ... but that doesn't make you weak. So don't change who you are. At the same time, you have to know when you've done all you can—when staying will only pull you down to his level. There comes a time when you have to stand up for yourself and for what you believe in and be an example for your daughter," said Anne.

The two best friends continued talking. Anne tried on the new clothes Cindi had designed for her *Winter Wonderland* collection. Anne liked how they hugged her body like a glove, and Cindi loved that her best friend looked like a fairy princess in her designs. One dress was a white sequined, bateau neck, sweep-brush with a long train that sparkled like jeweled snow under moonlight. The other was a light chiffon with a full skirt and white knit bodice that molded around Anne's upper body. It made her look willowy and rail-thin while at the same time accenting her breasts and defining her shoulders. Either dress could be worn on the red carpet or at a festive gala.

Cindi had worked night and day to get the pieces made. She had slept very little but still maintained razor-sharp focus. She had a feeling of accomplishment that she'd never felt before. She felt confident and empowered.

"Oh, please tell me I can have a couple of these when you've finished with your auditions for *Project Runway*!" said Anne.

"Of course, you can. I'm so happy you like them!" Cindi said.

"Cindi, your clothes are exquisite. The judges on *Project Runway* are going to fall in love with them."

Cinderella hoped so. If she couldn't be the princess of her own dreams, perhaps other women could wear her clothes and become princesses in their own real-life fairy tales.

While Cindi was fitting Anne in her clothes, Arielle's mother called. Margaret asked if Kaitlyn could spend the night with them because the two girls were having so much fun. Cindi was glad she offered. When they ended their call, she told Anne, "Looks like I have a free night. Kaitlyn's staying over at Arielle's."

"Look. Why don't we go out to dinner and see a movie? I'll call Trevor and tell him I need some girlfriend time. What do you think?" Anne asked.

"Oh, I don't want to interrupt your plans with Trevor tonight," said Cindi.

"Cin, it's no problem. We weren't going to do anything tonight, and to tell you the truth, Trevor wants to see the ball game on TV, and I don't care about watching it," Anne said.

"I would love that. I honestly don't feel like sitting around the house wondering if Paul is going to call, and I need a little break," Cindi said.

Anne called Trevor and told him she was spending the evening with Cindi.

"I can't tell you how much I appreciate your friendship," said Cindi.

"I appreciate yours, too. We're going to have a great night and celebrate you!" Anne said.

They freshened up and then headed to dinner and a movie. There was a half-moon that looked as though it was slowly sinking behind the trees. Cindi loved the moon, and watching it calmed her when she was troubled. Tonight, however, she couldn't help but feel as though the moon was about to fall to Earth at any moment.

Chapter 39

inderella stood on a high cliff overlooking jagged rocks and an endless sea that
stretched out far into the mist. "Help me!" she screamed to the sea and the air.
But she knew that no one was listening. She remembered that there was never
anyone listening in this dream. And just as in her other dreams, her footing gave way,
and she started sliding down the cliff, unable to stop, falling fast.

Cindi told herself, I will be all right. I will be all right. As she descended, she
suddenly began floating. She safely and softly landed on the seashore. She saw herself
standing there, smiling with a bundle of beautiful clothes in her arms. Serene music
surrounded her, and she felt calm and peaceful. And empowered.

On Sunday, Cindi woke up slowly from the dream. Sunlight filtered
through the bedroom window. She lay in bed for a few moments and thought,
What a soothing dream! At first, it had been scary when she realized she was on
a high cliff. And she remembered that she had experienced the dream before
and almost died in it. But this time, she felt empowered and safe. *What was the*

message of the dream? she wondered. Maybe it was telling her that she could take care of herself and save herself. Maybe it was telling her that she did not need to be afraid. Whatever it was, it made her feel more confident about herself and her life.

The evening before, Cindi and Anne had experienced a fun "girls' night out." After dinner, they ate buttered popcorn at the movie—a romantic comedy that made them laugh until tears ran down their cheeks. It was just what Cinderella needed. They vowed to have more "girls' nights out" and not to let work, boyfriends, or husbands get in the way.

Kaitlyn arrived home on Sunday, and they spent a quiet day in the house. Cindi felt buoyed by her goal of making her *Project Runway* deadline. Kaitlyn played quietly in her room. She'd had so much fun at the Cirque du Soleil show and the impromptu slumber party that her heart seemed mostly healed from Paul's outrageous behavior. She did not mention Paul, and Cindi did not say anything about him, either.

Cinderella tried to keep busy on Sunday and not think about how Paul hadn't called yet. But she couldn't help becoming upset when she thought about the fact that she was paying half the mortgage on the new home as well as her everyday expenses at her current house. And she had taken out a home equity loan for the Jet Skis Paul had insisted on buying and helped pay for the ridiculous palm tree. Lastly, she covered half of the exorbitant bill from the ski trip in Colorado. Her savings were quickly depleting. She was still receiving checks for the ready-to-wear designs she'd sold to an apparel company in New York a few months ago. Thank goodness she had that money coming in. She vowed she would let Anne help her get her finances in order.

On Sunday night, Kaitlyn asked Cindi if they could eat dinner somewhere fun.

"How about pizza, Mommy? We haven't had it in a long time," Kaitlyn said.

"Pizza it is," said Cindi.

"Will Paul come, too?" asked Kaitlyn, her voice trembling just a little.

"Oh, I don't think so, honey. I haven't heard from him, so I imagine he's still with his children," Cindi said. She noticed a troubled look on her daughter's face.

Cinderella and Kaitlyn drove to California Pizza Kitchen in the early evening. Both liked to eat early on Sunday because of school on Monday. They shared a pizza and a salad. Cindi didn't have much of an appetite, but Kaitlyn was famished and ate two big pizza slices.

During dinner, Kaitlyn reminisced about the Cirque du Soleil show and mentioned that she might even want to become one of their dancers someday.

Cindi smiled. Kaitlyn was forever a dreamer and an eternal optimist. Cindi hoped her little girl stayed that way.

When they finished, they took their leftover pizza and headed home. It was dusk, and the sun was setting in shades of salmon and red. This was one of Cindi's favorite times of the day. She was still extremely upset about the whole weekend but felt that she had salvaged it as best she could. She and Anne had fun on Saturday evening. But Cindi's heart was aching, and she was still furious about the way Paul had treated her. The thought that their marriage might be over was devastating. She needed emotional support and looked forward to meeting with Dr. Thompson the next day.

They drove past Paolo's Italiano Rustico Restaurant, where Paul had taken Cindi one evening and where he had abandoned her after getting angry. Cindi slowed her car as they neared it. The restaurant was so beautiful and charming inside, and she had been so happy when they first entered—little did she know at the time how it would come to such a dreadful end. It was one of the first times she realized that Paul had a serious problem and that their marriage could be in trouble.

Lost in thought, Cindi almost ran into the car in front of her. Suddenly, she saw the unimaginable. Her hands shook, her heart thudded like a thousand drums, and her mouth went dry. Walking into the restaurant were Paul, his children, and ... Andrea Parks. *What the ...?*

Paul had his hand on Andrea's back, guiding her toward the door, and the four of them were laughing as if they had just shared the funniest joke in the world. Then she saw Paul take Andrea's hand as they followed the children inside.

Cindi wanted to march right over to Paul and Andrea and confront them. She wanted to scream at them. She wanted Paul to know that she saw them. But she couldn't. Kaitlyn was happily talking about Arielle and their day at Cirque du Soleil, and luckily, her daughter had not seen Paul and his kids.

That night after Kaitlyn had gone to bed, Cindi drank a glass of wine and sat on her patio. She watched the half-moon and cried softly, not wanting to wake her daughter. She was doing her best to calm down, but inside, she was furious.

On Monday, Cinderella arrived at her appointment with Dr. Thompson; they had scheduled the session at the end of their last meeting. Cindi was full of uncertainty and anxiety about her marriage, so the timing couldn't have been better.

"It's been a while since you've been here," said Dr. Thompson when she entered his office.

"I know. It's been a whirlwind the past few weeks," she said.

"Would you like a cup of coffee or tea?" he asked, always the gentleman. She sank into the overstuffed sofa and crossed her legs. Her heart was pounding, and her hands were shaking. She sat there awkwardly, not knowing where to start.

"How are things with you and your husband?" asked Dr. Thompson, smiling, the lines crinkling around his eyes.

"Not so good," she said as she burst into tears. "I'm sorry, but I feel like I'm in a nightmare!"

"Here," he said, offering her a box of tissues. "Just start wherever you feel most comfortable."

Cindi took a tissue and blew her nose. She hated when she cried in front of others, but she couldn't help it. She proceeded to tell Dr. Thompson about the ski trip to Colorado, how she had to pay half the bill, Paul's temper tantrums, the way his children treated Kaitlyn, his lies, the injections, his verbal abuse, how he forbade her and Kaitlyn from spending the weekend at their new house, and seeing Paul and his children with Andrea at a restaurant last night.

"That is inexcusable behavior. Have you asked Paul to come with you to see me?" asked the doctor.

"No, I haven't. I've been meaning to talk to him about it, but things were really good for a while, so I postponed it. I've put off talking about our finances or problems, too ... I know I should have addressed these things with him head-on, but I've just been trying to keep the peace," she said.

"Why do you think you've let Paul treat you like this?" asked Dr. Thompson gently.

"Are you saying this is my fault, Dr. Thompson?" she asked.

"No, not at all. It's not your fault that he abuses you emotionally or financially. But it's your responsibility to put a stop to it. It's up to you to decide what is acceptable behavior and what is not. When you let him treat you that way and then fall back in his arms when he turns on the charm, you're sending him a message. And that message is that he can abuse you and talk to you any way he wants, and simply come back with flowers and charm you right back into his arms—completely on his terms. He glosses over his overspending and then saddles you with the bills. And now, it seems like he might be taking this abuse a step further. It's typical of some men who have these tendencies to cheat on their wives—it's another way of acting out, of having their cake and eating it, too, so to speak," he said.

"The thing is, I have this programming in me that says I should share his bills because we're married, but if he's cheating on me, I can't accept that," she said.

"But you're covering bills that he initiated. That's not your responsibility," he said.

"And what's wrong with me when it comes to sex with him? I seem to be addicted to him. All he has to do is whisper in my ear and hug me, and I crumble. Why is that, Dr. Thompson?" she asked.

"It's an addictive relationship—just like your husband may have an addiction to anti-aging methods, buying expensive things, or the spa. Even compulsive working can be an addiction. And then, some men have addictions to women. To the conquest," he said.

"Why am I addicted to him, though?" asked Cindi.

"You have some trauma in your past. You mentioned the death of your mother. Your first husband also cheated on you. It's possible that you've felt abandoned and this trauma carries into your relationship with your husband. You may be trying everything you can to keep from being abandoned in this relationship, and the sex may provide a false sense of intimacy for you," he said.

"From what I know, Paul's mother spoiled him with constant attention while putting him on a pedestal. But I know that's no excuse for the way he's treating me. Why can't I be more assertive and set boundaries with him? Why haven't I stopped his behavior toward me sooner?" she asked.

"You're a survivor, Cinderella. You've always landed on both feet. On one hand, survivors are tough, strong people. On the other, they have a vulnerable side, which often means they don't set boundaries when it comes to relationships. Without even knowing it, they frequently find themselves surrounded by exploitive or abusive people," he said.

Cindi nodded and blew her nose.

"You realize the extent to which he's mistreated you—and now you're mad as hell about it. Your anger is a natural part of the grieving process; it's normal," he said.

"Yes! Anger is exactly what I'm feeling. After he subjected my daughter to his blow up, I told him to get out. I can't accept him hurting her and swearing at me— or making me feel like a fool while he's taking Andrea to dinner *with his children*. I don't know if this marriage can be salvaged, or if it's even worth trying to save," she confessed.

"Only you can make that decision. You don't know for certain he's cheating on you, but what you saw with him and Andrea at the restaurant is an indication that he's at least considering it. Honestly, the first step to resolving your marriage problems would be to have him come to see me. But you need to decide if this is what you want. He has issues to work on if he wants to make this relationship with you work," he said.

"Philip, are those injections causing his behavior?" she asked.

"I can't be sure. Although I'm trained in pharmacology, I have no idea of the dosages he's taking. I do know that the long-term side effects of testosterone in men—including cognitive and behavioral changes—are well documented. They can experience confusion, mood swings, and aggression. It sounds like Paul already had these problems, and his meds might exacerbate what was already there. Again, this is just speculation. Right now, let's focus on you and determine what you want to do and what steps you want to take," said Dr. Thompson.

"I have a lot to think about. I don't even know if I want him anymore. Just the thought of his infidelity is infuriating, embarrassing, and insulting. I haven't heard from him all weekend, so he may have decided for me," she said.

"Your uncertainty is understandable. You've made the right move by seeing me. You clearly want to work on your own issues. You can't save this marriage by yourself—it takes two. But you need to think of yourself first and decide what you want," he said.

"This time, I do know. And right now I really hate him," she said.

When Cinderella left Dr. Thompson's office, she checked her phone and saw that Paul had texted her, *Let's talk tonight. I am so sorry for everything. XO, Paul.*

Typical, she thought.

She texted back, *Okay. See you tonight.*

But her heart was not in a forgiving mood.

Chapter 40

$\mathcal{I}$t was early spring—a time in south Florida when the days were pleasantly mild and mellow, and the evenings refreshingly cool. It was exactly one year ago when Cinderella had attended the Brave Cherubs Charity Ball at Vizcaya Museum and Gardens, and when she felt like the real Cinderella from the famous fairy tale who went to the ball and met her Prince Charming.

Cindi had fallen in love, quickly married her prince, and was whisked away to a fantasy wedding and honeymoon in Italy and Paris, and shortly thereafter jetted to a decadent Christmas ski trip with her family. She and her prince bought a mansion, and their life together was full of memories she would cherish for the rest of her life. At the same time, her dream world unraveled as reality reared its ugly head, exposing the cracks and flaws in her beautiful prince.

So much had happened in one short year, she couldn't believe it. She went from being blissfully in love to being completely crushed. Cindi went home feeling torn up inside and worried after her time with Dr. Thompson. She was still furious with Paul. She was angry at the way he treated her—the lies, the verbal abuse, the manipulation, and the cheating. She was angry with herself for repeatedly forgiving him just to smooth things over and for letting things slide by. And she was heartbroken at his betrayal. *What had happened? How could he treat me like a princess, write me poems, make love to me as if I was the most beautiful woman in the world, and lavish me with attention one moment, only to be deceitful the next?*

She could not understand his personality swings. He was like Dr. Jekyll and Mr. Hyde: two different people in one. And she felt humiliated and foolish for succumbing to his charms every time. Yes, she loved him—she couldn't deny that. *But there are times when love isn't enough, when sacrificing my self-esteem for love doesn't make sense, especially when the other person doesn't love or treat me with respect in return,* thought Cindi.

Cinderella planned to talk to Paul in the early evening while Kaitlyn was at her ice-skating lesson. While she was working on her designs and thinking about what she was going to say to Paul, Max called from New York. "My dear Cinderella, how are you?" he asked.

"I'm hard at work," said Cinderella, glad for the distraction. "And I'm pleased to report I'm almost finished. My friend Anne is serving as my model, and honestly, Max, she looks beautiful in the clothes."

"That's why I'm calling. Stefan and I would like to fly down this week and do a photo shoot with your clothes. Are you available?" he asked.

Cindi thought about her week and the difficulties she was having with Paul. She was inclined to tell Max to wait because she had so many things to deal with, but she decided that she wouldn't put her life and dreams on hold for Paul. Not after the way he had treated her. She needed to have the photos shot for her *Project Runway* audition.

"Yes, I'm available. When do you want to come?" she asked.

"Is Friday good?" Max asked.

"Perfect. I'll make sure Anne can be here to model the clothes," she said.

"Wonderful. Talk to you soon," said Max.

Cindi called Anne and asked her to be ready to model her clothes.

"Got it. It's in my calendar. Hey, everything okay, Cindi?" Anne asked.

"Yes. Hey, can we meet for coffee tomorrow? I need to talk to you," Cindi said.

As the afternoon sun started to drift down and the sky turned from red to black, Cindi's stomach churned and knotted as she waited for Paul. She drank a cup of tea, then a glass of wine. She nibbled on brie and paced the floor. She put a load of laundry in the washing machine and then brushed her hair.

She hated confrontation more than anything. She hated everything about this situation. *I am all right. I can survive this. I deserve better. I deserve a man who will love me and respect me. I do not deserve his abuse. I deserve so much more,* she told herself.

At 5:00 p.m., while Kaitlyn was at ice-skating practice, Cindi stood at the kitchen window. She watched Paul walk up the sidewalk. He wore a slightly crumpled suit, his dark hair was disheveled, and he looked tired and haggard, as if he hadn't slept much. He had a bottle of wine in his hands. *It's probably a peace offering,* thought Cindi as he walked in the door.

"Cinderella, I'm home!" he said.

Home? Whose home is he talking about? He hasn't really been living here lately, she thought. She sat at the kitchen table with her hands clasped together.

"I'm in the kitchen," she said.

"Cinderella, I want to say I'm sorry for the fight we had on Friday," said Paul as he entered the kitchen.

He avoided eye contact as he set the bottle of wine on the table. Instead of sitting down, Paul leaned on the table, looking down at the floor.

"I sometimes let my temper get the best of me and fly off the handle before I think," he said.

"'Sorry' won't fix it this time," said Cindi, flatly. "Kaitlyn heard every word."

"I know," said Paul, running his hand through his hair. "And I hate that. I'd take it back if I could."

"It's too late now. You not only hurt me, but you also hurt Kaitlyn, and she's never been anything but wonderful to you and your kids," she said.

"Look, I said I'm sorry. I want to make this up to you and Kaitlyn. Let me take you girls out to dinner tonight, and we'll all make up. I can fix this, Cinderella," he said.

"I'm not sure you can," she said, looking him straight in the eye.

"What do you mean? We've always worked things out, and we can work this out. I want this to work. Don't give up on us, Cinderella," he said.

"You called me a f**king bitch, Paul!" she said, her voice rising. "And you refused to let Kaitlyn and me spend the weekend in *our* house—a house that I own, too—and you said your kids hated me and Kaitlyn after all she and I have done for them and YOU!" she said.

"Look, I'm sorry, okay?" Paul said. He had never heard Cindi sound so forceful ... so angry. Generally, she was a softie and was easy to manipulate into a good mood. "I don't know how many times you want me to say this—I want this marriage to work. After all, I wouldn't have given you the wedding and honeymoon of your dreams if I didn't. And I wouldn't have taken you and Kaitlyn to Colorado for a vacation. I've given you the best, and I work hard so I can do that for you."

"If you really want this to work—if you really mean what you're saying—then we need to seek professional help," said Cindi.

"Like a headshrinker?" asked Paul, shifting on his feet.

"Yes, if that's what you want to call it. I've been seeing a psychiatrist for a while now," said Cindi.

"Why would you be seeing a shrink? Most of them are nuts," he said.

"You're wrong. He's extremely knowledgeable, and I needed to talk to someone about how you treat me and the problems in our marriage," she said.

"You've been talking to a total stranger about our relationship?" he asked.

"He's a professional, so I don't consider him a stranger. He's qualified to help, and yes, I've been talking to him about our problems. We have a lot of issues, and I have to take responsibility for things I need to change, and you should, too. So my question still stands: Will you come with me to marriage counseling? You say you want to 'fix' this. Well, this would be a start," Cindi said.

"Look, I don't believe in sharing our problems with a stranger, even if he is a professional. It's like you're admitting you're crazy if you go to a shrink. Do you want everyone to think you're crazy, Cinderella?" he asked.

"You're wrong. I think it shows that you're mature and committed to resolving problems and growing as a human being. There's nothing crazy about that," she said.

"People think you're nuts if you see one. I hear attorneys talk about it all the time," Paul said.

"Well, attorneys aren't mental-health experts," said Cindi.

"Let's just forget this voodoo therapy stuff right now. What can I say to make you believe I want this marriage to work?" Paul asked.

"No, I'm not going to forget this 'voodoo therapy stuff,' as you call it. Aside from that, you can stop lying to me, as well," said Cindi.

"I don't lie to you," said Paul. By now, he had opened the wine, had poured Cindi and himself each a glass, and was taking big gulps.

"Oh, yeah? Like you didn't lie about Andrea going with you to California?" she asked.

"Are we still talking about that?" asked Paul. Beads of sweat collected on his forehead. "That's ancient history. She's a colleague—my paralegal—and I needed her on that business trip."

"I can understand that, but you lied about her being there. You said you went alone," she said.

"I *meant* I was the only *attorney* who went to LA. You read into everything I say because you can't get over this paranoia jealousy thing," Paul said.

"I'm not ordinarily a jealous person. But, then this weekend ...," Cindi said.

"I know. I should have let you and Kaitlyn come to the house with me and the kids. I know ... I know ... you don't have to go on and on about that ... dammit, I said I was sorry," Paul said.

"Are you getting angry again? Because if you are, you can leave," she said.

"No, no, not at all," Paul said.

"And what *about* Andrea?" asked Cindi, her cheeks burning, her heart pounding.

"What about Andrea?" said Paul. His jaw clenched, and his eyes turned black. "You've got to let this jealousy go, Cindi. I'm sick of it."

"So, you're saying Andrea wasn't with you and the kids this weekend?" asked Cindi, coolly and smoothly.

Paul stared at the floor, took another big swig of wine, and said, "No, as a matter of fact, she wasn't. I don't know what she did this weekend."

Is he really outright lying and denying it to my face? she thought.

"I find what you just said very interesting because when Kaitlyn and I drove by Paolo's—you remember, that beautiful little restaurant where you and I had dinner one night, and oh, yes, that place where you walked out on me and I had to call a taxi to get home—I saw you with your kids, and lo and behold, Andrea was right there with you, too!"

"Yes, she was because we ran into her in the parking lot. And we've been working together on the case for our new LA client, and I told her she was welcome to have dinner with us. But she wasn't *with* us this weekend like you're accusing," he said.

"Since when do you hold hands with—and probably have sex with—an associate who's just helping you on a case? And didn't you just tell me that you didn't know what she did this weekend?" asked Cindi in anger.

"I don't know what you *think* you saw," said Paul, raising his voice and making a poor attempt at controlling his aggressive demeanor. "But it was just an innocent dinner. I have not slept with Andrea. We're just friends and coworkers, and I shouldn't have to be explaining this to you. I don't question you when you go off to New York and spend the entire weekend with your agent."

"Oh, come on. Stop deflecting and spinning this around. I know what I saw. I'm not imagining things. Whether you're sleeping with Andrea is not the only issue. You're a liar, Paul Francis, and a cheat. And if you can't take responsibility for your problems and see a professional with me to save our marriage, then we're done," she said.

Cindi could almost see steam rising from Paul's eyes. He was so angry he was shaking. His eyes were shining like black coal, and sweat poured off his forehead.

"You are the most insecure, paranoid, jealous bitch I have ever known!" Paul said. He hurled the half-empty bottle at the wall. Glass and wine spread across the kitchen floor. He then kicked a chair beside Cindi and knocked it over. She held her breath. She had never seen him this angry.

"F**K YOU! Just remember, this is all your fault! You're blowing it big time!" Paul said as he bolted out the door.

It's over. It's done. He just doesn't want to work on his problems. He's lying about Andrea. He lies about everything, he won't take responsibility for any of it, and he's completely out of control! she told herself.

Cindi shook so hard her teeth chattered. She sat at the kitchen table with her head in her hands and sobbed. When she didn't think there were any tears left, she began cleaning up the kitchen. Part of her wanted Paul to come back and tell her that it was all a mistake—that he would go to marriage counseling with her and that he would be hers forever. But another part of her said, *To hell with him!* Her heart ached more than she had ever known possible. It was a physical pain that was so real she thought she was having a bona fide heart attack.

The next day, Cindi met Anne at Las Palmas, where pomegranate margaritas were waiting.

"Honey, what happened?" asked Anne. Cinderella looked almost like a ghost. She was pale and thin, and her blue eyes looked hollow and very red and swollen from all the tears.

Cindi took a long sip of her margarita, savoring the sweet taste. "It's over, Anne. It's over," she said.

"Oh, honey," said Anne, reaching out for Cinderella's hand.

Cindi told her everything that had happened.

"It will be okay, Cinderella. You're a strong, confident woman, and you're going to be okay. You did the right thing. He wasn't going to change. Unfortunately, this prince is not so charming," Anne said.

"I know," said Cinderella, welling up with tears. "But this is the hardest thing I've ever had to do in my life—to accept that it's over and that Paul will never change."

"Honey, let's focus on the good things to come. You have a lot of wonderful things happening in your life right now. And you don't need to waste any more time on Paul. You gave him chance after chance. He is too arrogant and selfish to realize you are the best thing he will ever find," Anne said.

"I know I have problems to work on too. I need to know why I was so attracted to him in the first place, and why I allowed him to abuse me emotionally the way he did," Cindi said.

"Look. You're working on yours, and you're doing fantastic. We all have issues—none of us is perfect," Anne said.

"You're right. God, how I hate this, though," Cindi said.

"I'm here for you, and we'll get through this together," said Anne.

Later that day, Cindi picked up Kaitlyn from school. While they were having dinner, she told her that she and Paul were getting a divorce.

"Mommy, I'll miss Paul—Daniel and Isabella, too—but he wasn't very nice to you a lot of the time," Kaitlyn said.

This surprised Cindi. She didn't realize that Kaitlyn had known. "What do you mean?" asked Cindi.

"I know he hurt your feelings," said Kaitlyn, matter-of-factly. "And he was nice sometimes, too. But I didn't like it when he made you cry."

"Paul has problems with his temper. And he isn't willing to work on those problems, so you and I will be happier on our own—like we were before I met Paul," Cindi said.

"Paul was never my real daddy anyway. I don't like it when Paul yells at you ... or me," Kaitlyn said.

"So, you're okay?" asked Cindi.

"Yes, Mama. And Danny and Bella didn't play nice, anyway. They hurt my feelings all the time," Kaitlyn said.

Cindi marveled at her daughter's maturity. She was an "old soul." One really couldn't fool children, Cindi realized. *They always know what is happening— even when you think you are protecting them from it,* she thought. She gave Kaitlyn a hug.

"We're going to be great and have fun together—just like we always have," Cindi said.

Chapter 41

The rest of the week was a blur. Cindi stayed as busy as she could to keep her mind off her heart's fragile state. She contacted her lawyer— the same one she had worked with when she divorced Richard. She filed the necessary paperwork, and her lawyer set a court date in three months' time. Meanwhile, Cindi asked her attorney to force Paul to sell the new house. She did not want it nor the payments associated with it.

There was no word from Paul.

On Thursday night, Stefan and Max arrived from New York for the photo shoot. Cindi picked them up at the airport, and her heart lifted as Max hugged her and told her how happy he was to see her. He had very good energy—a wonderful aura surrounded him. One could not help but feel uplifted in his presence.

Stefan was handsome and charismatic, and his French accent was charming. Best of all, he was friendly and sweet. "So happy to see you, *la belle femme!*" he told her. He then kissed both her cheeks.

"It's good to see you and Max. I hope you had a good flight," she said.

"Oui. It was nice," he said.

She had worked so hard on the dresses, and now she could finally relax. At least this part of her life was good.

Jacquie came over to babysit Kaitlyn, and Cindi went out to dinner with Max and Stefan. They talked about New York, the fashion industry, and *Project Runway*. "I have no doubt you'll be accepted on the show. Tim Gunn thought your clothes were exceptional, sophisticated, and elegant," he said.

"I hope I make it to the show. This is my dream," she said.

"And the best thing is that if you win first prize, you'll receive $100,000 in cash to continue building your own line, a spread in one of the main fashion magazines, a new car, a technology suite, and the opportunity to design and sell an exclusive collection at one of the top stores in New York," Max said.

"I hadn't even thought about the money or winning," said Cindi.

"Whether or not you win—and I definitely think you can—your name will be known among all the major celebrities. It'll be a great boost to your career, my dear Cinderella," said Max.

Cindi could barely finish dinner she was so excited.

The next day, Cindi had all the dresses ready for Anne to wear in the photo shoot. Both Stefan and Max asked if there were any shorelines with white sand nearby. Anne suggested Paradise Beach. Even though it was private property owned by one of the lawyers at Paul and Trevor's firm, Trevor had taken Anne there a couple of times, so she knew it was open and available.

Cindi didn't really want to shoot photos there because she associated the location with Paul, but at the same time, she couldn't deny that it was one of the most beautiful beaches around. When they arrived, it was deserted and perfect. They spent the day taking photos of Anne wearing Cindi's designs on the sparkling white sands. The beach was so white it looked like snow that glittered in the sunlight. The afternoon brought in dark clouds, which served as a magnificent otherworldly backdrop to Cindi's white and "barely there" blue dresses.

"We can also overlay these photos on snow scenes if they don't turn out the way we want them. That will make a unique collection—the sandy white beach and snow," Stefan said.

"Whatever you think will look best," said Cindi. She was overwhelmed with emotion at how lovely the clothes looked on Anne. It helped to have a stunning model. Anne's long brown hair glistened and flowed down her back like a horse's mane. Stefan told Anne over and over again, "You're so beautiful, you should be a model."

Anne just shrugged her shoulders and said, "Nonsense!" She was much too practical to think of anything like modeling. As Anne slipped on each dress, Max and Stefan were both awestruck at how magnificent she looked, exclaiming that Anne was a heavenly vision.

With soft, shimmering whites and pale, "barely there" blues, Cindi had created a *Winter Wonderland* collection that comprised a floor-length, white sequin, shimmer knit dress; a strapless, bustier satin gown; a sparkling stardust, plunging-neck evening gown; a white, long-sleeved mermaid jersey gown; a draped chiffon, ivory, strapless gown; and an organza-over-Chantilly-lace gown. The clothes were ethereal.

As much as she was enjoying herself, Cindi couldn't help but reflect on the time she'd spent with Paul at Paradise Beach. It was there that she and Kaitlyn had first met his children. At that time, everything had been so magical and wonderful. *Well, Cinderella, think of this as an opportunity to replace those magical memories of Paul with new ones. Paradise Beach is now the place you showcased your designs,* she told herself.

Chapter 42

Two months after Cindi filed for divorce, she received a call from Max.

"My darling, are you sitting down?" he asked.

"What is it?" asked Cindi.

"You made it, my dear! You're going to be on *Project Runway*."

"Oh my gosh! Oh my gosh!" squealed Cindi. "Are you serious?"

"Yes, my dear, I'm completely serious. The judges loved your designs and can't wait to have you on the show," Max said.

"When is the show? When do I have to be there?" she asked.

"In one month. That will give you time to get organized and make arrangements to have someone stay with your daughter," he said.

After the photo shoot, Cindi had, over time, revealed to Max the details behind her impending divorce, which would soon be final. In fact, she hoped it would be settled before she traveled to New York to compete on *Project Runway*. *What a wonderful way to start a new life,* she thought.

Since working together, Max had been the strong, supportive father figure she needed, and she had cried on the phone with him more than once. Stefan had been supportive as well. He had flown to Florida a few times to take more photos of her designs and tutored her on how to use accessories and fabrics to create the mood and theme of the dress. They had developed a close friendship, and she trusted his fashion sense. Even Kaitlyn was fond of him. Whenever he visited, he took photos of Kaitlyn and coached her on how a model should pose. She loved it so much that being a fashion model had become one of her latest career dreams.

Despite emotions that were still raw and ragged regarding Paul, life overall had been on an even keel for Cindi. She had arranged for Jacquie to stay at the house full-time while Cindi was gone and had created a weekly schedule for them. If things went well, Cindi might be on the show for two months or more, so she had to be prepared. Anne had referred Cindi to her friend Sharon, a CPA, who would manage Cindi's bank account and take care of paying her monthly bills. Anne promised to check on Kaitlyn every day to make sure everything was okay. As a result, Cindi could travel to New York with peace of mind and be assured that all was well on the home front.

Max sent out press releases announcing that Cinderella would be a *Project Runway* competitor. It embarrassed Cinderella, but Anne told her to enjoy the limelight and that it was good for her career. She was on several morning talk shows and had even been featured in *South Beach* and *Southern Living* magazines.

One Saturday night, while Cindi was busy in her design studio, there was a knock on the front door. When she opened it, her heart stopped. There stood Paul. Since the moment he had walked out, she hadn't heard anything from him because all communication had been handled through their attorneys.

She couldn't deny it. His strong presence still unnerved her and gave her the feeling of butterflies in her stomach.

"Hello, Cinderella. Can we talk?" he asked.

"What are you doing here?" she asked, shocked, not knowing what to say.

"I wanted to see you. I wanted to talk to you."

"Come in," said Cindi.

She led him into the den and motioned for him to sit down on the sofa. She could not believe how fast her heart was beating. He looked so sweet and— despite her better judgment—*humble*. His luscious black hair was a bit long and swooped down over his forehead, which brought memories of their first encounter. His eyes were the blue-green that she could always get lost in. At the same time, he seemed thinner. He wore jeans and a white T-shirt that looked even whiter against his tanned, bronzed skin.

"You're looking well," he said a bit sheepishly.

"Thank you." Cindi had begun working out to relieve her stress and had also put on just enough weight to reclaim her curves. "Can I get you something to drink?" she asked. She honestly didn't know what to say. *Aren't we supposed to go through our attorneys if we want to communicate?* She couldn't remember.

"Sure ... if it's no trouble," he said. "Wine would be good."

Cindi went into the kitchen and opened a bottle of Dancing Bear. *How long has it been since I've seen Paul? Two months? Three?* Her mind was a blur, unable to think clearly.

She took the wine and two glasses back into the den. She poured it and then sat down across from him and asked him again, "Why are you here?"

"Well, I want to congratulate you on making it to *Project Runway*. I know that was your dream, and now you've made it happen," he said.

"Thank you. But it doesn't mean I'll win or anything. It's just a great opportunity to get my name out there," she said.

"I've always known you'd be successful," said Paul.

"Yes, you always did believe in me. What about you? How are things?" she asked.

"Work is good ... and busy ... as usual," said Paul. He took a big gulp of the wine. He was nervous, and Cindi could see that.

"Well, that's good for you," said Cindi.

They proceeded to talk about Paul's work and *Project Runway*. It was the first time Cindi could ever remember Paul really listening to her when she talked about the reality TV show. She felt herself relaxing and enjoying his company. *That's all it is,* she told herself, *two old friends enjoying each other's company. After all, we shared a lot in the year we were together.*

Paul turned on the gas fireplace, and it brought back memories of when they were first married and life had been a fantasy.

"We have an offer on the house—our house. I don't know if your attorney told you that, but a friend of the real estate agent is buying it," he said.

"I haven't heard yet, but that's great news," said Cindi.

"Yes," said Paul. He set his glass down and looked off into the distance. "I had such hopes and dreams for us there."

"Where will you live?" Cindi asked.

"I'm not sure. I have a few options, I guess," Paul said. "Cindi, I want you to know that you were right about everything. I know it's too late, but I'm truly sorry. I miss you, and I love you."

"I ... I ... I don't know what to say, Paul," she said.

"Can you ever forgive me?"

"Perhaps in time. But I don't really know," said Cinderella.

"Did ... did you love me, Cinderella?"

"Yes, Paul," she said.

"Do you *still* love me?" He looked at her with eyes that were full of pain and self-doubt. She had never seen this side of him before.

She turned her eyes away from his and looked at her hands and at the floor. *How can I tell him that my heart has ached for him every night since he left? That I worked as hard as I could to keep my thoughts on anything but him? That I miss him—I miss the loving Paul—more than I ever thought I could miss anyone. How can I tell him how much I want him to touch me, to kiss me, to make love to me?*

"Cinderella, do you still love me?" Paul asked again.

"No," said Cindi, blushing. "Well ... maybe ... I'm trying not to." *I can't believe I'm feeling this way after all he has done. Is it the wine?*

Paul quickly moved next to her on the sofa, pulling her close to him. His eyes mesmerized her—clear and blue-green like a warm, tropical sea. He brought his face close to hers, and their lips touched with hot, electric intensity. She grabbed his broad shoulders and held him tightly. *I have missed his touch so much! I have missed his lips. His arms. His chest.* She could feel his heart beating against hers as his warm, wet tongue probed her mouth. *I don't want this to end ... but it has to.*

He started to unbutton her blouse, but she pushed him away from her and said firmly, "No, Paul. This is a mistake. I can't do this anymore." She stood up and walked to the fireplace.

Paul followed her and put his arms around her.

"Paul," said Cindi. "Don't—"

"Let's stop this divorce. I love you, Cinderella, and I need you in my life. We can start over. Come on, baby, let's rethink this," he said.

"I *have* thought about it ... and I can't go back. You have some serious issues."

"But I love you, Cinderella. I want you ... I *need* you."

"Paul, I'm not sure you know what love is. I am sorry, but I think you should leave," said Cindi firmly, even though inside, she felt deep heartache. "I have a lot to do, and you need to go."

"Are you sure?" asked Paul. There was no anger in his voice—only sadness and regret.

"I'm sure," said Cinderella. It was one of the hardest things she had ever done—to tell him to leave when her heart, her body, and her soul wanted him to stay. But she knew that he could never be the person she wanted him to be.

He kissed her on the cheek and then walked out the door.

Chapter 43

O ne year after her separation from Paul, Cindi found herself preparing for
   the Brave Cherubs Charity Ball. Once again, the gala was being held at
   Vizcaya Museum and Gardens. The timing of the event seemed fitting—
life had come full circle. She had met her Prince not so Charming at this ball two
years ago. And only a year after she had met him, she filed for divorce, which was
finalized in May, just before she went to New York to compete on *Project Runway*.
Now it felt strange that two years after it all began, she was attending the ball again.

But tonight was different. She wasn't a shy, lonely woman who was attending
the ball solo to network with potential clients. She wasn't worried about whether
anyone would dance with her. She wasn't concerned whether she looked beautiful
enough to mingle with blue bloods. For one thing, tonight, Stefan was playing the
part of the prince. He would accompany her, along with Trevor and Anne, who had
recently moved in together. Things were going very well between them. "This is just
a trial living arrangement," Anne said. "We love each other, but we're realistic, and
we want to make sure our financial, career, and personal goals align."

Anne is always the prudent one, Cindi thought, smiling.

Cindi and Stefan were still just good friends, although he clearly wanted more. Max often teased them that he was going to have to set a date for them to get married and that was that! Max had adopted both her and Stefan and fretted over them as if they were his children. It warmed her heart.

Cindi told Stefan that she had been through two divorces and that the next time around, she would have to really invest time in learning about someone before getting intimately involved. She wanted her next romance to be a "forever" union. Stefan was good-natured about it and promised her that he was one of the good guys. And she knew he would not wait forever; she would have to decide soon whether to take this relationship to the next level.

They would always be friends, no matter what. And yes, she was attracted to him—she had no doubt about that. But it was refreshing just to be friends *for now*. She had been too hurt by Paul—and, unfortunately, she still loved him. There was no denying it. But he had too many issues and had hurt her and Kaitlyn. He had a lot of growing up to do, and she did not know if he would ever be capable of maintaining a committed relationship. She also often reminded herself of how Paul deluded her into believing he was one of the good guys. *And look how that turned out!*

Life had not gone well for Paul since the breakup. She recently learned from Trevor that, in addition to a string of meaningless relationships, Paul had to file bankruptcy, and he was living in a small apartment near his office. His lifestyle had finally caught up with him. Thank goodness they sold the house. Otherwise, he might have bankrupted her, too! She was lucky she left him just in time—before he took her down with him.

Not long after Paul had filed for bankruptcy, she also heard that he had suffered a mild heart attack. Cindi was not surprised. The stress of supporting his family, his lifestyle, and his hormone-injection habit had taken its toll. Trevor also shared that Paul had moved in with Andrea not long after the divorce was finalized. Eventually, however, she left him once she discovered he was insolvent and not the "financial knight in shining armor" who could rescue her. Her real motives were quite transparent.

Upon hearing about Paul's misfortunes, Cindi reflected on their last interaction. When he visited her just before the divorce was finalized, she now thought that perhaps the reason he wanted her back was that he realized her career taking off.

The fact that she questioned his motives revealed how much she mistrusted him. After all, he was such a great actor. He did have endearing qualities and could be absolutely perfect and loving when he wanted to. He just could not maintain the façade in his professional or personal life for very long. There was no question he adored Cinderella, but not enough to commit to working on his issues.

While in her kitchen, Cindi shared her thoughts with Anne as they sipped Dancing Bear and celebrated Cindi's her new freedom and self-empowerment. The two of them danced around the house to Katy Perry's song "Wide Awake" as it blasted through the home speakers. "This should be your new anthem!" Anne said.

They sang along with the top-40 hit:

> *I'm wide awake*
> *Yeah, I was in the dark*
> *I was falling hard*
> *With an open heart...*
> *And now it's clear to me*
> *That everything you see*
> *Ain't always what it seems...*
> *Yeah, I was dreaming for so long*
> *I wish I knew then*
> *What I know now...*
> *Gravity hurts*
> *You made it so sweet*
> *'Til I woke up*
> *On the concrete...*
> *I picked up every piece*
> *And landed on my feet...*
> *Yeah, I am born again...*
> *The story's over now, the end*

Cinderella still met with Dr. Thompson once a month and found the sessions rewarding and enlightening. She learned to set boundaries, and the more clearly she understood herself, the more clearly she understood everyone else. If she ever married again, it would be to the right man. Cindi also learned that Prince Charming shouldn't be someone to rescue her. She promised herself she would discuss money and finances before becoming too involved and committing to a long-term relationship.

Cindi felt sympathy for Paul concerning his bankruptcy, but she didn't dwell on it. Perhaps this was what he needed to go through in order to grow.

She appeared on *Project Runway* and won first place. Throughout the competition, she slept little, barely ate, and worked her fingers until they were numb. In the end, it was all worthwhile. After she won the competition, Cindi was featured on NBC, CBS, ABC, and numerous cable channels to discuss her designs and inspiration. One prominent fashion critic described the *Cinderella Couture Collection* as "a stunning and magical architectural creation that mystified and inspired."

Just when Cindi thought things couldn't get any better, Max called and told her Anne Hathaway saw her designs on *Project Runway* and wanted her to create a special piece for the red carpet. *Ah, yes, life is exceptional these days*, she reminded herself.

Tonight, Cinderella wore one of her creations to the ball. It was a champagne lace backless gown with a plunging neckline that accentuated her breasts. The dress was long and flowing and trailed behind her in gentle ocean-like waves. It hugged her hips and made her waist look tiny. Anne also wore one of her gowns—a teal silk chiffon dress that billowed out from the waist. Kaitlyn told them that they were both royalty and would be the most beautiful princesses at the ball.

It seemed like so long ago that Cinderella went to the first ball by herself and met the man she thought would be her prince. *Was it only two years ago?* Time flew by so quickly, and yet it seemed almost as if a thousand years had passed.

When Cindi, Stefan, Anne, and Trevor entered the ball, people turned to look at them. They were a stunning group, and by now Cindi was well known. The paparazzi immediately swarmed around them, snapping pictures. "Are these your creations?" yelled one journalist. "What inspired this look?" asked another.

Cindi and her friends simply smiled and walked into the main ballroom at Vizcaya. As always, it was full of elaborate decorations and decadent food. This year's theme was *Alice in Wonderland*. The famous book described Alice's bizarre and utterly unpredictable travels down a rabbit hole and the personal growth she experienced through overcoming a series of whimsical obstacles. *Life with Paul was like my own extended trip down the rabbit hole*, she thought to herself.

After dancing a bit, Cinderella slipped away to the ladies' room to freshen her makeup. Afterward, she grabbed a flute of champagne from a waiter as she headed back to Stefan. She decided to walk to the gardens for some fresh air. It was crowded and stuffy in the ballroom, and the night air felt refreshing on her skin.

As she walked through the gardens, her dress trailed effortlessly behind her. All of a sudden, someone caught her eye. Her heart stopped, and she held her breath. A tall man, over six feet, with luscious, thick, dark hair, stood under an archway of roses. A lantern hung next to his face, highlighting his sculpted features. Cindi was close enough to notice the Zegna dark gray suit. She couldn't believe it. *Was this some kind of hallucination? A dream? Déjà vu?* Instantly, she felt those butterflies that only he could make her feel. He walked over to her.

"Hello, Cinderella. You are a vision of exquisite beauty tonight."

"Hello, Paul. What are you doing here?" she asked.

"I was hoping to see you," he said.

"Did you come alone?" she asked.

"Of course. I wouldn't attend this ball with anyone other than you," he said.

"Well ... I am here with someone," said Cindi, speaking the words as quickly as she could.

"Congratulations on your success," said Paul, ignoring what she had just said. "I've been following you on the news. You've become quite the celebrity."

"Thank you. Things are going well. I feel blessed and grateful. How are you doing, Paul?" Cindi asked.

"I'm no good without you, Cinderella. My life has fallen apart. I'm broken and lost without you. We were made for each other," he said as tears welled in his eyes.

"I'm sorry for your misfortune, Paul," she said. "I really am."

He got down on his knee, took his iPhone out, and played a song for her. She listened closely to "The Story" by Brandi Carlile.

All of these lines across my face
Tell you the story of who I am...
But these stories don't mean anything
When you've got no one to tell them to
It's true...I was made for you...
Because even when I was flat broke
You made me feel like a million bucks...
And all of my friends who think I'm blessed
They don't know my head is a mess

No, they don't know who I really am
And they don't know what I've been through like you do
And I was made for you...

"Please, turn it off," Cindi said as tears rolled down her cheeks.

"I still love you, Cinderella," he said. He stood up. "I think about you every minute of every hour of every day. I made a mess of things, I know, but I take responsibility for what I have done... and I'm seeing a psychiatrist now ..."

"You're seeing a what?" asked Cindi, quite surprised. She wiped the tears from her cheeks. "I thought you said they were quacks."

"I guess I'm growing up because I no longer believe that. The one I'm seeing has helped me quite a bit. I've had a lot of time for introspection. I'm trying to be a less selfish version of me, Cinderella," he said.

"Did you love Andrea?" asked Cindi.

"No," he said. "That didn't last long. She had been pursuing me for a long time, and after one of our fights, I just gave in. But I never loved her, Cinderella ... I swear," Paul said.

"I don't know if I could ever believe anything you say. You lied constantly," she said.

"I did. But that's over. I know you'll only believe in actions—not words," Paul said.

Then, before she could stop him, Paul knelt down again on one knee.

"Cinderella, you'll always be the love of my life—my one and only princess. I am broken without you. I need you in my life. I promise to love you, cherish you, respect you, honor you, and be faithful," he said.

"Paul, what are you doing? People are looking. Get up from there!" said Cindi.

"Will you give me another chance ... marry me, Cinderella? I know you still love me," he asked.

"Yes, I do love you, Paul. But real self-awareness and change take time—it doesn't happen overnight. And in all honesty, I don't think I could ever trust you again," Cindi said.

"All I know is that I love you more than the moon and stars. And I promise to spend the rest of my life proving it to you. Please, Cinderella ... I love you. Please come back to me," Paul said.

Cinderella felt an old familiar tug at her heart—the pain and ecstasy of what once was, and the emptiness that surrounded the love she felt for him. It was true that she still loved Paul, and maybe she always would. But deep down, she could not believe that he had truly changed. She had learned that sometimes love isn't enough especially when the relationship wasn't good for her.

Right then, a voice called out to her, "Cinderella, is that you out there?" She looked up at the terrace and saw Stefan, smiling and holding a glass of champagne. She turned toward him and waved.

"Yes, it's me! I'll be right there!"

She turned back around to look at Paul. But in his place, there was only darkness and an empty champagne glass. Paul Francis was gone.

Cinderella's Guide to Financial Independence

I recall the first phone conversation I had with a potential client. A husband, dad, and CEO of a successful company, he asked me to provide financial advice for his family. During our talk, I shared what we would cover during our face-to-face appointment that would take place the following week. "I look forward to meeting your wife," I said.

"Oh, she doesn't have to be there because I take care of all the finances," he said.

Clearly, this is an extreme case of a woman putting her financial well-being in someone else's hands. At the same time, what he said succinctly illustrates how—too often—women allow someone else to take charge of their financial lives.

I wrote *Prince Not So Charming* as a call to action for all women. After two decades of providing financial advice to clients from diverse backgrounds, I have learned that women have many strengths but face specific challenges when it comes to money. In the following sections, I have included recommendations and common pitfalls to avoid. The final part of this financial guide is the *Prince Not*

So Charming Series. Included in this three-part section are specific suggestions for those in their 20s, 30s, 40s, and beyond.

Whether you have found your so-called prince or are looking for the man of your dreams, the responsibility to take complete charge of your financial life is in your hands. Do not wait for a personal crisis to occur. By then, it may be Cinderella's Guide to Financial Independence impossible to undo whatever financial damage has taken place.

Single or married, when you can proudly declare, "I don't need Prince Charming, I can learn to manage my money myself, I can do it myself, and I want to do it myself," you are on the road to independence.

Prince Charming Pitfalls

As you recall from *Prince Not So Charming*, Cinderella was still languishing from her messy divorce when Paul entered her life. Prior to meeting Paul, she and her best friend, Anne, spoke candidly about the myth of Prince Charming. Anne believed that before starting a new relationship, Cindi needed to be "a whole person who already has a fabulous life." She implored her best friend to begin any new romance from a place of personal power.

But seeking relief from her present-day problems overshadowed Cinderella's ability to follow her best friend's advice. She was overwhelmed with being the main caregiver for her daughter, the desire to be the best mom possible, a stagnant career, and uncertainty about the future. She was looking for her prince—someone who would love her unconditionally, ease the burden of being a single mom, help inspire her in her fashion career, and provide the peace of mind she longed for.

When she met Paul, she was instantly convinced that the man of her dreams had arrived. Seduced by his charm, Cindi's emotions clouded her ability to make good financial decisions.

As a result, she neglected to recognize the following:

1. **Giving Prince Charming full financial control also hands over your power.** When someone has control over your financial future, you are vulnerable to a financial crisis. Counting on Prince Charming to pay the bills exposes you to being controlled financially or otherwise. Knowledge and involvement in the daily expenses and income will help prevent becoming a victim.

2. **Anything can happen to Prince Charming, so be prepared.** He can die, become disabled, be a spendthrift, or simply turn out to be a

jerk. Relationships may be perfectly romantic in the beginning. The unfortunate truth, however, is that they often come to an end—given the current divorce rate is over 50 percent.

3. **When you are financially independent, you are better equipped to deal with the emotional devastation of a breakup.** Getting over the loss of Prince Charming, in and of itself, is tough enough. But it is exponentially more difficult when you are dealing with a breakup and being broke.

Failure to understand these three truths nearly led to Cinderella's financial demise. Her predicament is familiar to anyone who has been swept off her feet and consumed by the euphoria of a budding romance. Indeed, my over 20-year career as a financial adviser has taught me that we are all vulnerable to being deceived by someone who really isn't the person they claim to be.

In fact, I have met countless women—rich and poor, educated and uneducated, business leaders and stay-at-home moms—who, like Cindi, are convinced that Prince Charming exists. Experience has taught me, however, that *no man will ever save you*. Thus, it is our responsibility as women *to save ourselves*. But rather than place blame on Cinderella for making poor financial decisions, I encourage you to use her example to identify possible warning signs that can prevent you from putting your financial well-being at risk.

Money Is Power

An essential step in saving ourselves is to understand money's role in our lives. *Money gives you choices.* Once you give up your financial independence in a romantic relationship, you are now left with fewer options. When you maintain financial independence, however, you have choices. And choices give you the freedom to *not* allow anyone to mistreat you. In this way, financial independence is a powerful way to help increase your self-esteem.

In addition, it is not wise to rely on husbands, significant others, or partners for your financial security. Doing so is hazardous to your financial health. Consider the following statistics:

- Nine out of ten women will be solely responsible for their finances at some point in their lives.
- The historical average age of widowed women is 56 years old; one in four of these women is *broke within two months of being widowed.*

- Only 41% of women participate in their employer's 401(k) plan.
- Of poverty-stricken elderly Americans, 87% are women.

In order to thrive, despite these gloomy statistics, we must take charge of our finances. When feeling frustrated and uncertain about how to develop financial freedom—or if it's even possible—look to high-profile women today who, married or not, are financially independent: female business leaders such as Facebook Chief Operating Officer Sheryl Sandberg; XEROX Corporation CEO Ursula Burns; Sara Blakely, founder of Spanx; and Tamara Mellon, co-founder of Jimmy Choo shoes. There are other public figures who helped pave the way for women in the media, such as Barbara Walters and Oprah Winfrey. Many of these women experienced heartbreaking setbacks and were raised under difficult circumstances, and yet through hard work and perseverance, they overcame adversity and rose to national prominence.

General Guidelines for All Cinderellas

Our beliefs about money and our emotional attachment to it strongly influence how we spend and manage money. In fact, for most of us, money is never just about money; it is a tool that helps us accomplish other goals. Thus money is love, power, happiness, security, control, independence, freedom, and more.

In *Prince Not So Charming*, Paul, Cinderella's husband, used money as a way to feel better about himself. For example, he was insecure about his age, and used money to fuel his anti-aging regimen. In addition, as Cinderella's psychiatrist, Dr. Thompson described, her husband's desire to display a pretense of affluence with reckless spending on personal luxuries, vacations, dining out, home furnishings, and landscaping was a façade to make him look and feel wealthier than the reality.

By understanding the following four principles, you will be able to improve your decision making, regardless of the emotional role that money plays in your life:

1. The key to creating wealth is to live well below your means and save the rest. The mindset of "paying yourself first" will help you do this. It simply means to put your money in a savings account (thus "paying yourself") before you spend and possibly accumulate debt.

For instance, if you pay yourself first, you will have less discretionary cash overall and most likely will spend on necessities first. Only after you have an emergency fund, contributed the maximum to your retirement plan, and fully eliminated credit card balances and other unsecured debt, should you *even consider* the Chanel bag or expensive vacation.

Here are some ways to "pay yourself first":

- Create an emergency fund equal to between six to twelve months of your expenses.
- Contribute to a retirement savings plan monthly. To start, save at least 10% of your net income.
- Do not count on the next bonus. Until the money is in your account, it is not there to spend.
- When budgeting and planning for saving, begin with the end in mind. First, determine how much money you will need saved in the future in order to meet your retirement and other savings goals. Then figure out the amount required annually to reach that goal. Next, reduce your annual after-tax income by that required amount. What you're left with is the pot of money you have available to spend each year. This amount is your spending budget. Now you can determine how much of that budget is used for regular, necessary expenses (e.g. rent/mortgage, food, gas, insurance, etc...) and how much remains for discretionary expenses (entertainment, cell phone service, gym fees, etc...). These steps allow you to develop a budget that pays yourself first.
- Once you begin a retirement plan, do not review your investment performance daily; this will lead to unnecessary stress. Instead, have confidence that your portfolio will grow over the long term. Think of it this way: When you buy a home, do you calculate your home's value every day? Such information is irrelevant and will only cause you unnecessary anxiety.

2. Do not use money to make yourself feel good.
The psychological high that comes from a purchase, like other vices, is fleeting. There is nothing wrong with buying designer handbags and shoes as long as you are living well below your means and not using the purchases as a way to make you happy. But when you find yourself consistently practicing "retail therapy" or any other type of behavior that relies on spending money in order to feel good, replace it with activities that promote self-reliance and self-respect.

If money worries you, try taking control of your fear by using it to motivate you into taking action. For instance, if your response to financial anxiety is to procrastinate, especially when it comes to addressing the most important aspects of your financial life, invest time in figuring out the root causes of your tendency to delay making major decisions. Part of this process may entail working on your self-esteem. And never be ashamed of consulting with a mental-health expert in order to eliminate self-sabotaging behaviors.

The good news is that when women boost their self-confidence, typically their attitudes and feelings about money improve as well. The suggestions below may help you maintain a disciplined approach to money:

- Allocate time every month (preferably every week) to manage your money. Take this time to track your cash flow and to implement and create a budget using Quicken, Mint.com, or other personal-finance software.
- Maintain accurate records to help you file your taxes.
- Meet with a professional accountant to develop ways to pay the least or no tax. Take advantage of your eligible itemized deductions and exemptions by planning throughout the year.
- Maintain proper insurance coverage for the following: life, health, disability, long-term care when applicable, auto, home, personal, and an umbrella liability insurance policy.
- Think before buying. Statistics show that consumers base 95% of their spending decisions on emotions and 5% by the numbers. Impulsive buying due to emotions can create financial stress and hardship. High-pressure sales incentives are designed to short-circuit your rational decision-making process, creating a fight-or-flight response where you instinctively make decisions based on immediate short-term emotion. Keeping yourself out of that environment can also help prevent overspending and help you stay on track to your overall financial goals. In order to avoid succumbing to your emotions, which often leads to "buyer's remorse," delay large purchases by waiting a week before buying. After seven days, you may no longer find the purchase desirable.
- Shop with a list. In most instances, shopping *without a list* is more expensive than shopping with one. Unless necessary, resist making purchases that are not part of the list.
- When it comes to your car, buy rather than lease (unless your employer is leasing it for you). And when you purchase a car, buying it pre-owned with an extended warranty may be cheaper in the long run than buying brand new.

3. Be in control of your money. In other words, do not let money control you.
Once you've placed your money in a retirement fund or other portfolio, learn about your investments. If you are working with a financial adviser or broker, make sure you understand how he or she is managing your money. Your involvement will help identify any questionable activity that could negatively impact your finances.

The world of finance is complicated and can seem overwhelming. But with the guidance of a qualified professional, you will most likely find it fascinating. To learn more about your investments, consider enrolling in a class taught by a professional with solid financial credentials. Also, I suggest reading basic investment books such as the *Wall Street Journal's Guide to Understanding Money and Investing.*

Think about hiring an expert to provide financial guidance. Work with a CERTIFIED FINANCIAL PLANNER™ professional (CFP®) who is preferably fee based or fee only (compensated by only the client). You can verify his or her credentials for free on the following sites: www.cfp.net, www.imca.org, www.FINRA.org, www.SEC.gov, and www.adviserinfo.sec.gov.

During your meeting, request financial and retirement plan projections using future inflation assumptions, as well as reasonably conservative future rate-of-return calculations based on your risk tolerance. The financial plan should also provide you with suggested asset allocation for your retirement accounts and any other savings accounts you have. For example, the adviser should recommend diversifying your investment portfolio into multiple asset classes and sub-asset classes, such as fixed-income (government, corporate, and foreign), small-cap (value and growth), large-cap (value and growth), and international equities (developed countries). By adding asset classes that typically do not move in tandem with one another, risk and volatility are potentially minimized.

If you have a team of consultants, such as an accountant, estate-planning attorney, and CFP®, they should work together to evaluate and coordinate your complete financial plan. Each one should encourage you to consult with the others in areas related to their expertise.

4. Be smart and savvy with credit card debt.
Always use credit judiciously. Pay your balances on time and in full each month. In other words, do not incur late payment penalties and do not accumulate unsecure revolving debt.

If you have debt, paying off balances should be your top priority and an important step in gaining control of your finances. Remind yourself that credit-card debt is *completely within your control.*

First, determine whether you would benefit from using cash instead of credit. Using cash to prevent overspending is a powerful tool. Limiting yourself to a predetermined amount of cash on hand, creates a barrier to how much you can spend. Next, if you have debt, develop a plan as to how and when you'll pay the balance. Your strategy should include a specific amount you will pay each month. In addition, apply for a credit card with a twelve-month introductory low or zero percent interest rate. The objective is to consolidate your high-rate debt and transfer it to the new low-rate card. Be certain, however, to read the fine print of your new credit card's service agreement—you may be required to pay hefty interest rates in the event you have a late payment or the balance is not paid within the contract's terms.

Do not co-sign a loan with anyone. In fact, depending on the circumstances, it may be best for spouses to have separate credit.

Obtain your credit report annually. Aim for a FICO score above 700 (850 is the highest). Broadly speaking, a high FICO score indicates good financial health, solid verifiable income and a manageable amount of existing debt, all of which will help you qualify for favorable offers on credit cards, auto loans, and refinances.

Guidelines for Cinderellas Planning to Marry

Prior to Marriage

In *Prince Not So Charming*®, Cinderella was suspicious about Paul's spending from the beginning of their courtship. Although she was enraptured by his extravagant, "money is no object" spending, her gut felt otherwise. Even her best friend, Anne, shared her deep concern about his spending habits. But rather than becloud her fairy-tale romance, Cinderella chose to avoid confronting the issues, as well as the warning signs.

Instead of following Cinderella's approach, if you think you have found your prince, it is a good idea to be certain that both of your beliefs and habits about money align *before marrying*. During the dating period, determine if you both have the same values when it comes to money. In addition, observe the other's actions: Do they live within their means, and what are their spending habits like?

Furthermore, I encourage clients to ask their partners or fiancés questions such as, "Have you ever created a financial plan or a budget?" and "Do you have debt?" I also recommend that they share credit reports and consider discussing prenuptial agreements.

At one point in *Prince Not So Charming*, Anne suggested that Cinderella discuss a prenuptial agreement with Paul. Cindi thought it was absurd. "I don't have enough to warrant one of those," she said.

Anne responded, "You have more assets than you think: You own your home and have a sizable savings and an account earmarked for Kaitlyn's college education. But more important, the subject of the prenup will facilitate a frank discussion regarding each of your financial situations. I can't stress the importance of full disclosure."

There are many benefits of having a prenuptial agreement. It provides a framework for how to organize a family's finances, it protects each partner from the other's debts, and it defines assets that belong to each of you prior to marriage, which could protect claims on assets that would otherwise pass to children from previous marriages. If you have your own business, the agreement would protect your ownership should the marriage dissolve.

In the end, Cinderella did not follow her best friend's advice. There is no doubt conversations about money and legal arrangements may be uncomfortable and tense. But consider them as preventative maintenance. Choosing a fiscally irresponsible mate is hazardous to your finances and your relationship. After all, arguments over money are one of the leading causes of divorce. Therefore, you need to think about protecting yourself and your family.

As a CFP®, I frequently meet with couples that, prior to our work together, have failed to discuss what money means to each of them. When couples fail to share their feelings and beliefs when it comes to money, it leads to misunderstandings and conflict. In addition, partners may become defensive when they feel that their spouse's perspective is directly opposed to theirs. As a result, couples may become polarized, which puts their relationship at risk.

Instead, you should discuss the role of money in your lives before marriage, purchasing assets together, or commingling assets. Also, it is unwise to merge finances right away. By having a frank conversation about money, you are taking an important step toward building a financial future based on mutual respect.

During Marriage

In *Prince Not So Charming*, Cinderella's reluctance to discuss her concerns with Paul led to a series of decisions that nearly led her to financial ruin. For example, she agreed to buy a house that they could not afford, and when she expressed her apprehension, such as her anxieties over buying a $15,000 palm tree, Paul became indignant. In order to avoid future conflict, Cinderella convinced herself that relationships required compromise. She was committed to make her marriage last, so she avoided possible confrontations with Paul.

Regardless of the divorce statistics or how solid your marriage, the reality is you still need to plan your financial future as if you will be on your own. After all, Prince Charming may die, become disabled, or turn out to be not so charming.

Therefore, I recommend that when it comes to your finances, you take the belief, "I need to always protect myself." One way to do this is to be involved in all the financial decisions. Also, maintain your own credit by having separate credit cards and bank accounts. Next, understand how your family's savings are being invested. Finally, work with a CFP® who values your opinions and encourages you to participate in the decision-making process.

During or after Divorce

Once Cinderella courageously decided enough was enough and filed for divorce, her heart fell into a fragile state. But despite feeling despondent, she was determined to remain strong for her daughter and focused on her financial future without Paul.

There is no doubt that divorce hurts emotionally and financially. It often feels as if you are in the middle of a storm, surrounded by chaos, filled with fear, and uncertain about the future outcome. Meanwhile, during a marriage's breakup, you are required to make countless decisions right away. Unfortunately, you are most likely in the worst possible emotional state to do so. This may result in underestimating or overlooking expenses, both of which can threaten your ability to receive a fair settlement agreement.

In addition, when you are in the midst of a divorce, there are countless matters that are important to you, but only a few you can control. As a result, where you should focus your attention may not always be clear. In order to avoid making poor decisions, consider surrounding yourself with a team of seasoned experts who will recommend a course of action that will protect your interests and provide the much-needed support to make better decisions.

I refer to this team as your personal "Board of Directors." Whenever you are uncertain about the legal, financial, and emotional implications of any decision you make, consider seeking the advice of the appropriate member of your Board. Your Board may include all or some of the following professionals:

- CERTIFIED FINANCIAL PLANNER™ professional
- A lawyer, such as family law attorney and estate planner
- Certified Public Accountant (CPA)

- Mental-health expert, such as a marriage and family counselor or psychiatrist
- Nutritionist
- Health and fitness consultant
- Friends and family
- Spiritual guide

You may already have some form of a personal Board of Directors but have never defined it as such.

Next, establish a separate financial life before you file for divorce. To start, ask your attorney if closing joint credit accounts will benefit you. In addition, consider establishing your own:

- Credit cards
- Investment accounts
- Bank accounts

When it came to meeting the financial obligations you had as a couple, you might now find yourself inadvertently left paying the bills. To avoid this, develop a plan outlining each person's financial responsibilities. A legal document between you and your soon-to-be ex-spouse is preferable to a verbal agreement.

Keep in mind that life *after* your divorce may be dramatically different from what you have grown used to. In the weeks, months, and years ahead, you will most likely need to make important financial decisions. In order to maintain objectivity and evaluate the benefits and drawbacks of the choices in front of you, it is important to have a solid understanding of your divorce's settlement terms, your budget, and your financial needs and obligations. In the event that you are uncertain about a particular course of action you need to take, consider consulting the appropriate member of your Board.

Lastly, make sure your financial plan reflects your post-divorce needs. This includes updating your beneficiary designations and estate planning documents.

Death of a Spouse or Partner

The death of a spouse or life partner is one of the most stressful life events people experience. There are many issues to address while you may still be in shock. Contacting those that need to know and can support and assist you emotionally and financially is critical. As discussed in the prior section, it is important to consult your "Board of Directors" in this situation as well. Whenever you are uncertain about the legal, financial, and emotional implications of any decision you make, consider seeking the advice of the appropriate member of your Board. Having a trustworthy, competent team to assist you while you are not in the best possible emotional state is paramount during this time.

We recommend having a "family legacy book" in place in advance of a crisis and while both parties are in good health. It should address everything you would need or want to know in the event you suddenly become widowed. It provides an orderly framework on the specific steps to take, where important documents are located and the advisors who can help with cash needs and obtaining life insurance death benefits or other benefits you may be entitled to.

The next section, the *Prince Not So Charming Series*, provides general financial planning recommendations as they may apply to specific age groups. Remember, we all have our own distinct needs. Thus life's milestones—such as college graduation, marriage, mothehood, death, and maybe divorce—occur at different times (or do not occur) for everyone. Consider your own circumstances and how the suggestions in the *Prince Not So Charming Series* apply to your particular life stage. Similarly, there is no "one-size-fits-all" financial plan. In order to create a plan tailored to your situation, seek professional advice.

Prince Not So Charming Series for Women in Their 20s

You may have recently earned your undergraduate or graduate degree. Now, you are beginning your life as a full-fledged adult with its accompanying responsibilities. But despite having a college degree, the "real world" requires a skill set that no institution of higher learning can teach. As a result, you probably have very little experience in the world of finance.

After all, even those who majored in business may not have learned the day-to-day tools necessary to manage debt, to make wise investment decisions, to create a personal budget, or to develop and maintain a financial plan. So whether your degree is in art history or economics, educating yourself is key to improving your financial life.

In addition, there are many significant transitions that mark this stage in your life. Maybe you are planning to marry your college sweetheart. Or perhaps you have a full-time job and have decided to return to school to earn an advanced degree. As a result of these scenarios and more, critical questions may keep you up at night: Is it too soon to tie the knot? Or, how will I juggle completing coursework *and* working full time?

Unfortunately, there are no easy answers. For example, considering current divorce rates, the decision to marry can fill you with trepidation. And while earning a master's degree may appear attractive, it may be worthwhile to perform a cost-benefit analysis first. Ask yourself, "Will the degree (or certificate or credit) provide additional future income?"

Clearly, life also presents us with innumerable circumstances that are out of our control. But the good news is that we have areas in our life we can manage. The following recommendations are based on facets of our lives that we can control.

- Obtain solid healthcare coverage. If you are healthy and expense is a concern, look for low-cost, high-deductible plans. Most important, consider catastrophic coverage.

- Maintain excellent credit. In order to do this, think about using only one credit card. Another way to use credit responsibly is to deduct each credit card purchase from your checking account register. That way, your credit card bill will never surprise you because you have accounted for every charge. This will help you avoid spending more than you have. Also, use credit sparingly, pay your balance in full each month, avoid keeping high balances, and review your credit report annually.

- Carefully review the financial pros and cons of employment offers and benefit plans.

- If you have student loans, develop a plan right away to pay them off.

- Be sure to start contributing to an "emergency fund," which will cover at least three to six, but preferably six to twelve, months of your expenses.

- If you are thinking about returning to school for advanced degrees, certificates, or other training, consider the costs and perhaps find an employer willing to share or cover your expenses.

- Create a will, trust (if appropriate), power of attorney, and healthcare directives (requirements vary from state to state so be sure to identify the estate-planning documents that apply to your particular situation).

- Maintain proper insurance coverage for the following: life, health, disability, auto, home, personal, and an umbrella liability insurance policy (if appropriate).

- Allocate time every month (preferably every week) to manage your money. Take this time to track your cash flow and to implement and create a budget using Quicken, Mint.com, Manilla or other personal-finance software.

Prince Not So Charming Series for Women in Their 30s

In the United States, 46 percent of households have less than $5,000 in liquid assets. As bleak as this statistic sounds, the fact is that we live in a consumer-driven economy. Thus it is all too easy to spend more than we earn.

The thirties in particular, can be a costly decade. There are many potentially expensive transitions that mark this stage in your life. Perhaps you have waited until your thirties to marry and are in the midst of planning your wedding. Or, if you're married, you may be raising children. Or, perhaps you're planning to purchase a home. As a result of these scenarios and more, critical questions may keep you up at night: Can I afford the wedding? How can I best provide for my family? How much of a mortgage can I afford?

As difficult as this decade can be, the thirties provide may opportunities as well. If you are healthy, educated, and employed, this can be a period of significant income generation. If you're planning to purchase real estate or already own a home, you'll evaluate the tax and investment benefits of homeownership. And if you are married or are planning to be, there are many economic expenses and also advantages associated with marriage and having children.

Clearly, life also presents us with innumerable circumstances that are out of our control. But the good news is that we have areas in our life we can manage. The following recommendations are based on facets of our lives that we can control:

- Make it a high priority to contribute as much as possible to your company's 401(k) or other retirement plan or at least meet your employer's maximum matching amount.

- If you receive bonuses, raises, or both, use these to pay off debt first. Then, with the amount that remains, spend a little on yourself as a reward and save the rest.

- Plan ahead for major purchases, such as homes, cars, vacations, and education, by creating a specific savings plan or account to cover these large expenditures.

- Maintain excellent credit. In order to do this, think about using only one credit card. Another way to use credit responsibly is to deduct each credit-card purchase from your checking account register. That way, your credit card bill will never surprise you because you have accounted for every charge. This will help you avoid spending more than you have. Also, use credit sparingly, pay your balance in full each month, avoid keeping high balances, and review your credit report annually.

- If your career is stable, consider purchasing a home. A financial planner can help you determine what you can afford and the type of mortgage that is best suited for you.
- If you plan to have children or currently have kids, there is no doubt that raising a family is expensive. Therefore, have realistic expectations regarding *when* you'll have children and how many. In addition, part of maintaining a healthy partnership means that both you and your significant other make family-planning decisions together.
- If you have children, explore prepaid college tuition plans.
- Create a will, trust (if appropriate), power of attorney, and healthcare directives (requirements vary from state to state, so be sure to identify the estate-planning documents that apply to your particular situation).
- Maintain proper insurance coverage for the following: life, health, disability, auto, home, personal, and an umbrella liability insurance policy (if appropriate).
- Allocate time every month (preferably every week) to manage your money. Take this time to track your cash flow and to implement and create a budget using Quicken, Mint.com or other personal finance software.

Prince Not So Charming Series for Women in Their 40s and Beyond

Your forties and beyond are a period of reflection. You have paid your dues, so to speak, through hard work and discipline. As a result, you may have accumulated significant savings. There are many major transitions that mark this stage in your life. The reality of retirement may leave you trying to save as much as possible. You also may be considering the legacy you would like to leave your family, your community, or the world at large. Your legacy may be volunteering your time and expertise, philanthropy, or both. If you have children, you may be wondering how you will fund their college educations. Or perhaps you have divorced. In which case, you may be deciding if remarriage is in your future.

As a result of these scenarios and more, critical questions may keep you up at night: How and when can I retire? What legacy do I want to leave? Can I afford to pay for my children's education? And, should a prenuptial agreement play a role in my next marriage? Meanwhile, any number of catastrophic events could have put your financial future at risk. A difficult divorce may have left you with a smaller nest egg. Or, you or your close family members may have suffered from illnesses that have impacted both your financial well-being and your bottom line.

Clearly, life also presents us with innumerable circumstances that are out of our control. But the good news is that we have areas in our life we can manage.

The following recommendations are based on facets of our lives that we can control:

- If you haven't already funded a retirement plan, do it now! Consider minimum contribution of 20% of your income, and even more, depending on when you plan to retire and your projected living expenses throughout your retirement.

- If you are a corporate executive and have acquired company stock, grants, or warrants, evaluate the tax consequences of stock options prior to the exercise or sale. If you do hold concentrated positions, consider risk-management strategies.

- Develop a solid estate plan. Create or update your will, trust (if appropriate), power of attorney, healthcare directives, and—if applicable—estate and gift tax planning. Keep in mind requirements vary from state to state, so be sure to identify the estate-planning documents that apply to your particular situation.

- If marrying, remarrying, and/or contemplating a "blended household" consider a prenuptial agreement.

- Maintain proper insurance coverage for the following: life, health, disability, auto, home, personal, and an umbrella liability insurance policy (if appropriate).

- Allocate time every month (preferably every week) to manage your money. Take this time to track your cash flow and to implement and create a budget using Quicken, Mint.com, Manilla or other personal-finance software.

Happily Ever After

As you read in *Prince Not So Charming*®, Cinderella met Paul, who seemed to fulfill every item on her soul-mate checklist. He was well educated, successful in his career, hopelessly romantic, exceptionally handsome, and loved her daughter. Unfortunately, as their relationship progressed, his flaws began to outweigh the strengths that he brought to Cinderella and their marriage. While Cinderella initially responded to Paul's abuse and emotional instability by placating her temperamental husband, she soon realized that no amount of conciliatory gestures would improve his erratic behavior.

There is no doubt that the events within *Prince Not So Charming*® are entirely fictional. But at the same time, they embody the countless stories I have heard from women across the country who have found themselves financially and emotionally trapped in abusive relationships.

Cinderella's personal evolution represents the power we all have within us. Although many women have insecurities regarding money management, statistical research indicates that—when compared to our male counterparts—women make better investment decisions, are more organized, and are highly goal oriented.

The bottom line is that there is no secret to managing our finances. What it takes is the same dedication and commitment we have to our families, our communities, our careers, and our health.

When Cinderella found her inner strength, it signaled a dramatic shift from powerless to empowered, from dependent to self-sufficient, and from frustrated to happy. As a result of her personal transformation, she courageously confronted her husband, filed for divorce, and took control of her financial life. When you take charge of your finances, you take charge of your life.

Resources

www.cfp.net

www.imca.org

www.FINRA.org

www.SEC.gov and www.adviserinfo.sec.gov

National Domestic Violence Hotline: 1-800-799-SAFE(7233) or
TTY 1-800-787-3224 www.ndvh.org or www.thehotline.org

Sources:

National Center for Women and Retirement Research

Financial Education Center for Women Entrepreneurs

To learn more about *Prince Not So Charming* and to order additional copies, visit
www.princenotsocharming.com.

You may also email us at princenotsocharmingbook@gmail.com.

Nothing contained in the book *Prince Not So Charming*® should be misconstrued
as investment, financial, legal, tax or other professional services advice, but is
general information only. Nor is the information provided in the book being

A portion of the net proceeds from the sale of this book will benefit Women In Distress of Broward County, Inc.

Women In Distress is a nationally accredited 501(c)(3) domestic violence center serving Broward County for more than 38 years. With a mission to stop abuse for everyone through intervention, education and advocacy, services include a 24-hour crisis line, emergency shelter, outreach and supportive services for women, men and children.

In 2013, the Starfish Circle was launched by philanthropic individuals committed to making an impact on the lives of survivors of domestic violence. The purpose is to recruit 200 founding members each making a gift of $2,500 to raise $500,000, which will provide 5,300 nights of safe shelter and supportive services to women, men and children fleeing from domestic violence. To learn more about Women In Distress and how you can become a founding member of the Starfish Circle, please visit www.womenindistress.org or call 954-760-9800.

www.womenindistress.org
P.O. Box 50187, Lighthouse Point, FL 33074 954-760-9800

About the Author

Kathleen Grace, CERTIFIED FINANCIAL PLANNER™ (CFP®) professional, Certified Investment Management Analyst (CIMA®), is a Managing Director of *United Capital Financial Advisers*. Ms. Grace advises affluent families, *Fortune 500* executives, entrepreneurs, and institutions throughout the country on all facets of financial and estate planning, helping them chart a financial course for lifetime wealth creation.

Ms. Grace earned a bachelor's degree in Business Administration in Finance from the *University of Miami* and completed her CFP® curriculum at *Nova Southeastern University School of Business*. In addition, Ms. Grace was awarded the CIMA® designation presented by the Investment Management Consultants Association with education and curriculum through the *Wharton School of Business*. The CIMA® designation is a professional designation exclusively for investment management consultants. Ms. Grace served as a subject matter expert for the CIMA® certification exam.

Ms. Grace is a frequent contributor to print, radio, and television media. She currently serves on the Foundation Board and Chair of the Investment Committee of Florida Atlantic University, as Board Member and Co-Chair of the Starfish Circle initiative of Women in Distress of Broward County, Inc., and actively supports Make-A-Wish® Southern Florida and the Unicorn Children's Foundation.

CPSIA information can be obtained at www.ICGtesting.com
Printed in the USA
BVOW02s1527100116

432408BV00002B/16/P